SLA and the Literature Classroom: Fostering Dialogues

American Association of University Supervisors, Coordinators, and Directors of Foreign Language Programs

Issues in Language Program Direction
A Series of Annual Volumes

Series Editor
  Sally Sieloff Magnan, University of Wisconsin–Madison

Editorial Board
  David Benseler, Case Western Reserve University
  Diane Birckbichler, Ohio State University
  Heidi Byrnes, Georgetown University
  Yukiko Hatasa, University of Iowa
  Charles J. James, University of Wisconsin
  L. Kathy Heilenman, University of Iowa
  Carol A. Klee, University of Minnesota
  Celeste Kinginger, Pennsylvania State University
  Claire Kramsch, University of California–Berkeley
  John Lalande II, University of Illinois
  James Lee, Indiana University
  Timothy Light, Western Michigan University
  Judith E. Liskin-Gasparro, University of Iowa
  Judith Muyskens, Colby-Sawyer College
  Alice Omaggio Hadley, University of Illinois
  Benjamin Rifkin, University of Wisconsin–Madison
  Wilga M. Rivers, Harvard University
  H. Jay Siskin, Cabrillo College
  Albert Valdman, Indiana University
  Joel C. Walz, University of Georgia
  Mary Wildner-Bassett, University of Arizona

Style for the AAUSC Series
  This publication follows the *Chicago Manual of Style* (Reference Style B). See pages 215–222 in this volume for details about preparing manuscripts for submission.

SLA and the Literature Classroom: Fostering Dialogues

Virginia M. Scott
Holly Tucker

HEINLE & HEINLE
THOMSON LEARNING

United States • Canada • Singapore • Spain • United Kingdom

HEINLE & HEINLE

THOMSON LEARNING

AAUSC
SLA and the Literature Classroom: Fostering Dialogues

Virginia M. Scott and Holly Tucker, Editors

Publisher: Wendy Nelson
Marketing Manager: Jill Garrett
Production Editor: Eunice Yeates-Fogle
Manufacturing Coordinator: Kerry Burke
Cover Designer: Sue Gerould/Perspectives
Designer/Compositor: Roberta Landi
Copyeditor: Susan Jones-Leeming
Printer: Odyssey Press, Inc.

Library of Congress Cataloging-in-Publication Data

SLA and the literature classroom : fostering dialogues / Holly Tucker and Virginia M. Scott, editors.
  p. cm.
  Includes bibliographical references.
  Contents: The Gordian knot, language, literature, and critical thinking / Jean Marie Schultz -- Developing literary and literary competence / Heidi Byrnes and Susanne Kord -- Crossing the boundaries between literature and pedagogy / Joanne Burnett and Leah Fonder-Solano -- Rethinking foreign language literature / Diana Frantzen -- Reading the patterns of literary works / Janet Swaffar -- Teaching literary texts at the intermediate level / Stacey Katz -- A stylistic approach to foreign-language acquisition and literary analysis / William Berg and Laurey K. Martin-Berg -- Researching into the teaching of literature in a second language / Elizabeth Bernhardt.
  ISBN 0-8384-2466-X (alk. paper)
  1. Philology, Modern--Study and teaching. I. Title: Second language acquisition and the literature classroom. II. Tucker, Holly. III. Scott, Virginia Mitchell.

PB35 .S56 2002
418'.0071--dc21

Copyright © 2002 Heinle & Heinle, a division of Thomson Learning, Inc.
Thomson Learning^{TM} is a trademark used herein under license.

All rights reserved. No part of this work covered by the copyright hereon may be reproduced or used in any form or by any means—graphic, electronic, or mechanical, including photocopying, recording, taping, Web distribution or information storage and retrieval systems—without the written permission of the publisher.

For permission to use material from this text or product, contact us by:
Tel   1-800-730-2214
Fax   1-800-730-2215
Web   www.thomsonrights.com

Text credit: pp. 160–61, Jacques Prévert, «Déjeuner du matin», *Paroles*, © Editions Gallimard, 1949.

For more information contact Heinle & Heinle, 25 Thomson Place, Boston, MA 02210, or visit our Web site at: http://www.heinle.com

ISBN: 0-8384-2466-X

Printed in the U. S. A.
1 2 3 4 5 6 7 8 9   04 03 02 01

Contents

Acknowledgments vii

Introduction ix

Renewed Debates

The Gordian Knot: Language, Literature, and Critical Thinking 3
Jean Marie Schultz

Colleagues in Dialogue

Developing Literacy and Literary Competence: Challenges for Foreign Language Departments 35
Heidi Byrnes and *Susanne Kord*

Crossing the Boundaries Between Literature and Pedagogy: Perspectives on a Foreign Language Reading Course 75
Joanne Burnett and *Leah Fonder-Solano*

Language, Literature, and Pedagogy

Rethinking Foreign Language Literature: Towards an Integration of Literature and Language at All Levels 109
Diana Frantzen

Reading the Patterns of Literary Works: Strategies and Teaching Techniques 131
Janet Swaffar

Teaching Literary Texts at the Intermediate Level: A Structured Input Approach 155
Stacey Katz

A Stylistic Approach to Foreign Language Acquisition and Literary Analysis 173
William Berg and *Laurey K. Martin-Berg*

From Scholar to Teacher

Research into the Teaching of Literature in a   **195**
Second Language: What it Says and
How to Communicate it to Graduate Students
Elizabeth Bernhardt

About the Contributors   211
AAUSC Style Sheet   215

Acknowledgments

Collaborative effort and intellectual exchange mark every page of this volume. We could have not completed it without the generosity of many colleagues and friends. We wish first to thank Sally Magnan for her enthusiasm for the initial proposal and her unwavering advice and support as the project developed. We are also grateful to all of our authors for their fine work and cheerful cooperation as they helped us take their contributions through the publication process. Each manuscript was read, anonymously, by at least two members of the AAUSC editorial board. Our thanks to David Benseler, Diane Birckbichler, Yukiko Hatasa, Charles James, L. Kathy Heilenman, Carol Klee, Claire Kramsch, John Lalande, Timothy Light, Judith Liskin-Gasparro, Sally Magnan, Judith Muyskens, Alice Omaggio Hadley, Ben Rifkin, Wilga Rivers, Jay Siskin, Joel Walz, and Mary Wildner-Bassett. We are also sincerely appreciative of Ben Rifkin's helpful tips as a former AAUSC editor. At Heinle & Heinle, Wendy Nelson and Eunice Yeates-Fogle did a superb job shepherding the manuscript through its various manifestations.

Closer to home, our colleagues and graduate students at Vanderbilt University shared our interest in the project and offered insightful comments and encouragement: Tracy Barrett, Barbara Bowen, Dan Church, Heather Garrett, Julie Huntington, Bérénice Le Marchand, John McCarthy, Anthère Nzabatsinda, Lara Semones, Margaret Splane, and Patricia Ward. Holly Tucker also thanks Leonard Hinds, Buford Norman, Jeffrey Peters, Deborah Steinberger, and other good-natured *dix-septiémistes* for many pleasurable and fruitful conversations about teaching the *Grand Siècle*. Finally, to our families for filling our lives with wonder, joy, and boundless inspiration.

Introduction

The title of this volume, *SLA and the Literature Classroom: Fostering Dialogues*, challenges us to establish communication between two groups. The identity of each of these groups, however, is not immediately apparent. The first group, SLA (second language acquisition), is particularly vague because it has come to include researchers who explore how a second language is acquired (both in the field and in the classroom), specialists in foreign language (FL) teaching and learning (K–16), and finally university teaching assistant (TA) supervisors.[1] While our use of the term SLA includes all of these roles, we are particularly concerned with American university professors who teach foreign languages and FL methodology courses and who supervise graduate TAs. With regard to the second group, namely those included in the reference to "the literature classroom," we consider them to be American university professors of foreign language literature with a wide variety of training, approaches, and fields of research. In most institutions, these two groups operate quite independently and have different responsibilities. Occasionally, literature professors may teach language—in particular, professors at four-year liberal arts colleges. The converse, however, is rarely the case; SLA practitioners do not generally teach literature. So, the two groups, often housed within a single department, operate separately.

The divisions between SLA and literature are not superficial. Rather, they may be as profound as the divisions between colleges of education and programs in the liberal arts, between the natural sciences and the humanities, between those who value applied research and those who honor research in theoretical domains. This division cuts through to how "real intellectualism" is defined: Do real intellectuals wrestle with concrete and practical phenomena? Or do they grapple with abstract and transcendent notions?

At the heart of these debates lies an unspoken belief that, in the academy, the two groups are divided into second-class citizens and the "elite." The second class citizens, or members of the SLA group, may have clear ideas about what is involved in learning/acquiring and teaching FL; the elite, or the literature group, may wish to preserve their place among their colleagues in disciplines such as English and

Philosophy. While the division between SLA and literature practitioners has many dimensions—ideological (how we think about issues), linguistic (how we talk about issues), and/or curricular (how we conceive of the teaching enterprise), there is no doubt that these two groups are united in their shared commitment to students. As we look for a new professional discourse that will allow us to transcend disciplinary territorialism, we should keep in mind that students in foreign-language departments are, at any level, language learners. Whether in the lower-level classroom or the literature classroom, teachers guide their students in an exploration of how meanings are expressed and communicated through a target language. This common focus on language and language learners is, in our view, where the dialogue must begin.

The title of this volume also indicates that we want to "foster" dialogues, a term that suggests something has been left to languish and requires nurturing. Indeed, in the past, language and literature were not considered separate disciplines. Rather, literature was at the core of the language curriculum and was generally used to teach language (see Schultz, this volume). However, with the advent of the audiolingual method, of the notion of communicative competence, and, more recently, of proficiency-oriented instruction, literature has been increasingly removed from the language-learning enterprise.[2] Practitioners of language and literature have gradually moved into separate camps, each with increasingly distinct ways of articulating their academic endeavors. Many scholars in our field recognize the degree to which this rift can be counterproductive—particularly as it impacts morale, promotion and tenure, distribution of service responsibilities, gender issues, and much more. We believe that only a collaborative approach will help to bridge *a priori* distinctions between practitioners in both fields. That is, there must be an increased focus on how existing SLA research can inform the teaching of literature and, conversely, what literary theory and practice might bring to SLA research. This volume serves, therefore, as a forum for fostering dialogues between practitioners in SLA and in literary studies in order to identify those commonalities that unite us.

Our own experience provides a model that we, the editors of this volume, would like to share. Virginia Scott has taught college-level French for nearly twenty years. Her job description at Vanderbilt University includes directing the first- and second-year French language program, supervising the graduate teaching assistants, teaching the graduate-level FL methods class, and teaching advanced-level French grammar, composition, and conversation classes. Holly Tucker has

Introduction

taught college-level French for ten years. Her primary area of expertise is seventeenth-century French literature, and she teaches undergraduate and graduate courses in her specialization. She also regularly teaches intermediate-level French language, introduction to reading, and graduate-level research and bibliography. Because we are in a relatively small department, our conversations about teaching and learning began soon after Holly joined the Department of French and Italian at Vanderbilt University. However, it was not until Virginia directed the Vanderbilt-in-France program and Holly took over the direction of the language program and TA supervision that our collaboration began.

While directing the study abroad program, Virginia taught a course on twentieth-century literature to advanced-level students of French. Although most of her coursework in graduate school had been in literature, she had rarely taught upper-division literature courses and felt somewhat daunted by the challenge. Wondering if she would measure up to the standards set by her colleagues who regularly teach literature, she asked those colleagues for help in deciding which works to study. Once the theme of the course was decided (the image of the solitary figure in the twentieth-century novel) and the reading list was established (Beauvoir, Camus, Colette, Duras, Gide, Mauriac, Sartre), she felt the work was mostly done. The actual teaching experience, however, was not that simple. Unlike the language course, which is frequently dictated by explicit content (grammar structures, vocabulary units, short readings with guiding questions, culture capsules, current events, etc.), she found that the literature course has little in the way of a prescribed support system for the teacher. She was faced with two embarrassingly simplistic questions: What do teachers of literature actually do during a fifty-minute class period? And, by extension, what should students do? In her recent article (Scott 2001), Virginia describes the essence of her dilemma:

> The most important work I did during that semester was trying to answer questions that plague many of us in foreign language and literature departments. Do students have the necessary proficiency in the target language to read and discuss literary texts? How can the literature classroom serve as a place where students' needs for utilitarian relevancy are met? Why do language teachers and literature teachers often feel that they are in different "camps"? And, most importantly, how can the study of literature (re)claim favor (or popularity) among foreign language students (p. 539)?

Ultimately, she returned from the experience wanting to talk to a colleague in literature. How had her experience been typical? The challenges of the literature classroom were very different from those in the language classroom, and she felt a need to analyze her approach(es) critically.

Meanwhile, with a one-course load reduction, Holly faced her new responsibilities as language coordinator. Syllabi had to be revised and lecturers teaching language courses had to be integrated into the TA groups. During the semester, she met regularly with TAs to develop lesson plans, discuss teaching strategies, explore computer software applications, and write tests. One of the most challenging aspects of her work involved mentoring TAs who were teaching courses that she, herself, was not teaching. And, to add to her already full set of obligations and her research program in literature, she regularly observed classes taught by the TAs; all observations were followed by a post-observation conference and a written report for the student's file.

Although Holly had done course work in SLA theories and foreign language pedagogy while in graduate school, nothing had actually prepared her for the many time-consuming tasks involved in this job. Moreover, she was unprepared for the sense of isolation that often comes with coordinating language courses. While supportive, her colleagues did not seem to recognize the amount of "behind-the-scenes" work that went into the job, nor did they understand how much energy was required to foster the TAs' professional development. She wondered what strategies Virginia used to carry out this kind of responsibility every semester. The challenges of the language supervisor were very different from those she faced as a literature teacher and, like Virginia, she felt a need to analyze her work critically.

The conversations that followed Virginia's return to the department reinforced the mutual respect that had come from "wearing each other's hats." We began to collaborate as teachers in several ways: Holly gave presentations on teaching reading and literature in Virginia's methods class; Virginia gave presentations on empirical research design and bibliographical style in Holly's graduate course on research methods; we discussed the qualities and shortcomings of various texts, including literary texts, for the elementary- and intermediate-level courses; we talked about Holly's use of communicative, small group activities in her literature course on the age of Louis XIV, and Virginia's use of challenging literary texts in the grammar and composition class.

In addition, we collaborated in scholarly ways by reading each other's work and presenting papers jointly at professional meetings. In particular, Holly's interest in the *Standards for Foreign Language Learning* (hereafter referred to as *Standards*) brought several curricular issues into focus. In her recent article (Tucker 2000), Holly reconsiders the position of literature in the *Standards* and questions whether the new curriculum promotes the acquisition of interpretative skills necessary for literary exploration or whether it uses literature simply as a "springboard" for something else (linguistic production, historical-cultural lessons). She concludes that much of what makes a literary text "literary" is overlooked in the *Standards* and suggests that this could pose important obstacles in efforts to articulate K-12 foreign-language instruction within higher education.

In all, our conversations about curriculum and about teaching language and literature have deepened our understanding of each other's work as well as of our own work. This volume represents the culmination of our collaboration to date. Our enthusiasm when sending out the call for articles led us to imagine that our colleagues would be as motivated by the topic as we were, and this was confirmed by the many submissions that we received. Although nearly all of the submissions are from applied linguists—most likely because they are most familiar with this publication—we are convinced that the dialogue has begun. The articles in this volume confirm our sense that we are not talking about dissolving categories. We are interested instead in respecting differences while seeking unity in mission.

We have divided the articles into four categories: renewed debates; colleagues in dialogue; language, literature, and pedagogy; from scholar to teacher. While the themes of each division are different, all the articles echo the same call: literature belongs in the FL curriculum from the elementary through the advanced levels.

We begin the volume with the section called *Renewed Debates* to acknowledge that discussions about the place of literature in the FL curriculum are not new in our profession. In "The Gordian Knot: Language, Literature, and Critical Thinking," **Jean Marie Schultz** underscores the fact that these debates have a long history. She argues, however, that the renewed attention to literature in the FL curriculum represents a radical shift in approach. Rather than being another phase in an historical cycle of inclusion/exclusion of literature from the language curriculum, she believes that the era of the *Standards* ushers in the possibility of a dynamic new approach to teaching literature. Schultz provides a succinct historical review of the place of literature in the FL curriculum, moving from the "text as cultural artifact" prevalent in grammar-translation period, to the "text with plural meanings and multiple interpretive possibilities" issued by semiotics and reader-response theory. After defining her notion of critical thinking, she describes how FL literature can foster the development of these skills by destabilizing prior knowledge and restructuring experience. In order to illustrate her point, she describes a second-year program that uses short literary texts to teach students how to engage in close readings as well as to interpret larger cultural issues, thereby developing the kinds of critical thinking skills that are endorsed by the *Standards*.

The second section of this volume, *Colleagues in Dialogue*, reflects the collaborative spirit of this volume in that it includes two articles written jointly by colleagues in SLA and literature. Their dialogues provide models for developing collegial understanding about ideological issues related to literacy as well as models for curricular reform based on a revised understanding of teaching language and literature. In the first article, "Developing Literacy and Literary Competence: Challenges for Foreign language Departments," **Heidi Byrnes** and **Susanne Kord** engage in a dialogue that challenges philosophical and practical divisions both inside and outside the academy while also describing the curricular revisions at their institution that address these divisions. Byrnes crafts a powerful argument for reform based on the notion that a thorough rethinking of our understanding of the nature of language is required. Rather than continuing to support educational practices that separate language and knowledge, she proposes that pedagogical approaches must reflect an understanding of language as a humanly constructed meaning-making model of reality. This understanding of language as a social semiotic presumes an integration of language and knowledge that can shape a thoroughly new understanding of the nature of language and literacy. To illustrate how these concepts play out in the classroom setting, Kord outlines a course that achieves a symbiosis of content and language instruction—a course in which students are encouraged to evolve beyond communicative goals to achieve nuanced interpretations of literary texts and, by extension, human experiences. Byrnes and Kord weave a convincing argument for curricular reform that integrates language and content at all levels of instruction.

In the second article of this section, "Crossing the Boundaries Between Literature and Pedagogy: Perspectives on a Foreign Language Reading Course," **Joanne Burnett** and **Leah Fonder-Solano** present a methodical comparison of their beliefs and practices with regard to teaching a third-year introduction to reading and literature course. They review their different educational backgrounds—one in foreign language acquisition and the other in literary study—and describe their different approaches to teaching the same kind of course. In confronting both their similarities and differences, Burnett and Fonder-Solano demonstrate how engaging in dialogue leads to discovery, appreciation, and collegiality. Ultimately, their dialogue provides concrete evidence of the positive results of opening up one's classroom to a colleague with a different background and approach.

The third section of this volume, called *Language, Literature, and*

Pedagogy, includes different theories and approaches to teaching language and literature in an integrated way. The first article, "Rethinking Foreign Language Literature: Towards an Integration of Literature and Language at All Levels" by **Diana Frantzen**, reviews recent research and provides an introductory argument for incorporating literature in the language classroom as well as language in the literature classroom. Frantzen discusses how students can learn to analyze the ways that certain grammar structures are used in literary texts in order to understand how grammatical choices affect meaning. She also argues for developing language skills—particularly reading, speaking, and writing—through the advanced levels of study.

The next three articles in this section propose pedagogical approaches to teaching literature, from the earliest to the more advanced stages of language learning. Much research and scholarship has been devoted to teaching FL, however, comparatively little has been done to address the teaching of literature.[3] That is, the "how to" for teaching literature is often limited to learned strategies (i.e., what our own literature professors did) and to personal preferences (i.e., what works best for us individually). These articles identify pedagogical approaches to the teaching of literature that are founded on a sound understanding of how language is acquired.

In "Reading the Patterns of Literary Works: Strategies and Teaching Techniques," **Janet Swaffar** presents an approach for teaching literature to beginning students that creates readers equipped with strategies to interpret literature. She endorses top-down processing that teaches students to attend to patterns of textual messages. In her "r+1" approach, students learn to reconstruct macropatterns through a discovery process that explicitly encourages them to try out their own hypotheses. In this discovery process, which involves language exercises that are in textual context, the teacher serves as a guide and not as an expert. Swaffar emphasizes that there are no right answers, just right processes of reading. She shows how students can learn to consider objectively the space between what a text says and what a reader perceives it to say. She argues that using this approach makes novice readers aware of the possible discrepancies between their expectations and the information in a literary text, thereby integrating literary study into language acquisition.

In the next article, "Teaching Literary Texts at the Intermediate Level: A Structured Input Approach," **Stacey Katz** proposes a model for sensitizing students to the richness of literary texts based on Lee and VanPatten's (1995) structured input/ouput approach to teaching FL. She begins by discussing the difficulties and challenges of intermediate-level FL courses. In particular, she notes that the concept of "bridge courses" may be faulty as it ignores the students who do not pursue language study beyond the intermediate level. Her model, using structured input and output activities, focuses on a communicative approach to teaching literary texts that can enhance the language learning experience for students with different levels of language proficiency and with varied reasons for studying FL. Katz provides examples of her approach by presenting several input and output activities for teaching a poem and a narrative text. She concludes her article by affirming the importance of incorporating student-centered communicative strategies when teaching literary texts. In addition, she challenges the profession to develop these kinds of activities for the benefit of both novice and experienced teachers.

In the last article of this section, "A Stylistic Approach to Foreign-Language Acquisition and Literary Analysis," **William Berg** and **Laurey K. Martin-Berg** discuss an approach to teaching third-year "bridge" courses. They show that students in a course that focuses on language and culture as well as students in an introductory course on literary analysis can benefit from using a stylistic approach to literary texts to understand both form and content. According to their definition, "style" refers to the choices a speaker or writer makes from among many possible expressions. The "stylistic approach," by extension, teaches students how to look for and interpret stylistic dimensions of a text. Berg and Martin-Berg illustrate their approach by showing how students can compare two versions of the fairy tale, *Sleeping Beauty* (a seventeenth-century version and a modern version for children), in order to uncover grammatical and semantic differences between the texts. In another example, Berg and Martin-Berg demonstrate that by comparing the first sentence of Flaubert's short story, *Un Coeur simple*, with a teacher-generated reformulated first sentence, students in an introduction to literary analysis class can learn how to use semantic analyses to gain a deeper understanding of literature.

The final section of this volume, *From Scholar to Teacher*, addresses the important issue of teacher preparation. In many graduate programs, teaching assistants are required to take a methods course in which they review SLA theory and research as it applies to FL teaching. The focus of these courses is generally on developing competence in the four skills (listening, speaking, reading, and writing) at the elementary and intermediate levels. While most graduate students will go on to teach literature, they are rarely prepared to do so in an intentional fashion. In response to this problem, **Elizabeth Bernhardt**, in her article "Research into the Teaching of Literature in a Second Language: What it Says and How to Communicate It to Graduate Students," states that graduate students need to be prepared to teach language and literature. She argues that in the traditional literature class there is a focus on content rather than a focus on the students; graduate students can be taught to adapt the student-centered approaches typical of the language classroom to the literature classroom. Even more important, she challenges us to be aware that graduate students are often socialized into the "lang-lit split" in the traditional methods course and that we must help them "to see that the acts of language and literature teaching are far more alike than they are different" (p. 191). Finally, Bernhardt's article provides an excellent conclusion to this volume by proposing that the collaboration between language and literature can begin with a change in approach to training teachers of the future.

We are hopeful that this volume will help inspire further reflection on how FL programs can be viewed, not as the sum of two parts, but rather in terms of a continuum in which all levels of instruction are interconnected. Given the dearth of research models for FL literature in the classroom, the potential for innovation is great. The need is all too pressing.

Notes

1. In her recent article, "Second Language Acquisition, Applied Linguistics, and the Teaching of Foreign Languages," Claire Kramsch (2000) describes the confusion that abounds regarding the term "SLA." She concludes that the term "applied linguistics" is most apt to describe what is typically meant by "SLA" because it includes the varied understandings most often ascribed to this field of inquiry.
2. In his article "W(h)ither Literature? Reaping the Fruit of Language Study Before It's Too Late," John McCarthy addresses the problems of removing literature from language learning.
3. In her introduction to *Learning Foreign and Second Languages: Perspectives in Research and Scholarship*, Byrnes (1998) discusses this issue, arguing that FL teachers and applied linguists omitted the literature classroom from their inquiry. Implicit in her argument is the notion that the kinds of pedagogical approaches inspired by the proficiency movement were limited to language acquisition.

Works Cited

American Council on the Teaching of Foreign Languages. 1986. *ACTFL Proficiency Guidelines*. Hastings-on-Hudson, NY: American Council on the Teaching of Foreign Languages.

Byrnes, Heidi. 1998. Constructing Curricula in Collegiate Foreign Language Departments. In *Learning Foreign and Second Languages: Perspectives in Research and Scholarship*, edited by H. Byrnes, 262–95. New York: The Modern Language Association.

Kramsch, Claire. 2000. Second Language Acquisition, Applied Linguistics, and the Teaching of Foreign Languages. *Modern Language Journal* 84: 311–26.

Lee, James F., and Bill VanPatten. 1995. *Making Communicative Language Teaching Happen*. New York: McGraw-Hill.

McCarthy, John. 1998. W(h)ither Literature? Reaping the Fruit of Language Study Before It's Too Late. *ADFL Bulletin* 29: 10–17.

Savignon, Sandra J. 1983. *Communicative Competence: Theory and Classroom Practice*. Reading, MA: Addison-Wesley.

Scott, Virginia M. 2001. An Applied Linguist in the Literature Classroom. *French Review* 74: 538–49.

Standards for Foreign Language Learning: Preparing for the Twenty-First Century. 1996. Yonkers, NY: National Standards in Foreign Language Education Project.

Tucker, Holly. 2000. The Place of the Personal: The Changing Face of Foreign Language Literature in a Standards-Based Curriculum. *ADFL Bulletin*, 31: 53–58.

Renewed Debates

The Gordian Knot: Language, Literature, and Critical Thinking

Jean Marie Schultz
University of California at Berkeley

In his 1990 article entitled *Bandwagons Revisited: A Perspective on Movements in Foreign Language*, Frank Grittner discusses what he sees as the cyclical nature of SLA theory and pedagogy. In response to disappointment with the results produced by a given language teaching approach, new methodologies are developed to replace it. These at first generate a great deal of enthusiasm and are promoted as the new "key" to effective pedagogy. When results fail to meet expectations, the new methodologies fall into disfavor, soon to be replaced either by new ones, or, more often than not, by a return to former ones (p. 14).

The current renewed attention to the incorporation of literature into the foreign language curriculum might at first blush seem to fit into Grittner's cyclical paradigm of teaching methodologies. It is undeniably true that for literally generations of students, the study of literature constituted the cornerstone of language learning. As Grittner himself points out, for various grammar-translation methods, which can trace their origins back at least to ancient Greece, a significant amount of time was devoted to the translation of literature as a means by which to develop linguistic skill and to convey knowledge about the foreign culture (p. 19). However, with the rise of the oral proficiency movement and the development of communicative methodologies, which emphasize speaking skills in real-life practical situations, the focus on the literary text fell into disfavor. Not only did literature seem not to respond to the need for authentic, contemporary, primarily oral linguistic input, but the often highly stylized and sophisticated language of the literary text, which formerly had been seen as providing examples of refined linguistic structures to emulate, came to be considered far too difficult and therefore inappropriate for the language learner. In fact, the 1986 version of the ACTFL Proficiency Guidelines does not include literature in its curricular recommendations until learners' language abilities are at an "advanced" level (ACTFL Proficiency Guidelines, 1986). Now, however, seemingly in keeping with Grittner's analysis, methods emphasizing oral language skills, and particularly those excluding literature from the curriculum, are being called into question. Under pressure primarily from literature faculty, who often find their students unprepared in terms of their ability to deal with texts, language faculty are again focusing their attention on the effective use of literature in their curricula in order to provide their lower division students the linguistic and analytical skills necessary for success at upper division levels. There is a very real concern that if students do not have some experience in dealing with literature fairly early in their language studies, they might not be able to pursue more advanced work later. Regarding communicative methodologies and the need for literature in the language curriculum, Heidi Byrnes (1997) writes:

> that students need to be led in a well-motivated fashion, beginning with their first college language courses, away from the highly contingent language use in largely interactional oral communication of meanings that has in recent years become the momentum driving their language acquisition; faculty members must introduce students to the linguistically considerably more elaborated environments of written language and particularly to literary texts. In other words, language instruction must attend to the formal appropriateness, accuracy, and complexity of students' interlanguage and must assume that students' language use reflects the ways in which highly differentiated meanings are constructed in extended discourse and texts (Byrnes 1997, p. 9).

In regard to literature's place in the curriculum, SLA theory does indeed seem to be on a "literature-no literature-return to literature" cycle.

The seeming alignment of the current SLA explorations of literature's potential with Grittner's paradigm of the cyclical nature of foreign language methodologies is at best a superficial one, however. Although the effort to grapple with the most effective ways of incorporating more literature into language study may seem to be yet again another attempt to reinvent the proverbial wheel, the current motivation to do so derives from an understanding both of the literary text and of what it means to learn a foreign language that is radically different from those that drove either the grammar-translation or communicative approaches. By coming to grips with a revitalized language/literature dynamic we can work toward an understanding of what in fact is so radically different about the renewed call for more literature in the language curriculum, particularly in light of recommendations set forth in the recently published *Standards for Foreign Language Learning in the Twenty-First Century* (1999). Moreover, such an understanding will help both to further current goals for greater articulation along the language/literature continuum and to contribute to the development of strategies for the effective incorporation of literature in language programs.

Part I: Historical Overview of the Literary Text in the Language Curriculum

As mentioned above, for many generations of language learners, literature served as the cornerstone of their studies, which tended to be based on various grammar-translation approaches. The use of literature within this context had a very clear rationale. With oral and aural skills relegated to a position of significantly less importance than reading skills, the focus of instruction fell heavily on the accurate mastery of grammar and vocabulary (Brauer 2000). The literary text served very well the pedagogical goals of this approach, providing authentic material consisting of a rich vocabulary and often complex grammatical constructions. In terms of practice in translation, the literary text could prove a rigorous exercise in the accurate rendering of meaning, either in going from the original language to L2 or vice versa. The effective translation of texts was, in fact, often considered a hallmark of linguistic mastery, if not an art in itself (see Benjamin 1955). However, literature's role was not simply to supply material designed to foster the acquisition of vocabulary, sophisticated grammatical constructions in context, and texts for advanced translation exercises. The study of literature itself was, indeed, the ultimate goal of language learning (Brauer 2000, p. 5).

This conception of the primary goal of language learning had a very decisive effect on the pedagogy of the literary text. Aside from the significant attention to translation activity, discussion of texts came to play a prominent role in more advanced language classes. The discussion was very narrowly focused, however, with questions concentrating on vocabulary and grammar from a linguistic or rhetorical point of view and on comprehension checks. For example, one very well respected French textbook published in 1968, and intended as a reader for advanced students, presents excerpts from the "classics" of French literature (Maman, Helstrom, Abel, Bourque, Hull, and Politzer 1968). Prereading material situates a given text in terms of literary history and the author's biography. Postreading questions check for comprehension of plot and of the subtleties of the French language, asking, for example, what the author means by a given figure of speech. What is significant about this approach is that it posits the literary text as a fixed object of study with a correct answer to each question posed. In this view, literature is relegated to the status of a cultural artifact that mirrors both the historical period during which it was written and various aspects of the author's life. To understand a literary text in the language classroom was to understand all the words and the grammar and to be able to summarize the plot. Moreover, in many advanced literature courses prior to the sixties, when we see a significant change in sensibilities, texts were taught as products of their time and of the individual author's experiences and as essentially closed entities best handled by specialists. The lay reader's direct interpretative interaction with texts was generally discounted as invalid.

Part II: A New View of Literature; A New View of Language

Although it is not within the purview of this article to review the evolution of modern literary criticism, an overview of two intertwining trends, semiotics and reader-response theory, can help clarify for both language and literature teachers how certain shifts in the understanding of literature, particularly pertaining to the nature of the text and the reader's relationship to it, can affect the use of literature in the language classroom. Simply put, both trends in contemporary theory signaled a movement away from historical and biographical criticism, which required knowledge outside the text itself, and opened up the appreciation and interpretation of literature to all readers. It was not that literary studies became less demanding, soliciting a kind of free-for-all in terms of the subjective interpretation of texts (see Hirsch 1976). On the contrary, the tools necessary for the effective interpretation of literature, particularly at advanced levels, could be extremely rigorous, often necessitating a firm grounding in linguistic theory, which is not without relevance for foreign language study (see Culler 1975). However, there was a very definite demystification of literature that was accompanied by the tacit understanding that interpretative skills could be taught to students and that texts could be appreciated as entities in and of themselves, even if the reader had no particular knowledge of their historical context or the author's life. The text now was no longer seen only as a closed historical and sociocultural artifact for imperialistic study, where readers have the impression of understanding it because they are privy to hard facts concerning it and can situate it within its historical and biographical contexts. Rather, the emphasis in literature centered on the text as autonomous and as an open and dynamic entity of plural meanings and multiple interpretative possibilities. Moreover, individual readers, through a combination of their own intellectual skills and personal experiences, were seen as capable of generating interesting and original interpretations of texts, albeit with guidance from teachers.

This view of literary texts has radical implications for the study of literature in language courses. Perhaps one of the most provocative critics to play an early pivotal role not only in changing our concept of literature, but also in reconciling it with linguistics is the French semiologist Roland Barthes, whose distinction between "readable" and "writable" texts is crucial to understanding the dynamic interpretative role that readers play in coming to terms with literature. Barthes's theory is perhaps best outlined in the introduction to *S/Z* (1970). Here he defines the readable text as the text that is fundamentally closed to multiple interpretative possibilities. It consists of formulaic stories written according to accepted conventions, or even the "classic" whose interpretation has become fossilized within its often canonical literary category. According to this view the reader is fundamentally a passive consumer of literature (p. 10). The "writable" text, on the other hand, is the work that directly involves the reader's interpretative skills, making him or her an active producer of meaning through individualized interactions with the text (p. 10).

Barthes's view of the reader as writer derives from a radically different view of literature itself. Rather than the closed "readable" text defined by literary history and authorial biography and by its denotative elements, the "writable" text depends on its connotative potential. Barthes envisions the text as a whole that nevertheless radiates an infinite number of connotations that invite dynamic, multiple interpretative possibilities. According to Barthes, "Topologically, the connotation assures a (limited) dissemination of the meanings, spread as gold dust on the apparent surface of the text (the meaning is the gold). Semiologically, the entire connotation is a departure from a code (which will never be reconstituted), the articulation of a voice which is woven into the text (p. 16)."[1] Instead of one fixed interpretation attributed to the text, it consists of approximations of meaning that create a work that is always redefining itself with every reading and every reader (pp. 16–17). Readers themselves are thus seen as bringing to texts their own individual, complex views consisting of diverse experiences and previous readings. "The more the text is plural the less it is written before I read it ... This 'self' that approaches the text is already himself a plurality of other texts, of infinite codes ..." (p. 16).

Barthes's pioneering work on the nature of texts and readers holds numerous resonances with other semiotic and reader-response views, many of which have contributed to SLA and applied linguistic theory (see Davis 1989; Shanahan 1997). Michel Riffaterre (1979), Jurij Lotman (1973), Umberto Eco (1979), Louise Rosenblatt (1978), and

Wolfgang Iser (1978) all deal with texts as plural entities of multiple interpretative possibilities always in the process of evolving and with readers as highly complex individuals whose schemata (see Rumelhart 1981) consist of vast repositories of personal experiences that influence their interactions and interpretations of texts. For the French semiotician Michel Riffaterre (1979), for example, literary meaning can only be a product of interactions between readers and texts. "The literary phenomenon is not only the text, but also its reader and the collection of the reader's possible reactions to the text" (p. 9). Louise Rosenblatt (1978) insists that readers "must bring a whole body of cultural assumptions, practical knowledge, awareness of literary conventions, readiness to think and feel" to the text (p. 88) and that "Not the words, as uttered sounds or inked marks on a page, constitute the poem, but the structured responses to them" (p. 14).

The Russian semiotician Jurij Lotman (1973) espouses a complex theory of literature, seeing the text as a multiplanar entity of intersecting constructs of signifiers, all of which can be understood in terms of linguistic systems. For him, the text is a highly condensed form of artistic information; and in order to have access to this information, the human conscious, which Lotman defines as a linguistic conscious (p. 37), must also possess its unique "language." Once engaged in the decoding "game" of literature, readers' interactions produce very powerful effects on them, enabling them to live vicariously an infinite range of experiences, to access worlds and cultures no longer existent or that may never exist, to define themselves more fully, and ultimately to control better their reactions to unknown and even threatening experiences.

> The game possesses an enormous significance during the learning process of a type of behavior, for it allows for the modeling of the situations in which the unprepared individual would be threatened with death . . . he learns to model this situation in his consciousness, since under the guise of the game he represents an amorphous system of reality whose rules can be formulated. . . . the game gives man the possibility of a conventional victory over the invincible. . . . it helps him overcome fear when faced with identical situations and forms an indispensable structure of emotions for practical activity (p. 105).

Like Barthes, Lotman also emphasizes the unique individuality of all readers and the consequent multiplicity of interpretative responses. ". . . the artistic text . . . gives to different readers different information —to each according to his understanding—it also gives the reader a language from which he can assimilate the next portion of information during a rereading. It acts as a living organism which finds itself in an inverse relationship with the reader and which instructs him" (p. 55).

The German reader response critic Wolfgang Iser (1978), whose theories have had an important impact on the work of Janet Swaffar and other applied linguists in understanding the reading processes of foreign language learners (Davis 1989; Swaffar 1988; Swaffar, Arens, and Byrnes 1991), also reacts to the view of the literary text as a fixed totality to which one concrete, definitive interpretation can be attributed, insisting instead that "the meaning of a literary text is not a definable entity but, if anything, a dynamic happening" (p. 22), which allows us "to experience things that no longer exist and to understand things that are totally unfamiliar to us" (p. 19). For Iser, the interaction between the reader and the text is so complete and so intimate that both merge into one single situation where meaning can no longer be understood as existing outside the reader as an object to be known but rather as "an effect to be experienced" (pp. 9–10).

Although there are very real theoretical differences among each of these critics, they all intersect in their views of texts as intricate, multidimensional systems of connotative codes that are interpretatively realized according to the reader's equally complex and individual interactions. Moreover, the reader's participation in the dynamics of the text on an individual basis is important precisely for the *changes* textual interaction provoke *within* him. Iser perhaps best reconciles the subjective with the objective interpretative responses by emphasizing the restructuring of personal experience that reading engenders. He says:

> The experience of the text . . . is brought about by an interaction that cannot be designated as private or arbitrary. What is private is the reader's incorporation of the text into his own treasure-house of experience, but as far as the reader-oriented theory is concerned, this simply means that the subjectivist element of reading comes at a later stage in the process of comprehension than critics of the theory may have supposed: namely, where the aesthetic effect results in a restructuring of experience (p. 24).

The concept of change within the reader, of his or her restructured experience is crucial for understanding the dramatic impact of literature on the development of higher-level critical thinking skills, particularly as they relate to the endeavor of learning a foreign language. Daniel Shanahan (1997) makes explicit this relationship when he writes:

> Because of language's unique role as a vehicle for higher cognitive functions, which also makes it the ideal medium through which to

view some of those functions, discussion of language tends to focus on the cognitive ... it is quite clear that language has roots deep in the affective dimension of the human experience, and the nature of that relationship is critical to our understanding of the process of language learning, especially with respect to the role of literature and culture and to the way in which they can contribute to what we might call the "affective magnet," that is, the power to turn affect into an inducement rather than an obstacle to learning (p. 169).

It is precisely this relationship between language, literature, and cognition that we shall examine in Part III.

Part III: Literature and Critical Thinking

Although the topic of critical thinking skills enters frequently into general discussions of educational goals, and increasingly into deliberations concerning language pedagogy, specific definitions are difficult to pin down. John McPeck (1981) offers a number of insights into the term, defining critical thinking as "reflective skepticism," wherein norms or traditional ways of doing things are called into question. Ultimately, the conventional might be accepted, but never automatically without thought (p. 6). According to McPeck, critical thinking skills can be taught by inculcating in learners the intellectual skills, methods, and modes of reflection relevant to the discipline, by focusing on the cognitive processes set in motion in grappling with a problem and by helping learners to know what questions to ask. All of these notions will be important to keep in mind when dealing with the teaching of literature in the language classroom.

Paul Ramsden (1992) overlaps with McPeck's analysis but is more schematic in his definitions of lower- and higher-level critical thinking skills. In surface approaches to learning, students focus fundamentally on the superficial aspects of tasks. In dealing with texts, for example, learners concentrate on words and sentences without integrating them into the general context. They depend on memorized information and discrete facts but without reflecting on their relevance to deeper issues; and they fail to hone in on general theoretical principles, treating examples rather as separate units in and of themselves (p. 46). The result of surface learning for Ramsden is that it distorts material and texts by privileging the limited understanding of parts, which gives the impression of comprehension, over a complex understanding of the intricate whole. In deep learning, students are more synthetic and global in their approaches, since they draw on previous knowledge and theoretical principles, often from other disciplines, in their efforts to solve a problem or to grasp a text as a coherent totality (p. 46). The student who employs higher level critical thinking skills to problems focuses on the paradoxical and problematic and attempts to organize and reconfigure the diverse elements of content into a structured whole that casts the problem or text in a new and original light. Ramsden further subdivides his concept of levels of learning and text comprehension. On the first level are the "what" of learning, which is defined as the "meaning aspect: that which is experienced; the significance of the task," and the "how" of learning (p. 43), which is the "structural aspect: the act of experiencing, of organizing, of structuring." These are then further subdivided. The "what" of the task is divided into the "surface" aspect, where the focus is on the "signs" of the text or the word-sentence level. The "deep" aspect focuses on what the task is about or on the author's intention. The "how" category is divided into the "atomistic" aspect, which "distorts the structure, focuses on the parts, segments the whole," and the "holistic" aspect, which "preserves the structure, focuses on the whole in relation to the parts" (p. 42).

Ramsden's (1992) analysis, together with McPeck's (1981), contributes significantly to our understanding of the potential of literary texts to encourage the development of critical thinking skills. According to Ramsden's definitions, surface learning coincides with our previous discussions of grammar-translation and traditionalist approaches to literature in the language classroom, where the focus is on the word and sentence levels of language and on the accurate translation of texts from one language into another. Also within this category resides the impression of text comprehension based on access to historical and biographical facts and defined as the ability to summarize the plot.[2] Concepts of deep learning, on the other hand, articulate closely with approaches to literature that do not see the text as a closed and narrowly defined entity. The emphasis on synthesis and global approaches, drawing from other fields and previous knowledge, and on approaches to texts in terms of lived-through experience reverberates significantly with the definitions proposed by Barthes (1970), Riffaterre (1979), Lotman (1973), Rosenblatt (1978), and Iser (1978). The text, by its very nature, invites and even requires readers to engage in dynamic levels of deep learning, thereby developing their critical thinking skills. Furthermore, in that literature often calls into question the accepted, the traditional, and the prejudicial, the effective reader of texts must approach them with a measure of "reflective skepticism."

In their discussion of critical thinking, the French researchers Bourgeois and Nizet (1997) focus on concepts of change within the learner and on the restructuring of experience as key to understanding deep learning. They insist that prior knowledge is essential, because learning cannot take place in a void. However, according to their constructivist model, there is a certain inclination toward stasis on the part of the learner who tends to construct a closed articulatory loop around a specific configuration of knowledge, a loop that channels, and perhaps limits, other cognitive challenges. In order for true deep learning to take place, a conflictual element must enter the loop and destabilize the system. With this new element, preexisting structures of knowledge, which have been stored in memory, are activated and restructured to accommodate the new information and thereby to restore equilibrium within the knowledge structure. "If learning supposes . . . the preexistence of prior knowledge and the mobilization of this knowledge in the learning situation, this knowledge can only be transformed if it enters into conflict with new information or, in other words, if the confrontation between prior knowledge and the new information leads to a significant destabilization of the former" (p. 34). Because deep learning depends on change within the individual's cognitive structure, it is important that teaching methods not only introduce new information that will encourage students to question their previous assumptions, but also provide students the means to integrate this information into new knowledge structures, thereby fostering the development of critical thinking.

> [T]he only way to break a closed loop is the introduction of change. It is a question of making the subject gain access to a metatheoretical frame which will permit him to inscribe in a new perspective not only his own initial point of view but equally that of his partner, as well as their interrelationships. Such a frame constitutes therefore a very powerful fulcrum for getting out of a closed loop. This argument emphasizes therefore the importance, on the pedagogical level, of 'reframing strategies', which consist in leading learners engaged in cognitive conflicts to use these metatheoretical (or metacognitive) frames which allow them to get out of their own initial point of view (or mode of cognitive functioning) and to inscribe it in a new perspective, by articulating it in a coherent fashion with the alternative points of view (or modes of functioning) with which they are confronted (Bourgeois and Nizet 1997, p. 108).

Bourgeois's and Nizet's discussion is significant not only because it intersects with McPeck's and Ramsden's analyses of deep learning and critical thinking in terms of the emphasis on change and restructuring but also because it stresses the need for providing learners with cognitive strategies to mobilize new reflective modes in dynamic ways. Literature, and particularly foreign literature, provides an ideal vehicle for such destabilization of stagnant knowledge loops and the mobilization of alternative cognitive modes and points of view precisely because of its ability to engage readers in its "game," in Lotman's terminology, causing readers, replete with their own schemata, to merge with the text, to experience vicariously the unexpected, particularly in terms of the foreign culture, and to restructure their prior knowledge. Goals of restructured experience, expanded points of view, and significant change in cognitive frames and loops of knowledge are precisely among the objectives of contemporary theories of language learning and teaching as set forth in the *Standards*.

Part IV: Literature and the Foreign Language Standards

The *Standards* (1999) grew out of the *Goals 2000: Educate America Act* (Phillips 1999) and represent an effort to go beyond a limited four-skills view of language education, proposing in the process to change radically current teaching paradigms (Phillips 1999, p. 3). Rather than seeing language study as a fundamentally skills-oriented, self-contained enterprise that only tangentially includes culture in terms of practical competencies, the *Standards* encourage language instruction that focuses on its interdisciplinary implications and ability to influence learners in terms of developing an increased awareness of self and others and in terms of encouraging deep cognitive processing skills.

The explicit role of literature in a *Standards*-based curriculum is as yet problematic, however. Although the *Standards* include literature, its study can be seen as diluted among other language learning goals. Moreover, there is a lack of clarity as to how specifically to use literature in the language classroom and as to how sophisticated interpretations should be (Tucker 2000). Nevertheless, the philosophical and theoretical underpinnings of the *Standards* suggest a more dynamic use of literature than has been the case in the past, one that articulates well with reader-response and semiotic views of texts and with critical thinking goals. In addressing the significance of the personal in language and literature, Tucker sums up the issue in the following way:

> While the hermeneutic implications of this personal stake in literary criticism—and in literature itself—are far from uncomplicated, a better understanding of how the personal operates in both language and literary studies can serve as a productive point of departure for a critical rethinking of *how*—not *whether*—literature can be taught in a Standards-based curriculum (p. 56).

The *Standards* proposes five interlocking dimensions for language curricula: communication, culture, connections, comparisons, and communities. Although the first two may at first seem very familiar, their goals are designed to be more expansive than is the case in traditional approaches to language teaching. In terms of communication, classroom formats should veer away from the limited "I-R-E" pattern of teacher initiation—student response—teacher evaluation (Hall 1999, p.25) and instead encourage what Joan Kelly Hall (1999) calls "instructional conversations," which she defines as "... a developmentally rich pattern of teacher-student interaction whose purpose is to assist students' understanding of and ability to communicate about concepts and ideas that are central to their learning" (p. 29). This kind of expansive discourse is crucial to the student's development of complex, internalized knowledge systems, which can only come about through the negotiation of multiple and at times conflicting ideas. Within this context, Hall specifically posits literary analysis in the language classroom as particularly useful for encouraging this kind of deep processing on a communicative dimension (p. 29). Seen in this way, the communicative goal of the *Standards* resonates significantly with what we have discussed previously in terms of critical thinking skills development and a dynamic view of literature.

Literature also plays a crucial role in the teaching of culture according to the *Standards* revised definition of this language learning dimension. As indicated above, culture, which has long been considered an important aspect of instruction, has nevertheless only been superficially integrated into the language curriculum. According to Dale Lange (1999), this is partly due to the lack of consensus as to what constitutes culture, with all its implications of high and low culture, "C" and "c." Also contributing to the ambiguity of a specific pedagogy of culture is its constantly shifting nature (p. 60). Culture, according to Lange, is always in a state of transition. Given this, it is crucial to provide language students the linguistic and cognitive tools necessary to evaluate and interact effectively both with the native and foreign culture in their states of constant flux. This means not restricting the teaching of language to its formal features or to practical and often cognitively limited communicative activities. Instead, instruction must engage students in deep learning formats. Echoing Byrnes (1997), Lange notes that "The [National Standards] study suggests that **if** the emphasis in the progress indicators for these standards is only on cognitive knowledge and comprehension as well as only on affective receiving and responding, **then** students may not necessarily be able to compare, contrast, analyze, synthesize, and evaluate aspects of another culture" (p. 70). Moreover, Lange specifically mentions literature as a rich medium for encouraging the dynamic cultural interaction that fosters higher level critical thinking skills. In support of his contentions, Lange cites Michael Byram (1989) who ". . . argues that the full integration of language and culture comes . . . with the examination of literature—not only in the unique representation of the culture by the author, but also as the author represents that culture in general—as well as through experience" (p. 79). For Byram, "Artefacts of literature, music and the like are the expressions both of the idiosyncratic meanings of individuals and also of the systems of meaning which individuals share" (p. 84). In literature particularly, then, linguistics and culture meet in a form that encourages the learner to engage in deep processing activities, for by participating in the multiple textual representations of shared and individual meaning, learners must reconfigure their knowledge structures to incorporate this new information and thereby develop these structures in a more complex way (Byram 1999, p. 115).

Inevitably linked to the *Standards*'s cultural dimension is the goal area of comparison whose foundation, according to Alvino Fantini (1999), rests on the development of higher level critical thinking skills. In studying a foreign language, learners are inevitably forced to compare its underlying linguistic structure with that of their native language and in the process they become aware not only that meaning is expressed differently from language to language, but also that a seemingly stable content unit with a one-to-one correspondence between language signifiers takes on subtle connotative shades (p. 166). Benjamin (1955) eloquently addresses the richness of comparative cultural nuances in "The Task of the Translator" when he notes that the English "bread," German "brot," and French "pain" neither denote nor connote the same signified (p. 74). In comparing language differences, Fantini states that ". . . learners go beneath the surface structure to explore how language expression carries meaning, how meaning is construed in language, and how different languages construe meaning differently" (p. 166).

The effect of linguistic comparison on the individual is far more radical, however. Fantini points out that learners go through very complex translation processes in grappling with their new language. Precisely because of the connotative implications of language, these processes can at times prove both disorienting and enlightening, forcing the learner to consider language and meaning in a new way. According to Fantini:

> This process of converting perception to thought and thought to language . . . requires fragmenting holistic *experience* in accordance with

the existing *word categories* in one's own tongue, since the words of languages are discrete units, conveyed only one at a time . . . In this way, language serves as a basic classificatory system, segmenting and fragmenting our notions of the world into available word categories while also grouping and combining categories of words in other ways (p. 180).

Fantini's analysis of the fragmenting effect of language learning intersects significantly with McPeck's, Ramsden's and particularly Bourgeois's and Nizet's discussion of deep cognitive processing, where in order for learning to take place, the learner's knowledge structures must, in fact, first be shattered and then restructured to include the new disruptive information. And because the human conscious can be understood as a linguistic conscious (Lotman 1973), language learning itself indeed provokes a profound effect on cognition. For Fantini, this effect contributes significantly to the development of alternative ways of thinking, of zigzag thinking, of seeing the world anew (p. 183). Literature can play an important role in fostering alternative thinking and language learning precisely because it casts language into original forms, forms which, as we have seen with Barthes and others, multiply connotations and fragment and reconfigure words in new and creative ways.

The process of reading literature for the foreign language learner is a complex one, however. As Lotman points out, the literary text, which can be considered a secondary modeling system overlaid on the primary linguistic system of natural language (p. 36), engages the language learner in a dynamic double translation activity, first in interacting with the language itself and then with its artistic manifestations. In the literary text, therefore, the effects of language learning are multiplied because one of the goals of reading is ". . . to explain how a text becomes the carrier of a specific thought—of an idea—, how the structure of a text relates to the structure of this idea . . ." (Lotman 1973, p. 31). The skills of language learning are thus essential to analyzing literature, not only because the text exemplifies the linguistic features of grammar and vocabulary in context but also because these features create unique ways of meaning that the learner comes to understand. Moreover, as Fantini suggests, in working with literature the learner's knowledge and cultural structures also undergo profound changes, for in grappling with the text, students must also come to terms with a new culture as uniquely represented therein. A consequence of foreign language reading is, then, that learners also cast in a new light their comprehension of their own culture and their place in it.

Given our shifting understanding of the nature of literature, its effect on language acquisition, and the double effect of language and literature on cognition, it becomes clear that texts can no longer be taught in the language classroom as in the past—as an excuse for vocabulary or grammar work, or as a cultural artifact. Superficial approaches are no longer adequate to the educational challenges now set before us. However, in that literary texts are so complex, a major question presents itself, namely how to teach literature effectively within its dynamic context to students whose language skills are in process and avoid at the same time the cognitive overload that might make the reading and discussion of texts a disconcerting experience. It is the practical classroom implications of the literary text that we will explore in the next section.

Part V: The Pedagogy of the Literary Text

In "Constructing Curricula in Collegiate Foreign Language Departments," Heidi Byrnes (1998) outlines the weaknesses and dangers of poorly articulated college language/literature programs and the flaws of deferring pedagogical responsibility for learner outcomes to textbook choice (p. 271). Having encountered over fifteen years ago precisely the problems Byrnes recently delineates, the intermediate French program at the University of California at Berkeley was radically revised in 1986 in several ways. First, other than a reference grammar, textbooks were eliminated and replaced with course readers containing pedagogical materials specifically designed to target the language, critical thinking, and writing goals necessary for students' success in upper division courses at Berkeley. Second, the curriculum was based on a language-through-literature approach designed to provide students experience in dealing with texts such as they would be asked to do in upper-division courses. Third, intermediate program text selection was made both with the students' level of French and with the third-year advanced reading and composition course curriculum in mind. Fourth, a rigorous composition component was designed to target students' writing skills (see Schultz 1999, 1995, 1994, 1991a, 1991b). The revised program produced immediate positive results in terms of student language skills, critical thinking skills within a literary context, and in terms of smooth lower to upper-division program articulation. Faculty teaching the third-year course, who have been interviewed concerning student preparedness every semester since the program's inception in 1986, have consistently expressed satisfaction with their students' abilities to handle texts, discuss them, and write about them in French. The following discussion of the pedagogy of the literary text within the intermediate-level foreign language curriculum can thus be couched within the context of a program that has afforded much experimentation in the effective incorporation of literature.

The decision to use literature as the primary curricular component coupled with the elimination of any intermediate program textbook has radical implications for language pedagogy, particularly given that the majority of the multisectioned intermediate courses at Berkeley are taught by graduate student instructors, most of whom are working on doctorates in literature but who have limited training in language acquisition theory as well as limited experience in teaching. All sections must thus be parallel in terms of curriculum and yet take into account the differences of both instructors and students as individuals who will respond and interact uniquely to texts. Moreover, given the preceding discussion concerning the complex and multidimensional nature of the literary text, flexible and dynamic approaches are the only ones appropriate to "writerly" texts and at the same time capable of accommodating language/literature, departmental, teacher, and student goals. Pedagogical seminars at each course level are essential to the viability of an individually tailored program; and consequently, all instructors in the program are required to take the appropriate seminar for the French course they currently teach.

Both semesters of the intermediate French program are fundamentally organized around the reading of one short prose text per week, either a short story or a play, for the first seven weeks of the fifteen week semester. For the last six weeks, students read longer works, but over a two-week period for each text. Mid-semester, there is a two or three week poetry unit (see Schultz 1996). Classes meet five days per week. At each level, one day per week is devoted to grammar review, among other language activities, such as oral reports. The approach to literature can be conceived in terms of three basic principles with three substeps:

1. An introductory experiential activity designed to mobilize students' personal schemata and thereby increase receptivity to textual issues.
   a. A closing creative activity.
2. Training in techniques of close readings designed to target language issues not only as they pertain to form but more importantly as they pertain to meaning.
   a. Close reading group discussion activities.

3. General discussion of larger textual issues of theme, motif, setting, characterization, symbolization, and intentionality, etc.
   a. Group discussion of individual paper topics.

Because the approach is based on principles rather than on specific techniques, it is extremely flexible from multiple points of view. Various iterations of it can be used with virtually any text. Teachers can adhere to the principles and yet incorporate their own interpretations into class discussion, thus increasing their personal commitment to their teaching. They can also tailor general discussion to student interactions with the text, according more time as necessary to a topic that may particularly have sparked student interest. In close readings, students focus on language learning basics, vocabulary, and grammar, but go beyond traditional surface-level approaches by attending to how these elements create complex meaning. Moreover, they acquire both the linguistic and interpretive skills necessary to go on in French. In fact, the skills that students develop in the process of learning a new language, of focusing on the intricate relationship between form and meaning, of paying attention to linguistic detail and reconstituting meaning, contribute to the development of their interpretive reading skills. Finally, students are encouraged to enter into a phase of "reflective skepticism" in regard to their own culture and the target culture, and in the process they begin to define themselves differently.

In discussing the above six principles used in the intermediate French program at Berkeley, I will illustrate their application with activities designed to accompany Émile Zola's short story "The Attack on the Mill" (Baker and Cauvin 1995, pp. 107–30), which students in French 3 (first semester of the intermediate program) read during the last two weeks of the semester. The story, which centers on the tragic love story between the miller's daughter, Françoise, and her Belgian neighbor Dominique, who is ultimately killed, is set against the backdrop of the Franco-Prussian war.

The Value of Experiential Approaches

In her essay addressing the importance of an interdisciplinary approach to language teaching in a *Standards*-guided curriculum, Miriam Met supports her contention with research showing that learners do not construct meaning in a void, but rather use prior knowledge to access new knowledge (Met 1999, p. 138). The implications of this point, which intersects with work done by Bourgeois and Nizet (1997) and in schema theory (Rumelhart 1981; Swaffar 1988), is significant for language students. In their work with literature, students need to be able to relate initially to texts on their own terms, drawing on their personal schemata as a point of departure for more objective interpretation. For language learners, an initial personal reaction is particularly important precisely because they do not necessarily have ready access to the cultural underpinnings of the text. Grappling with the text from their own perspective first avoids the short-circuiting of critical reflection that can occur if, for instance, texts are first presented solely as a product of the author's life and times.

Each text used in the intermediate French program is thus first introduced using an experiential activity designed to mobilize students' personal schemata and to encourage their oral communicative skills. It is far less cognitively taxing for language learners to discuss personal experiences than to enter into analytical discussions where they must support and defend their interpretations (ACTFL 1986). These activities can assume many forms based on the dynamics of the specific literary text under discussion. Perhaps the most common activity used in the program is the "quick-write" in which students are given five minutes in class to write on a prompt related thematically to the text. If a text deals with childhood, students will be asked to write on an event from their past. For a fantastic text used in the program, students are asked to write about a supernatural experience they have had or that someone they know has had (see Schultz 1995). In the poetry segments, students routinely write on thematic prompts connected to the poem they will be discussing (see Schultz 1996). With all of these exercises, students are asked to share their writing with a group of three peers, thus encouraging their oral production as well as their written competence. After about ten minutes of discussion, each group selects one example that is shared with the entire class. At this point, the instructor works with the material presented, writes main ideas on the board, and tries to make connections with some of the textual issues students will encounter in their reading. This opening activity thus lays the groundwork for greater receptivity and ultimately better reading comprehension.

For Zola's text, the setting plays a significant role in highlighting the disastrous consequences of war. As the battle progresses, features of the countryside, as well as the mill and an old elm tree, are systematically destroyed. The story opens with a lengthy and rich description of the town and its surroundings, a description crucial to the narrative effect, but one replete with unfamiliar vocabulary that can prove linguistically challenging to intermediate-level students. Because Zola's text depends on the ability to visualize the scene, the introductory experiential activity is organized around a collaborative drawing exercise where students work in groups of three and mine the text for specific detail in order to come up with a sketch of what the setting might look like. Students, thus, must talk together in French and reach an agreement as to what visual information to include. Moreover, they must read very carefully for detail and accuracy. At the end of the designated time, about fifteen minutes, students share their sketches with the entire class. At this point, their work is evaluated for accuracy both by other classmates and by the teacher. This activity allows the instructor to check for basic comprehension and to address any surface-level vocabulary or grammar issues. More importantly, however, students have already begun the preliminary process of text analysis, using a sense, visualization, that is often neglected in language curricula (Schwerdtfeger 1994).

The closing experiential activity for the "The Attack on the Mill" takes its cue from the introductory exercise. In the course of discussion, instructors help students to take stock of Zola's visual techniques, which operate much like a movie camera, encompassing wide panoramas or zooming in to focus on small details. Moreover, the story is very action-packed and suspenseful, with Françoise scaling a wall at one point to save Dominique's life and later frantically searching the woods in which he is hiding in order to save her father, who will be shot in Dominique's place unless he returns. Students then are asked in their closing activity to assume the role of a movie director and to work again in groups of three to discuss details of how they would write the screen play for one of the five chapters in Zola's story. They must cast the various roles, go over the cinematographic techniques they would use for the filming, and discuss any other aspects necessary for their production. The fact that the activity taps into cinema, which is widely appreciated by American college students, together with its somewhat lighthearted orientation make this an appealing and creative exercise with which to close the text, placing students very much in the "writerly" role.

Close Reading Techniques

The experiential activities are very valuable for their personal appeal; they have a mobilizing effect on individual schemata and generate discussion crucial for oral skills development. However, because they tend to originate from a subjective base, they do not encourage deep learning to the extent that other textual approaches can (Bereiter & Scardamalia 1987). Moreover, in overlaying personal schemata on texts, students do run the risk of misreading, of relying too much on "'mnemonic irrelevances' or failure to follow texts closely because contingent memories and associations get in the way" (Durant 1996, p. 85; see also Rumelhart 1981). In order to guard against misreading and to encourage critical thinking, the most rigorous and fundamental of the pedagogical principles used in the intermediate French program involves close readings. This technique, which is key to sophisticated literary analysis, plays an essential role in bridging the gap between language and literary studies; for in focusing on discrete components of carefully selected passages, students analyze the vocabulary for both its denotative and connotative meanings and grammatical structures, not only as exemplars of linguistic rules but also as vehicles of unique significance.

For virtually every text in the program, instructors lead their students in a close reading of the introduction, which invariably establishes many of the themes and motifs in a short story. Moreover, in analyzing the introduction with the teacher, students from the outset feel grounded in their reading and better able to handle the rest of the text on their own. Because the drawing activity focuses on the first three paragraphs of Zola's text, students begin their teacher-guided close reading in the fourth paragraph. Here Zola presents a personified portrait of the mill built on paradoxes which highlight its crucial role in the story.

> Et c'était là que le moulin du père Merlier égayait de son tic-tac un coin de verdures folles. La bâtisse, faite de plâtre et de planches, semblait vieille comme le monde. Elle trempait à moitié dans la Morelle, qui arrondit à cet endroit un clair bassin. Une écluse était ménagée, la chute tombait de quelques mètres sur la roue du moulin, qui craquait en tournant, avec la toux asthmatique d'une fidèle servante vieillie dans la maison. Quand on conseillait au père Merlier de la changer, il hochait la tête en disant qu'une jeune roue serait paresseuse et ne connaîtrait pas si bien le travail; et il raccommodait l'ancienne avec tout ce qui lui tombait sous la main, des douves de tonneau, des ferrures rouillées, du zinc, du plomb. La roue en paraissait plus gaie, avec son profil devenu étrange, toute empanachée d'herbes et de mousses. Lorsque l'eau la battait de son flot d'argent, elle se couvrait de perles, on voyait passer son étrange carcasse sous une parure éclatante de colliers de nacre (Baker and Cauvin 1995, p. 108).[3]

Instructors proceed sentence by sentence though the passage asking students to respond to and to interpret what Zola might mean by specific lexical choices. In sentence one, what image is evoked in the combined vocabulary of "cheered up," "tick-tock," and "crazy vegetation"? In sentences two and three, what is the effect of the alliteration in "plâtre" and "planches" [plaster and boards] and of the hyperbolic

The Gordian Knot: Language, Literature, and Critical Thinking 23

metaphor that the mill is "as old as the world"? In the fourth sentence, why does Zola compare the cracking sound of the turning mill wheel to "the asthmatic cough of a faithful, old house servant"? In sentence five, what is the force of the personification designating a new wheel as lazy and not knowing the work as well? To what semantic category does the brick-a-brack the miller uses to patch the old wheel belong? Why is this important to the visual image created? In sentence six, why is the word "empanaché" "decked out with plumes" particularly appropriate? In the last sentence, what vocabulary is associated with precious jewelry? What metaphorical image underlies this vocabulary? How is the image paradoxical? How does the word "carcass" further differentiate the image? Finally, what past tense form predominates in the passage and why? These are just some of the questions instructors can ask their students as they work through this passage. Students' preliminary interpretations will eventually become all the more significant within the context of the rest of the story when the eventual battle will lay waste this idyllic scene. Zola's vocabulary evoking illness and death thus functions early on as a foreshadowing of tragic future events. In working through the text in this way, fragmenting it and reconstituting it, students thus learn important interpretative literary principles at the same time that they grapple with the elements of language.

In addition to the systematic analysis of introductions, principles of close readings can be incorporated intermittently throughout each literary unit to focus on significant passages that the instructor feels are important to emphasize. A second iteration of the close reading technique is moved to a small group format. For each text, the course reader contains sets of group discussion exercises pertaining to selected passages, each of which is divided into sections or movements and for which there is a set of detailed questions such as presented above. According to this format, students work together in small groups, asking and answering the questions in their assigned section. At the end of the designated time, they are asked to make a presentation to the entire class, always emphasizing the significance of their observations. Rather than simply repeat back their answers to the questions, however, the designated speaker for each group must, with the help of his or her peers, synthesize the collective findings, presenting an analytical and interpretative summary of them. The rest of the class is asked to take notes and to comment after each minipresentation. Students thus must work on their critical thinking skills at the same time that they develop their oral skills. The exercise is well structured to meet the cognitive demands of the class, moving from simpler tasks of answering questions with the help of a small group of peers to more complex ones of synthesizing and theorizing. An additional benefit of the group discussion exercises is that in terms of classroom management, they are extremely economical, allowing instructors to cover significant portions of texts in a relatively short time period.

Discussion of Larger Textual Issues in the Language Classroom

Instructors teaching in the intermediate French program report that student response to close reading techniques, which are new to American students, is very positive. However, inasmuch as close reading is intense and detail-oriented, when dealing with entire texts, it is neither practical nor does it maintain student interest over a prolonged period. American students simply are more experienced from previous English literature classes in dealing with larger textual issues and therefore welcome such discussion in the foreign language classroom. Moreover, broader-based textual discussion provides students with different types of analytical tools. Rather than the fine, detailed analysis of close readings, broader-based discussion encourages students to think synthetically, to generalize from textual evidence, to theorize, and to engage in Hall's (1999) "instructional conversations."

Because all texts are unique, general discussion of themes, characterization, setting, symbols, motifs, and the like is the most difficult area to deal with in terms of a systematic pedagogy common to all intermediate program sections. An important issue in one text simply doesn't exist in another; a rigid template for the pedagogy of the literary text would therefore be impossible to overlay successfully on every work. Moreover, even if such a template could be developed, it would violate the very underpinnings of the literary text, essentially turning a "writable" into a "readable" work.

In terms of Zola's text, characterization has proven a valuable starting point for general discussion in part because the author constructs the text around bipolar oppositions. The miller is described, for example, as being "happy on the inside but serious on the outside." In contrast, his daughter is "serious on the inside but cheerful on the outside." The initial presentation of Dominique is of the stereotypical handsome, lazy seducer. The reader soon discovers, however, that once engaged to Françoise, Dominique is a devoted companion and a hard worker. Perhaps the most telling opposition centers on the French captain and the Prussian officer. Here Zola both plays with national stereotypes, the French captain as dashing soldier and the Prussian as cold and rigid commander, and subverts those very stereotypes. The French captain becomes a buffoon by adhering rigidly to his orders to hold the mill until six o'clock sharp, whereas he should retreat much sooner to save his men. The Prussian officer is only too willing to violate his orders to accomplish his military purposes. In working with the characterizations in this particular text, then, students are constantly put in the position of McPeck's (1981) reflective skeptic, as they analyze characters in terms of their oppositions and eventually generate theories as to Zola's purpose in dismantling stereotypes, particularly within the context of a short story highly critical of armed conflict. Discussion of the text on this basis inevitably takes students into other areas. Connections can be made with the contemporary situation in other countries where conflict drawn along stereotyped ethnic or religious lines is a fact of life. Cultural stereotypes in general are an equally fruitful area for discussion. Students thus hone their analytical skills in terms of literature, as well as reflect on their own prejudices and stereotypes with regard to other cultures. In short, they are encouraged to integrate potentially disruptive material into their knowledge loops and, therefore, to restructure their experience.

Characterization is, of course, only one aspect of any text. In "The Attack on the Mill," the highly personified setting plays an important role. In addition to the visual, Zola also uses various sounds to highlight events. There is a motif of fate with which Zola, in fatalistic fashion, seems to indicate that characters are ultimately powerless to alter their destiny. The language itself, which is often highly metaphorical, provides an additional area of investigation. This list is not exhaustive, nor do each of these elements need to be covered during the two weeks that students work on Zola's text. The point is that instructors have a whole series of topics at their disposal. In approaching any one area, it is useful to start in summary fashion with the "what" of the topic. However, discussion cannot stay on this level of lower order questions (Long 1986, p. 48), which is characteristic of traditional approaches to texts in language classrooms where comprehension checks tend to dominate. As Ramsden's (1992) work demonstrates, instructors must quickly veer off the "what" to deal with the "how" and "why" of the text. How does Zola use sound imagery or the setting and why does he use it in this way? Can we go back into the text, particularly to the beginning, and see how symbols of fate are working? Why does Zola seem to be so pessimistic as to the positive effects of human effort? Responses to this last question can lead to a brief discussion of the Naturalist movement in France, which provides students additional, historical and cultural information, but only after they have dealt with significant portions of the text. Instead of filtering Zola's text through a literary category, as students are tempted to do if texts are presented as products of a specific literary movement, they have first interacted with the text on their own terms and thus now see the historical material as illuminating, but not the *raison d'être* of the text and the only explanation of it.

Additional thematic issues can be dealt with effectively in the final pedagogical principle outlined above. For each text read in the intermediate French program, students are asked to write a short analytical paper such as they would write in an English class and as will be expected of them in their upper division French literature and culture courses. Because of the problematic nature of argumentative writing (see Schultz 1991b), specific composition lessons are integrated into the curriculum. One way to provide students with preliminary direction for their eventual essays as well as deal with multiple textual aspects in an efficient manner is through discussion of the essay topics in a small group format. The day before the activity, students are asked to select the essay topic that interests them most and to think about how they would organize their paper. The next day, instructors group students according to the topic they have selected and ask them to talk about it for about fifteen minutes. At the end of the time, students share the highlights of their discussion with the entire class, again generating further debate about the issues raised.

The six principles outlined above are not presented in sequential fashion but rather are integrated in alternating fashion in order to vary the linguistic and cognitive skills targeted. The initial work on a text always begins with the low stress introductory experiential activity and is followed by the more intense close reading of the introduction. The movement is therefore from personal to analytical. Instructors then move to thematic discussion, incorporating additional close readings, often in the form of the group discussion exercises, as warranted. Students thus alternate between detailed, fragmenting work and synthesizing, theoretical efforts. Towards the end of the unit, attention turns to the paper topic discussion in small group fashion. The final wrap-up of the text involves again a more experientially oriented activity that addresses students' personal creativity in the foreign language, thus making them also, in a sense, producers of imaginative and artistic "texts."

Conclusion

I began this paper by referring to Grittner's (1990) work on recurrent trends in foreign language pedagogy precisely because the current interest in literature seems at first blush to hark back to a very traditionalist stance. Indeed, given that there is a large body of published material on the incorporation of literature in the language classroom (Carter and McRae 1996; Collie and Slater 1987; Lazar 1993; Simpson

1997), in addition to the existence of language textbooks that include selections from literature, the very logic behind a renewed discussion of the subject might be put into question. It may well be claimed that literature has always had some role in the language curriculum. However, in tracing the shifting view of literature from historical and cultural artifact to dynamic, plural text that comes into being via interactions with individual readers, and in outlining the potential effect literature can have on cognitive processing skills and on personal and cultural understanding, it becomes apparent that the current interest in literature derives from a very different spirit. As the *Standards* demonstrate, foreign language learning can no longer be seen as an isolated field. Instead, it is an endeavor with significant implications, complementing and adding to the dynamism of other disciplines and increasing our understanding of our own and other cultures on profound levels. In the process of working with a foreign language and its literature, moreover, students learn more about themselves and their personal identity. At the same time, as Fantini in particular suggests, they also develop their critical thinking abilities. For the cognitive strategies that come into play in the process of learning a foreign language—the fragmenting and reconstituting, the synthesizing and generalizing—are precisely the strategies that come into play in the literary text. The difference resides within the movement from micro to macrolevels, where in literature, readers extend their work with language on multiple dimensions, factoring themselves into texts through identification with and differentiation from characters, through plot participation, and through the experience of new or dormant emotions. In focusing on literature in the language classroom, then, we are not returning once again to the same old thing reconfigured in a new trend. Language curricula already have significant experience approaching texts in a "readerly" fashion. Now in order to respond to new developments on multiple educational planes, literature in the language curriculum must be approached from a "writerly" stance.

Notes

1. All translations from French are my own.
2. Although generally considered a lower order activity, plot summary is not necessarily so. See Nash 1986, p. 70.
3. And it was there that father Merlier's mill cheered up a corner of crazy vegetation with its tick-tock. The building, made of plaster and planks, seemed as old as the world. It half soaked in the Morelle, which formed a clear round basin in this place. A lock was fitted into the millstream, the waterfall fell from several meters onto the wheel of the mill, which cracked while

turning, with the asthmatic cough of a faithful servant who had grown old in the household. When people advised father Merlier to change it, he shook his head saying that a young wheel would be lazier and wouldn't know the work as well; and he patched the old one with everything that fell into his hands, with barrel staves, rusted iron fittings, zinc, lead. Because of this, the wheel seemed more gay, with its strange profile, all decked out with plumes of weeds and mosses. When the water would hit it with its stream of silver, it would be covered with pearls; people would see its strange carcass pass through a brilliant set of mother-of-pearl necklaces.

Works Cited

American Council on the Teaching of Foreign Languages. 1986. *ACTFL Proficiency Guidelines*. Hastings-on-Hudson: ACTFL.

Baker, Mary, and Pierre Cauvin. 1995. *Panaché littéraire*. Boston: Heinle & Heinle.

Barthes, Roland. 1970. *S/Z*. Paris: Seuil.

Benjamin, Walter. 1955. The Task of the Translator. In *Illuminations*, translated by Harry Zohn, 69–82. New York: Schocken Books.

Bereiter, C., and M. Scardamalia. 1987. *The Psychology of Written Composition*. Hillsdale, NJ: L. Erlbaum.

Bourgeois, Etienne, and Jean Nizet. 1997. *Apprentissage et Formation des Adultes*. Paris: Presses Universitaires de France.

Brauer, Gerd. 2000. *Writing Across Languages*. Stamford, CT: Ablex Publishing Corporation.

Byram, Michael. 1989. *Cultural Studies in Foreign Language Education*. Philadelphia, PA: Multilingual Matters Ltd.

Byrnes, Heidi. 1997. Governing Language Departments: Is Form Function? *ADFL Bulletin* 29: 7–12.

———. 1998. Constructing Curricula in Collegiate Foreign Language Departments. In *Learning Foreign and Second Languages*, edited by Heidi Byrnes, 262–95. New York: Modern Language Association of America.

Carter, Ronald, and John McRae. 1996. *Language, Literature & the Learner*. London: Addison Wesley Longman.

Collie, Joanne, and Stephen Slater. 1987. *Literature in the Language Classrooom*. Cambridge: Cambridge University Press.

Culler, Jonathan. 1975. *Structuralist Poetics*. Ithaca, NY: Cornell University Press.

Davis, James N. 1989. The Act of Reading in Foreign Language: Pedagogical Implications of Iser's Reader-Response Theory. *Modern Language Journal* 73: 420–28.

Durant, Alan. 1996. Designing Groupwork Activities: A Case Study. In *Language, Literature & The Learner: Creative Classroom Practice*, edited by Ronald Carter and John McRae, 65–88. London: Addison Wesley Longman.

Eco, Umberto. 1979. *The Role of the Reader*. Bloomington, IL: Indiana University Press.

Fantini, Alvino E. 1999. Comparisons: Towards the Development of Intercultural Competence. In *Foreign Language Standards: Linking Research, Theories, and Practices*, edited by June K. Phillips, 165–218. Lincolnwood, IL: National Textbook Company.

Grittner, Frank M. 1990. Bandwagons Revisited: A Perspective on Movements in Foreign Language. In *New Perspectives and New Directions in Foreign Language Education*, edited by Diane W. Birckbichler, 9–41. Urbana, IL: NCTE.

Hall, Joan Kelly. 1999. The Communication Standards. In *Foreign Language Standards: Linking Research, Theories, and Practices*, edited by June K. Phillips, 15–56. Lincolnwood, IL: National Textbook Company.

Hirsch, E.D. 1976. *Validity in Interpretation*. New Haven, CT: Yale University Press.

Iser, Wolfgang. 1978. *The Act of Reading*. Baltimore, MD: The Johns Hopkins University Press.

Lange, Dale L., 1999. Planning for and Using the New National Culture Standards. In *Foreign Language Standards: Linking Research, Theories, and Practices*, edited by June K. Phillips, 57–136. Lincolnwood, IL: National Textbook Company.

Lazar, Gillian. 1993. *Literature Through Language Teaching*. Cambridge: Cambridge University Press.

Long, Michael. 1986. A Feeling for Language: The Multiple Values of Teaching Literature. In *Literature and Language Teaching*, edited by C.J. Brumfit and R. A. Carter, 42–59. Oxford: Oxford University Press.

Lotman, Iouri. 1973. *La Structure du texte artistique*. Paris: Gallimard.

Maman, André, Jo Helstrom, Adeline Abel, Jane Bourque, Alexander Hull, and Robert Politzer. 1968. *Les Grandes heures littéraires*. New York: McGraw-Hill Book Company.

McPeck, John E. 1981. *Critical Thinking and Education*. New York: St. Martin's Press.

Met, Myriam. 1999. Making Connections. In *Foreign Language Standards: Linking Research, Theories, and Practices*, edited by June K. Phillips, 137–64. Lincolnwood, IL: National Textbook Company.

Nash, Walter. 1986. The Possibilities of Paraphrase in the Teaching of Literary Idiom. In *Literature and Language Teaching*, edited by C. J. Brumfit and R. A. Carter, 70–88. Oxford: Oxford University Press.

National Standards in Foreign Language Education Project. 1999. *Standards for Foreign Language Learning: Preparing for the the Twenty-First Century*. Lawrence, KS: Allen Press, Inc.

Phillips, June K. 1999. Introduction: Standards for World Languages—On a Firm Foundation. In *Foreign Language Standards: Linking Research, Theories, and Practices*, edited by June K. Phillips, 1–14. Lincolnwood, IL: National Textbook Company.

Ramsden, Paul. 1992. *Learning to Teach in Higher Education*. London: Routledge.

Riffaterre, Michel. 1979. *La Production du texte*. Paris: Seuil.

Rosenblatt, Louise M. 1978. *The Reader, the Text, the Poem*. Carbondale, IL: Southern Illinois University Press.

Rumelhart, David E. 1981. Schemata: The Building Blocks of Cognition. In *Comprehension and Teaching: Research Views*, edited by John T. Guthrie, 3–26. Newark, DE: International Reading Association.

Schultz, Jean Marie. 1991a. Mapping and Cognitive Development in the Teaching of Foreign Language Writing. *The French Review* 64: 978–88.

———. 1991b. Writing Mode in the Articulation of Language and Literature Classes: Theory and Practice. *Modern Language Journal* 75: 411–17.

———. 1994. Stylistic Reformulation: Theoretical Premises and Practical Applications. *Modern Language Journal* 78: 169–78.

———. 1995. Making the Transition from Language to Literature. In *The Foreign Language Classroom: Bridging Theory and Practice*, edited by Margaret Austin Haggstrom, Leslie Zarker Morgan, Joseph A. Wieczorek, 3–20. New York, NY: Garland Publishing.

———. 1996. The Uses of Poetry in the Foreign Language Curriculum. *The French Review* 69: 920–32.

———. 1999. Computers and Collaborative Writing in the Foreign Language Curriculum. In *Networked-Based Language Teaching: Concepts and Practice*, edited by Richard Kern and Mark Warschauer, 121–50. Cambridge: Cambridge University Press.

Schwerdtfeger, Inge. 1994. The Learner's Gaze. Paper presented at the Berkeley Language Center Conference, University of California, Berkeley, CA.

Shanahan, Daniel. 1997. Articulating the Relationship Between Language, Literature, and Culture: Toward a New Agenda for Foreign Language Teaching and Research. *Modern Language Journal* 81: 164–74.

Simpson, Paul. 1997. *Language Through Literature*. London: Routledge.

Swaffar, Janet. 1988. Readers, Texts, and Second Languages: The Interactive Processes. *Modern Language Journal* 72: 123–49.

Swaffar, Janet, Katherine M. Arens, and Heidi Byrnes. 1991. *Reading for Meaning: An Integrated Approach to Language Learning*. Englewood Cliffs, NJ: Prentice Hall.

Tucker, Holly. 2000. The Place of the Personal: The Changing Face of Foreign Language Literature in a Standards-Based Curriculum. *ADFL Bulletin* 31: 53–58.

Zola, Émile. 1995. L'Attaque du moulin. In *Panaché littéraire*, 3d edition, edited by Mary J. Baker and Jean-Pierre Cauvin, 107–30. Boston, MA: Heinle & Heinle.

Colleagues in Dialogue

Developing Literacy and Literary Competence: Challenges for Foreign Language Departments

Heidi Byrnes and Susanne Kord
Georgetown University

Locating Our Dialogue

Reflecting the collaborative spirit of the volume, this contribution is co-written by two colleagues. Our remarks continue in a public forum many conversations that have occurred between us in conjunction with a three-year effort in which all teachers of our home department, the faculty and graduate students of the German Department at Georgetown University, revised the entire undergraduate program. Entitled "Developing Multiple Literacies," the project constitutes an ambitious effort to link language acquisition and the development of literacy in a second language within a comprehensively conceived curricular framework that overcomes the split between language courses and content courses (www.georgetown.edu/departments/german/curriculum/curriculum.html); Byrnes 1999 and 2000). Naturally, the teaching of literature became part of this endeavor to re-envision the work of a collegiate foreign language (FL) department.

Our contribution is not a joint article in the customary sense but, with the exception of this introduction and concluding comments, takes the form of a dialogue of alternating voices that retains our respective interests and different knowledge bases and insights. Susanne Kord, as the literature professor, candidly investigates the enabling and disabling assumptions that characterize existing practices in the teaching of literature, particularly those in upper-level classes taught by literature professors. On that basis she proposes options for linking language learning and literature teaching within the context of an upper-level literature course, a German comedy course. The result can be characterized as a language-based pedagogy of literature, or content in general, a central feature of the restructured curriculum in our department. In turn, Heidi Byrnes investigates what insights adult instructed language acquisition (SLA) research has contributed that might translate into pedagogies for enabling students to engage substantively with literary texts. She concludes that surprisingly little attention has been devoted to this concern given its central role for collegiate FL departments. However, particularly perceptive work can be found within L1 literacy studies and a literacy-oriented pedagogy, especially in the multicultural context of Australian education that supports students' work with texts, oral and written, by using genre as a construct for organizing both curricula and pedagogy (Freedman and Medway 1994a, 1994b; Gee 1998; Halliday 1993; Jones, Gollin, Drury, and Economou 1989; Martin 1985, 1999). Its radical difference lies not merely in its focus on genre as contrasted with sentence-based grammar but in its underlying conceptualization of the relationship of language and knowledge and, by extension, its relationship of language acquisition and the learners' existing L1-based knowledge and their emerging multiple literacies. Such a reconsidered foundation both necessitates and facilitates the creation of an integrated curriculum for collegiate FL programs and necessitates and facilitates different pedagogical approaches for all faculty members in all courses, literature-oriented or not. In our experience it is an intellectual reorientation that is most appropriate for FL education in collegiate cultural and literary studies departments.

Never the Twain Shall Meet: Language, Literature, and Other Great Divides (Kord)[1]

Teachers of literature, particularly those housed in collegiate FL departments, find themselves facing several Great Divides when doing that for which they are supposedly best qualified, teaching literature. Those rifts can be defined by the polar opposites literature versus language, content versus form, literary scholarship versus the teaching of literature. The Great Divide manifests itself institutionally in the traditional rift in most FL departments between "language instructors" versus "literature professors" and the reward structure that privileges the scholarly over the curricular and the pedagogical; pedagogically in the sense that these structures inevitably shape curricula as well as in-class assumptions and behaviors. In scholarship, the literature-language-divide has found frequent expression in fearful comments by literature professionals on the increasingly uncertain status of literature in upper-level FL instruction, accompanied by worries that literature is being replaced with classes that target "communicative" competencies; in rather desperate attempts to reintroduce literature into this curriculum which is perceived as increasingly "foreign" to the FL literary scholar; and in a growing body of scholarship on the teaching of literature in the FL classroom that focuses more on courses than curricula and largely ignores both available scholarship in language acquisition and in literature.

It should come as no surprise, then, that models that attend to both language acquisition and acquisition of literary competence, however defined, are comparatively rare (cf., Haggstrom 1992; Holten 1997; Knutson 1993; Lazar 1993; Moeller and Kunczinam 1993; Murti 1996: Schultz 1996). On the one hand, scholarship on the teaching of literature frequently engages in pursuits that would be considered outdated and methodologically questionable in literary scholarship, concentrating, as it often does, on questions regarding plot and author biography. On the other hand, language acquisition in the literature classroom is not targeted, but implicit: in courses whose content focus is literature (as opposed to courses that target a specific second language (L2) acquisition goal, such as writing, and merely use literature to attain that goal), L2 acquisition is either ignored entirely or indirectly targeted by comprehensible input and unstructured "discussion."

Both approaches essentially perceive student difficulties in approaching the text as cognitive, not linguistic, and both are at grave odds with the conclusions drawn in parts of the SLA literature as to how L2 students read (Bernhardt 1991). If these depictions by teachers of literature are to be taken as accurate accounts for what goes on in their classrooms, we would have to conclude that nobody ever actually *teaches*. The implication is that students' language level automatically improves in a parallel curve to the increasing sophistication of the content or topics of discussion: students are "encouraged" to develop L2 "skills" in connection with their reading (Dykstra-Pruim 1998, p. 106); they "pick up" the language without the instructor "anticipating" this (Blickle 1998, p. 112); teachers are merely "setting the conditions" for student learning (Brumfit 1985, p. 114). Invariably, the assumption—carried over from the "mastery" model of L2 acquisition—is that students must already have a high level of L2 competence before they even can begin to read, an assumption that already seems to indicate that further explicit L2 instruction and learning will not take place in the literature classroom.

What little does take place is very often limited to "passive skills" like comprehension/recognition, vocabulary acquisition, or stylistic text analyses that are not followed up by active application. Quantity is privileged over quality: what matters is how much the student talks, not how. Reading is followed by comprehension questions; plot summaries are followed by cultural or literary history context questions; the content progression from Stage 1 (content questions and stylistic analysis targeting mainly comprehension) to Stage 2 (background knowledge with regard to author, history, culture attempting to provide the text with a context) is nowhere matched in terms of L2 acquisition, which is usually abandoned at Stage 1. "Knowledge" is defined initially as comprehension, later as recall of facts; interpretive, analytical, and discourse capabilities are not taught. Very frequently, the refusal to integrate linguistic and literary competence in a literature course results in communicative breakdown at the end: as soon as the discussion moves into the abstract or interpretive/analytical domain, students are permitted to revert to L1 and all attempts at L2 exposure, even on the "input" level, are abandoned. Text analysis in the target language is seen as invariably resulting in a lower level of ideation (Littlewood 1986; cf. also the survey conducted by Gray 1995); this fact is not seen as related to the absence of pedagogical interventions that target the development of analytical abilities in the foreign language, but as an inevitable fact of life in the FL literature classroom. Conversely, the many models for literature classes in which cultural, literary, historical context and the development of analytical skills are abandoned in favor of a near-exclusive focus on the students' personal response to the text (for example Benton 1996; Guidry 1991; Koppensteiner 1990; Moffit 1998) can stand as an indication of the extent to which content is edited out of the course to uphold even its meager L2 component, consisting of comprehensible input and discussion—an indication of the level of sophistication that must be sacrificed to *keep* that input comprehensible.

The Teaching of Literature and Language: Critiquing Received Practice (Byrnes)

The previous *mis-en-scène* regarding the teaching of L2 literature points to a number of issues that have burdened the FL profession for quite some time, in its institutional structures, programmatic choices, pedagogies, and even in the nature of its scholarship. While what Kord aptly describes as the Great Divide has all too often been interpreted as being "caused" by an undue research focus and the concomitant undervaluing of teaching on the part of the literature professoriate (James 1997; Response to Dorothy James 1998a and 1998b; Patrikis 1995; but see Byrnes 2001), more foundational divisions are at work. I interpret them as arising from a long-standing tradition in Western thought, of separating language from knowledge, a tradition that has not only affected major philosophical and linguistic approaches to the understanding of language but has pervasively shaped our educational practices, including most specifically our pedagogies.

Though recent developments in the FL field are not generally interpreted in this fashion, I characterize them as permitting a broader and more open discussion about the relationship of knowledge, language, and culture than has been possible over the last fifty years. These possibilities have long been available in the quieter recesses of scholarly thinking on both sides of another Great Divide, namely the one created and sustained by the Cold War. Until recently, and for very different sociopolitical and ideological reasons, however, they had little access to the center of the public forum of the profession's discourse. Specifically, our current practices rest, to a significant extent, on a normative and essentialist model of knowledge and language, in line with long-standing Western philosophical constructs that have presumed knowledge to be independent of language, pre-existing, "out there" as it were, in an idealized, even God-given metaphysical realm. Such knowledge is "discovered," usually in the form of rules, or as a way to God's Truth in the Logos of the Book, or in God's Second book, the Book of Nature, the project of the sciences. It is not generally understood as humanly constructed through language, where that linguistic semiosis responds to historical and cultural contingencies and intentionalities and becomes the key site for human cognition, affective and rational, even non-linguistic knowledge creation. Instead, beginning with Greek philosophy, language is primarily seen as the act of naming rather than of human meaning-making. It follows that, given the existence of many languages, a particular language system is therefore in its essence arbitrary and unrelated to the very shaping of that knowledge, and is teachable in the form of abstract rules.

In addition to the consequences arising from this kind of culturally independent understanding of language, twentieth century interpretations of the nature of scientific inquiry provided a corroborating heavy overlay of objectivist and value-neutral metaphors for understanding language as a system. This approach was well suited to the aspirations of the emerging field of American linguistics in its attempt to become an accepted player in the American academy and also a worthy recipient of significant funding resources in the post-war era. The high compatibility between such theorizing about language and the long-dominant model of learning, namely behaviorism, is as obvious intellectually as it is advantageous strategically. It helped to establish the unusual influence and staying-power of the kinds of understandings of language and language learning that have arisen in audio-lingualism and subsequently in the growing field of SLA research. That these are historically embedded constructs with enormous consequences in our educational conduct is well exemplified if one surveys the contributions in even one professional journal over close to a hundred years, as was recently done in retrospective articles in the *Modern Language Journal* (Issues 84, 4 [2000] and 85,1 [2001]).

Even so, I believe the contemporary scene allows for a decidedly different viewpoint, namely the possibility of considering language as a culturally embedded form of human meaning-making, of semiosis, in short, of language as a social semiotic. By that I mean taking knowledge to be intricately linked to the language patterns of situated language use, where the use of language is a way of knowing and a way of being that is historical in origin and directly related to social action. In the former communist-held countries such an approach was best explicated by Bakhtin (1981) and Vygotsky (1986); in the West, such an investigation of language has been referred to as "functional" and is prominently associated with the British-Australian linguist Halliday and his followers. It emphasizes a symbiotic relationship between human activity and language in which, as Hasan (1995) puts it, "the very existence of one is the condition for the existence of the other" (p. 184). By investigating key constructs of systemic-functional linguistics, namely context of situation, register, text, and text structure, it is possible to create a conceptual framework that can substantiate this claim.

For example, Halliday (1985) reverses the relationship between notions of language and notions of grammar that prevail in language instructional contexts. Instead of considering language to be "a system of forms, to which meanings are then attached," he considers language to be "a system of meanings, accompanied by forms through which the meanings can be realized" (p. xiv). In particular, two central meanings are addressed by language, namely "(i) to understand the environment (ideational), and (ii) to act on the others in it (interpersonal). Combined with these is a third metafunctional component, the 'textual', which breathes relevance into the other two" (p. xiii).

Dramatically different from the typical structuralist grammar which is a grammar of syntagmatic linearity—as stated, often with roots in logic and philosophy—this is a grammar not of normative rules but of choices and relations, where "the grammatical system as a whole represents the semantic code of a language" and "the context of culture determines the nature of the code" (Halliday 1985, p. xxxii). Thought-provoking even for our concern with adult instructed FL learning is Halliday's statement regarding child language learning: "As a language is manifested through its texts, a culture is manifested through its situations; so by attending to text-in-situation a child construes the code, and by using the code to interpret the text he construes the culture" (1985, p. xxxii).

To sum up, the relationship of language and knowledge that a systemic-functionalist approach to language foregrounds is that "... language as *social semiotic praxis* ... should be seen unequivocally as a *construer* of reality, not just as its *representer* ... it does not *represent* reality; it simply *construes a model* of reality" (Hasan 1999, p. 53). Therefore, while the relationship between language as a system may be considered arbitrary with regard to the species-specific potentialities of the human language-making capacity, the relation between meaning and that level of the language code which Halliday refers to as its lexicogrammar is far from arbitrary but, instead, constitutive. As Hasan (1999) summarizes this issue:

> The social context within which acts of meaning are embedded is an occasion for carrying out some **social action**, by **co-actants** in some **social relation**, placed in some **semiotic contact** (p. 62, emphases in original).

My historical excursus in no way suggests that the gradual shift in American FL instruction—interestingly enough primarily at the K-12 level—is an instance of the kind of thorough reconsideration of the relationship of language and knowledge that I have begun to sketch out and located particularly with systemic-functional linguistics and a sociocultural Vygotskian approach to knowledge and learning. Quite the contrary. Given the proceduralization of American FL education, particularly through the power of textbooks, various standardized testing practices, and generally insufficient programs for teacher education, that would be expecting too much.

So, what does all of this have to do with language and literature teaching in collegiate foreign language departments? As I contend, quite a bit. True, the profession's changing assumptions and emphases have generally been described in metaphors that are familiar to the field, namely in terms of grammar versus communication, or accuracy versus fluency, thereby suggesting that the old paradigm is intact: any shifting could then be construed in terms of addition—*add* communication to the foundation of grammar, or *add* fluency once students have acquired a certain level of accuracy. Yet, as the insufficiency of an additive approach came to light, we find, on the one side, high-profile professional skirmishes claiming incompatibility between fluency and accuracy while, on the other side, conciliatory voices pleading the case for both. In the end, they generally recommended little more for the attainment of fluent and accurate language use than the well established practices of skill-getting and skill-using of grammatical features, though now through more contextualized communicative activities.

As it turns out, both positions are deeply flawed. The issue is not, and cannot be, the status of grammar in language use: there is no language use without grammar, more precisely, there is no language use without a situationally accurate lexicogrammar, and that means without appropriate language forms. The issue, instead, is understanding the nature of language as a social semiotic, an understanding that inherently puts meaning-making, ways of understanding the world around us, at the heart of language use and not as an after-thought, and from there proceeds to ensure the development of local-level accuracy. Herein lies the enormous potential for FL education, particularly if we pursue dynamic change in three areas:

- through a reconsideration of curricula, understood not as a loose aggregation of courses (cf., Byrnes 1998), but as carefully conceptualized and planned encompassing frameworks that continually integrate content and language acquisition;
- through reconsideration of the nature of interlanguage development, understood not as an additive progression toward native-like norms, but as working toward a multi-competence that, at the college level, is best described in terms of multiple literacies;
- through a reconsideration of the nature and place of pedagogy, understood not as privatized sets of options "that work" for an individual instructor but as choices that have a public dimension because they manifest underlying assumptions and educational goals expressed within a previously agreed-upon curricular framework.

Language-Based Literature Teaching: Building Bridges (Kord)

To me the preceding issues have been of profound concern for some time, both as a language teacher and as a professional who has a vested interest in the representation of literature. Previous to my department's curricular reform, my classroom experiences were no different from those of most of my colleagues at other institutions; they can be distilled into the following three points:

- Traditional foreign language classes (by which I mean textbook-based four-skills courses aimed at developing language *skills*, e.g., "proficiency") are seen, by most students, as both less interesting than and intellectually inferior to "content" courses in other disciplines[2] for two reasons: the course emphasis on skills rather than intellectual development or acquisition of concrete knowledge, and the lower student (and instructor) interest in the subject matter of the course, traditionally a disconnected collection of themes haphazardly

Developing Literacy and Literary Competence

fashioned into the course content by virtue of their placement in the textbook;
- Traditional language training does not prepare students for reading and analyzing literature;
- Once these students "graduate" into the content part of the curriculum, very often the literature course, their inadequate language level limits expression of their cognitive and analytical potential. Very often it leads them to "dumb down" the text in their linguistically inadequate analysis to a degree that I find absolutely unacceptable and that I view as a stark contrast both to the complexity of the text and the students' cognitive abilities.

Since my department has made the decision to take up the challenge to redefine its curriculum in terms of a holistic model of language instruction that integrates linguistic and cultural knowledge right from the beginning (Byrnes 1996, p. 256), it has become more feasible for literature faculty teaching in this new context to develop courses that attend adequately to both "content" and "language." The course that I would like to discuss below is an example of how such bridges can be built. It has numerous advantages over the same literature course as I would have taught it only a few years ago:

- The course takes place in a *curricular context* of other courses on the same level that try to achieve a similar symbiosis of content and language instruction. It follows courses that adequately prepare students for the advanced level language and content work they will encounter in my course.
- The course *combines* intellectually challenging *content* (literature, literary and political history, and reception history) *with discourse training* that will enable students to discuss both the texts and the contexts in an intellectually adequate (scholarly) fashion. The language aspects of the course are *deliberately targeted and developed* in all four modalities, rather than left to chance; students are held responsible for both the content and the linguistic aspects of the course in assessment.
- Compared to other literature courses that I have taught, the course offers a broad and varied menu of activities and discourse and assessment practices which deliberately elicit different discourse skills (descriptive, narrative, organizational, performative, and analytical).

- Compared to other literature courses that I have taught, the course is exceedingly student-oriented, rather than teacher-oriented, without relinquishing or modifying the intellectual or "content" goals of the course.

Look Who's Laughing: German Comedies was developed as a fourth-year course in the context of our departmental curricular reform. It concerns itself equally with literary content (texts and historical/social/authorial/cultural contexts) and with academic/literary discourse about the larger philosophical and scholarly context (investigations of different stylistic and literary forms of humor, of different literary genres, of theoretical texts by the authors on the subject, historical development and differentiation of comic genres, and reception history; cf. syllabus, Appendix A). In an instructional approach that is equally concerned with literature and literacy, this content progression would necessitate an exactly parallel progression in the stylistic/linguistic aspects of the course, reinforced by adequate writing assignments. In *Look Who's Laughing*, these assignments progressed from the micro level (a scene analysis) to the macro level (a review of a play performance, which obviously requires not only concrete knowledge of the structure, content, authorial intentions, sociohistorical context, etc., of the original play, but also a considerable expert vocabulary and stylistic repertoire to mimic the stylistic conventions of professional review writing). For the final paper (on the meta-level), in which students were asked to provide a scholarly analysis of one author's complex relationship with comic genre (Lessing's "serious" comedy; Dürrenmatt's "tragicomedy" etc.), they were required to combine their acquired knowledge of texts and contexts with a solid foundation in relevant secondary literature and an ability to adequately employ scholarly conventions as well as language.

It should be readily apparent that instructors who expect students to deliver this level of reflection, and do it in a linguistically and stylistically adequate manner, must be willing to engage in carefully thought out pedagogical interventions over the course of the semester, with the goal of enabling students to acquire the language necessary to perform these tasks and of providing adequate reinforcement. While the themes remain the same as those of a traditional literature course (to wit, Kleist in the context of the Romantic movement; Kleist in the context of the French Revolution; Wilhelm Busch in the context of the Wilhelminian era; Lessing as a religious philosopher; Carl Sternheim and Nietzsche; Carl Sternheim and Expressionism; Dürrenmatt's adaptation of Aristotelian poetology, etc.), language acquisition is no longer limited to unstructured "discussion." The linguistic tools to discuss

Developing Literacy and Literary Competence

topics of this nature have to be deliberately and repeatedly offered to students (see Appendices B and C for examples, one from the beginning and one from the end of the course), in the form of extensive modeling by the instructor, directed discussion on the part of the students, and follow-up assignments (such as oral reports, see Appendix D for the relevant instruction sheet) and written assignments. Needless to say, students' success in acquiring the necessary vocabulary, style, and conventions was central to my assessment of all their work, written as well as oral. Throughout instruction I relied on instructor modeling (in the form of very deliberate usage on my own part of the language I wished students to acquire in the classroom, a model oral report delivered by me, as well as extensive written instructions for all tasks required of the students), repeated exposure, and deliberate stylistic direction of student discussion rather than memorization. Stylistic and lexical tools thus modeled and gradually incorporated into students' speech ranged from basic analytic vocabulary (how to discuss, describe, and analyze a text) to specific vocabulary dealing with theater and performance and finally to the adaptation of scholarly style (how to advance an argument or disprove, support, undermine or critique someone else's; how to write a professional review or place one's own work in the context of scholarly literature).

I would like to offer, at this point, two brief examples of student writing, both on the same theme: a review of the Emil Jannings' 1929 film of Kleist's *The Broken Jug*. The students are charged with incorporating both textual and contextual knowledge of the original drama and language and style adequate to literary analysis and professional review writing (my translation, all mistakes approximated):

> *Student A:* The film speaks much about this *[case error]* problem between the *[case error]* peasants and the [case error] autorities *[spelling error]*. The *[case error]* historical background, when *The Broken Jug* was written, explains this theme. The French [error: adjective instead of noun] had sudenly *[spelling]* their Revolution (1789) and ten years later came the French ocupation *[spelling]* in Germany (with Napolean *[spelling]* as Emperor). The German people were *[number error]* of course not pleased on this *[error: preposition]* and out of this feeling came *The Broken Jug*. A fitting *[ending error]* theme here is whether one should respect the authorities. Ruprecht did not do this, and for that he got his punishment.[3]

> *Student B:* The performance of this comedy, authored *[case error]* by Heinrich von Kleist, supposedly centers on the theme of injustice in society. Although differences between the written *[ending error]* and the performing *[participle and ending error]* comedies exist, the plot

of the comedy remains similar in both. The cultural background of the drama describes a Dutch village near Utrecht during the seventeenth century. At the center of the comedy Kleist places the role of a corrupt village judge. The plot of the film unfolds as follows: In the first scene, Village Judge Adam is portrayed as a corrupt and immoral person. Subsequently, an incident is brought before him. Frau Marthe, a funny old woman, accuses Ruprecht of having *[tense error]* broken her jug. This notwithstanding, Ruprecht, who is engaged to her daughter, claims that it was impossible for him to have broken the jug since he had not even been in Eve's room.[4]

In comparing these two writing samples, I would like to argue that while Student B clearly approaches the text with a considerably greater degree of sophistication, that sophistication is *almost exclusively linguistic, rather than cognitive*. In traditional literature classrooms, teachers would be inclined to interpret the difference between these two essays rather vaguely, indeed, fatalistically (Student B is simply a "better" student), as a difference in cognitive and interpretive ability or background "knowledge." In this case, however, both students acquired the same textual and contextual background. The differences in interpretive and analytical ability that these essays obviously reflect are inextricably bound up with the authors' (in)capacity to engage a language that would enable them to express their ideas on the high cognitive level on which they are situated. That level is rather high in Student A's essay: he accurately identifies several central background motives that are essential to an understanding of the play, for example the connection between the French Revolution and the philosophical and social debates it engendered on such principal organizational aspects of society as obedience to authority, as well as the changed aspect this debate must have taken on in Germany where it occurred in the context of occupation from without rather than revolution from within. The problem with Student A's essay is obviously neither historical background nor his ability to apply it to the text nor his level of reflection, but simply the fact that he is linguistically limited. His syntax, sentence structure, morphology, and lexical choices are limited to that intermediate level with which language teachers are so painfully familiar; his menu of verbs at times is limited to introductory material (the French *had* their Revolution; the occupation *came*; out of this feeling *came* the play, etc.). What that means is that it is impossible for this student, *despite the high cognitive ability* he clearly brings to his essay, either to structure his essay in a way that expresses a logical progression from introduction to argument to conclusion, or to express adequately the complex relationships between text, authorial intention, social and political context, and decipherable philosophical content. Student B, on the other hand, does all this rather successfully: he progresses smoothly from the introduction to the contrast between film and play to the historical background to a discussion of the film in which plot is intertwined with interpretation to his final (rather critical) assessment of the film vis-à-vis Kleist's original. His deliberate choice of discourse markers (supposedly, subsequently, notwithstanding) both structure the essay and pre-figure its student-author's critical and analytic stance: the "supposedly" in the first sentence, for example, skillfully announces the author's intention to review the film negatively in the final analysis, namely as having failed in its design to portray the theme of social injustice. In contrast to Student A, Student B relies rather heavily on linguistic structures and lexical items acquired in class (compare Student B's "The plot of the film *unfolds as follows*" with Student A's "The film *speaks much about...*"). He is producing complex syntax, with significant variation in occurrence and placement of different clause structures within a sentence. And finally, given the fact that most of us have been trained according to the "mastery" model which essentially assumes that error-free L2 production constitutes the desirable outcome, it is important to note that Student B's essay *is not error-free*, that it is, in fact, prone to very similar case, ending, and tense errors as the work of Student A.

My approach throughout the class was neither to insist on error-free language production, as a traditional language instructor might, nor to ignore language entirely, as a traditional literature instructor might, but rather to encourage a stylistic sophistication that eventually enables students to express the whole range of creativity and cognitive reasoning of which they are capable. In the context of their new-found stylistic elegance, scholarly analysis, and sophisticated reasoning, their errors seem a relatively minor concern so long as they impair neither understanding nor students' ability to sustain a sophisticated argument. The applicability of this work to a real-life as well as an academic context seems to support such an approach. While both students commit errors, Student B's opinions and interpretation of the play would be respected in the L1 context—in casual conversation with educated Germans as well as at a German university—; Student A's would not.

In addition to the more traditional writing assignments, which were performed and assessed individually, students were asked to engage in extensive group work either on oral reports or dramatic scripts of their own. Oral reports on each author we read were delivered in groups of two. These reports served a dual function: on the one hand, they moved the class focus from teacher to students (since this material, now presented as the result of student research, would traditionally have been delivered in the form of a lecture by the teacher); on the other, they constituted extensive oral practice in advanced discourse since they required students to work without notes, from an overhead that was composed in outline form only, and fill these content points with language which was both spontaneous and highly complex (see Appendices D and E for my instructions for the oral reports and an excerpt from a student-produced overhead). Somewhat less traditional, and also less restrictive of students' language use, were the script-writing exercises that completed discussion of each play (see Appendix F for instructions). In these script-writing exercises, students were asked, in groups of four or five, to write and perform a ten-minute version of the play we had just finished discussing while keeping all major plot strands and applying an L1 cultural context of their choice to the play. The results certainly far transcended the benefits traditionally accorded dramatic performances in the L2 classroom (cf., Ronke 1993, pp. 213–17, whose survey respondents listed as primary benefits gains in pronunciation and student confidence). For one thing, my students took the opportunity to incorporate relevant L1 culture as a chance both to be the "expert" (since I was considerably less familiar with these contexts than they were) and to illustrate aspects of the L2 literature through that context. In our bi-monthly in-class performances, Lessing's *Minna von Barnhelm* was revised as a 007-movie, Kleist's *The Broken Jug* as an American courtroom-drama modeled on the O. J. Simpson-trial, Carl Sternheim met Ace Ventura, and Dürrenmatt's *The Visit* metamorphosed into a jailhouse flick. These performances not only resulted in a considerable amount of creative energy and an increased tendency of students to rely on others in the group, they also furnished the basis for a great deal of self-reflexive discussion, centered around the question of what each team had to cut from the original to keep within the ten-minute limit and their reasons (interpretive, analytic, pragmatic, organizational) for making those choices. These performances also required, once again, both linguistic aptitude and a great deal of interpretive acumen. For example, Appendix G provides a short excerpt from one such student production: from within the adaptation of Lessing's original as a 007-movie, simultaneously a skillful parody of the genre itself, emerges a highly perceptive interpretation of the characters and their inter-relationships that is essential to an understanding of Lessing's original (Tellheim's humiliation as a disbanded officer, his generosity apparent in his treatment of the widow, Just's coarseness, his hatred of the innkeeper and his protectiveness of his master). Simultaneously, the exercise provided students with an opportunity to explore facets of the language otherwise rarely encountered in German language courses (in this case, code language) and to *use language* to create their own aspects of the comic, at times in surprising and innovative ways. Throughout the semester, language from elsewhere in the course was frequently incorporated into student scripts: an example is one production in which the scholarly meta-discourse *about* literature we had practiced in other contexts inserted itself into the lovers' quarrel in the production. I take these scenes, in which Kleist's Judge Adam, played by one of my students, speaks of his own "relativized justice," in which Lessing's Minna, in the best scholarly style, demonstrates Tellheim's opinions to be "riddled with inconsistencies," to be signs that my students were quite willing to explore this new language in both the pragmatic and the playful sense—both aspects that I would consider essential in the pursuit of language acquisition.

Linking Content and Language in Pedagogy: Exploring New Foundations (Byrnes)

To situate the kind of bridge-building that Kord has exemplified with her language-based pedagogy for literature even more explicitly, I return to exploring the three areas I had earlier identified as particularly suitable for linking literature teaching and insights regarding language acquisition. To understand the merits of Kord's example, it is important to point both to the curricular context in which she has created her innovative pedagogy of the teaching of literature and the nature of that practice in light of the possibilities created by that context. Such a deeper understanding is also necessary if her proposals are to be available for wider application in other settings. The guiding concepts I will use for that discussion are the nature of an integrated curriculum, interlanguage development toward multiple literacies, and a public pedagogy of choices within a curricular framework.

Establishing Curricular Foundations for the Teaching of Literature

The German Department's curriculum renewal effort, "Developing Multiple Literacies," is a comprehensive project that spans all aspects of the four-year undergraduate program. It takes a content-oriented and task-based approach in all courses. This means that it focuses on content from the beginning of the instructional sequence and explicitly focuses on acquiring German to academic levels of performance to the end of the instructional sequence at students' graduation. As it does away with the traditional dichotomy of language courses and content courses, it creates an integrated program which is expressed in terms of five instructional levels according to specific curricular goals.

The entire curriculum is divided into the sequenced courses of Levels I–III, so called because students must take them in sequence. A group of six courses follows at Level IV. Addressing different content areas, they nevertheless share similar acquisitional goals and pedagogical emphases. At least two of these courses (for majors one of these is *Text in Context*) are taken by anyone wishing to pursue further studies in the department. Finally, Level V offers an open-ended number of courses. Such courses reflect broad student and faculty content and research interests. They continue the explicit linking of content with acquisitional concerns within a genre-based pedagogy, an approach that is particularly well suited to exemplifying and negotiating issues of learner identity and voice as these define upper levels of ability in a second language.

Beginning with thematically clustered content areas that exemplify a range of textual genres and that are manifested in the actual texts chosen—and these, of course, include literary texts—the curriculum as a whole, and each course in turn, derives from these materials a variety of carefully sequenced pedagogical interventions. With the exception of Level I, all instructional materials for the central required courses were created by the faculty–graduate student teams. Though Level I uses a commercially produced textbook, actual instruction is refocused by the extensive incorporation of materials and pedagogical tasks that not only respond to the acquisitional goals of this level but in important ways lay the foundation for and anticipate the practices at the subsequent levels, particularly their basic discourse orientation.

A close link between theme, genre, text, and task provides the basis for the pedagogical and real-world tasks in which students engage at all levels in all courses (cf., Grabe and Stoller 1997; Long and Crookes 1993; Robinson 2001; Skehan 1998; Stoller and Grabe 1997). This approach, not a method in the traditional sense, is intended to enhance learners' attentiveness to meaning-form relationships as they characterize a particular topic or field of inquiry (Long and Robinson 1998). Students' actual engagement with the materials incorporates considerations of task complexity, task difficulty, and task performance conditions as psycholinguistically important notions pertaining to the nature of learner processing and, by implication, the nature of students' likely performance (Skehan 1998). By conceptualizing L2 development as a long-term process within a coherent four-year program that is designed to facilitate students' evolving accuracy, fluency, and complexity of language use in all modalities, the curriculum strives for continued efficient and effective interlanguage development toward advanced levels of competence, including those that we associate with literate language use, and quite specifically, the interpretive abilities that we consider to be at the heart of work with literary texts.

From the particulars of our experience with curriculum renewal, the following generalizations for relating literature and language learning in programs and pedagogies have arisen:

- the priority of content in instruction, a priority which, importantly, is established through and with an in-depth exploration of the language of texts *so that both content and language might be learned together*;

- an exploration of texts from two perspectives, as embodying the typified features of the genre they represent, and as showing particular, situated forms of social action which are made possible by and within the overall capacaties of the genre;

- an emphasis on deliberately relating changes in the classroom to the best knowledge in the field as we could discern it, but always referring back to our particular educational setting and teaching situation and to the kind of language learning it seemed to facilitate;

- a willingness to consider this an open process, as manifested in the many informal and formal occasions for reflective teaching practice with their recursive loops and iterative adjustments—from textual to curricular to pedagogical to assessment insights and back.

All four areas show that curriculum, our students' interlanguage development, and our pedagogies are intimately related to each other and can be evaluated and developed only within that nexus. Previous efforts to link literature and language acquisition have tended to treat these matters separately: they focused on individual courses, made diverse recommendations about materials, suggested successful pedagogies, and considered their students' language learning characteristics. By contrast, this genre-based approach focuses on all these aspects simultaneously and locates them within the framework of a curriculum that has been conceptualized in terms of the specific functional literacies that learners can be expected to attain at each sequenced instructional level. All educational decisions are negotiated within this nexus.

Rethinking Interlanguage Development toward Multiple Literacies

The notion of interlanguage—the learner's gradual and non-linear approximation of target language norms—is perhaps the most central concept in recent SLA research, both classroom-based and naturalistic. Given its appearance in the early 1970s, it has, by and large, been interpreted in psycholinguistic processing terms that retain strong traces of the separatist status of language and knowledge that is part of the discipline's heritage. However, more recently, directions are opening up in theoretical and empirical linguistic research that investigate the perennial question between linguistic determinism and linguistic relativism in language use and language acquisition. When they come from a cognitive semantics perspective they interpret interlanguage development not only as linking cognition and language use but also as relating to societal practices, particularly to generic textual practices (see particularly the articles in the edited volumes by Gumperz and Levinson, 1996; Tomasello 2000; also Slobin 1996a, 1996b, 1997, 1998; Talmy 2000). Recently this conceptualization has begun to be influenced by emerging notions of literacy in education, particularly from a sociocultural perspective (cf., Gee 1998; Miller 1984; Wells 1994, 2000; Wertsch 2000). The result is an understanding of interlanguage development that is reminiscent of a kind of cognitive apprenticeship, a description that fits the adult L2 classroom particularly well when its pedagogy is genre-based (Kern 2000).

Genre-based forms of literacy are taken to instantiate larger sociocultural patterns according to which we take knowledge from the environment (Heath 1982; Tannen 1982, 1992). That does not mean that education will not or may not target specific literacies, such as the essayist academic discourse, the discourse of literary texts, or the discourse of talking about literary texts, as specific learning goals. Indeed, such literacies would not be presumed to arise naturally for all learners but would need to be taught explicitly (Gee 1998; Kinsella 1997; Martin 1998; Mohan 1979, 1986, 1989), and they would be placed in the context of larger communicative practices in order to signal that different groups employ and prefer different semiotic strategies in their literacies. As Gee (1998) and also the New London Group (1996) note, when they refer to the exclusionary as well as empowering nature of privileged forms of discourse, such sophisticated levels of awareness into discursive behavior are no longer a luxury but are necessary in a global, multilingual, and multicultural environment because they prepare individuals and groups to create new designs for sociocultural action in different spheres of their lives. Ultimately, through such reflection, students have the possibility for a deeper appreciation of the nature of all human meaning-making as heteroglossic and multilingual, for the individual and for a whole society (Bakhtin 1981), with all that this implies.

One of the few treatments of these matters explicitly intended for the L2 classroom is that by Kern (1995, 2000), who integrates the relevant literature into his notion of an "active literacy." His choice of term is itself a good reminder of the extent to which static notions of language and of language learning—which are focused on the individual outside any social frame of reference—continue to dominate thinking in the L2 teaching profession. Instead, he recommends that:

> Literacy needs to be developed through multiple experiences, in multiple contexts, with multiple text genres (both oral and written), for multiple purposes. Moreover, attention must be paid to the *relationship* among the particular text types, particular purposes, and particular ways of reading and writing in a given literacy practice. Finally ... we need to encourage students to take an active, critical stance to the discourse conventions we teach them (1995, p. 67).

In our experience with such a teaching toward multiple literacies the following features stand out:

- the centrality of text and its intended meaning(s) via genres, as the most suitable unit of analysis, not the word as in most of Vygotsky's account, nor the sentence as a traditional formalist approach strongly suggests;
- the nature of meaning-making occurring in the form of "constructing and interpreting of texts, and this involves the interplay of different components of meaning—interpersonal, textual, and logical, as well as experiential" (Wells 1994, p. 70);
- a greater transparency between grammar and lexicon at all levels of instruction and in all our pedagogical efforts and a greater focus on their resource rather than their rules character or their idiosyncratic nature;
- a careful integration of the linguistic characteristics of both dynamic and synoptic textual genres and their linkage to different genres and registers;
- the need to provide guidance to students as they engage in the important restructuring of their language system to accommodate the more abstract and systemic meanings encountered in written texts, something that is likely to occupy

them as well in their expanding L1 literacy, albeit at a more elaborated level.[5]

Toward a Public Pedagogy of Choices

Excellent teaching has always in the past depended on and will always in the future depend on teachers who are able to make their own informed choices involving awareness, attitude, knowledge, and skills. For us, the significant added benefit of the curricular renewal was that it created a forum for shaping and informing individual notions about second language learning by adults *in terms of certain basic premises we had agreed upon as an entire department*. Once that agreement existed, the curriculum itself, as process and product, developed into a flexible system of teacher beliefs, "the information, attitudes, values, theories, and assumptions about teaching and learning that teachers build up over time and bring with them to the classroom" (Richards 1994, p. 385). In addition to constant informal contacts, this kind of shared "pedagogical reasoning" came about, among other events, through whole group workshops, through level-specific considerations of materials, pedagogies, and assessment issues, through mutual class visitations and semester-long mentored teaching, through the creation of central documents that summarized our beliefs and spelled out their implications for our practice, and through pedagogical materials sharing, the results of which are now available on a joint computer drive accessible to all teaching staff.

In other words, in contrast to the pervasive practice in higher education of privatizing teaching, our program as a whole and our individual teaching became public goods to and for ourselves, rather than private possessions. In a sense, our collaborative work became our joint learning and the real foundation for departmental knowing, gradually leading us away from notions of "rightness" and "wrongness" about adult foreign language learning, from the sacred sites of the professional discussion—grammar, accuracy, fluency, content knowledge—and from pedagogical interventions as codified and approved by "methods." In particular, we continue to develop more sophisticated levels of awareness of the relationship between genres, themes, texts, and tasks as we explore in greater depth those aspects of L2 learning that characterize the very advanced learner at our curricular Level V.

Exploring Implications and Applications

How might the considerations that have arisen in our curricular implementation play themselves out as we reflect on future opportunities and challenges posed by an integrated content-oriented and task-based curriculum that gives a prime role to discursive practices mediated by genres? On a microlevel, activities of particular promise are that we should:

- investigate even more closely the relationship between genres and language use (see Martin 1998), connecting genres more overtly to task (Swales 1990), emphasizing their cultural embeddedness (Paltridge 1995), and explicitly submitting them to crosscultural comparisons (Kern 2000);
- explore the relationship between knowledge structures, genres, and text structures by strategically employing the procedural approach to transferring comprehended text into produced text that characterizes Swaffar, Arens, and Byrnes' (1991) treatment of reading;
- foster a more explicitly language-based approach to reading that goes beyond the customary schema-theoretic approach and follows Kintsch's (1989) proposal for what he calls a *construction-integration* model which deliberately links meaning creation to appropriate attention to language from a textual perspective;
- extend our linkage of textual analysis, particularly the organization of texts according to larger discourse units, to the teaching of writing and speaking, potentially including some aspects of this work already in Level III courses;
- use assessment practices to reinforce and expand our awareness of the interaction of content, texts, and tasks. Our most recent change-over to task-based writing assessment practices in all sequenced courses is now being extended to the assessment of speaking in those courses (Byrnes in press).

On a macrolevel, our experiences challenge both the dominant assumptions of FL teaching and also those regarding the nature and role of literature in a FL department. On the one hand, such approaches see language learning as learning to mean and not so much as the application of rules within the confines of the grammatical sentence. On the other hand, they locate students' engagement with L2 literary texts within the broader context of a socioculturally constituted literacy, where the appreciation and interpretation of literary texts is a highly specialized and valued skill, but by no means the only way in which students engage with texts in the process of acquiring the second language.

Indeed, one way to summarize both aspects would be to conclude that the notion of L2 literacy or, more precisely, multiple literacies in L1 and L2, constitutes a particularly felicitous way of characterizing the entire enterprise of learning a foreign language in a college environment because texts and their imagined worlds, rather than the contexts of the "real" world, constitute the vast majority of language use in our classrooms. An elaborated ability to work with texts—in comprehension and production, orally and in writing—is not merely a precondition for substantial work with literary texts. It aptly describes all second language learning by collegiate foreign language learners, regardless of programmatic emphasis or individual student interest and regardless of the level of instruction. Because a sophisticated literacy is essential for attaining advanced levels of performance, the construct of genre and the pedagogical approach arising from it support the integration of all undergraduate FL instruction that has heretofore eluded FL departments. Even if students are unable to invest the necessary time to attain such performance abilities we, as teachers, will have done everything while these students were in our classrooms so that their language use *at a time* would lead to continued and balanced language development toward multiple literacies *over time*.

Notes

1. I would like to thank my thirteen comedians for all they've taught me about teaching, for their hard work and for their willingness to let me use some of it here: Hanne Wegner, Cy Griswold, Dan Oldroyd, Ivan Parkinson, Fred Waelter III, Vivien Dude, Jeremy Higginbotham, Suzanne Johnson, Pat Hanniford, Michelle Corona, Ryo Hasegawa, Frank Salamone, and Kirsten Schwarz.

2. That there is an implicit hierarchy between "language courses" and "content courses," between courses perceived as teaching skills and those perceived as addressing intellectual development, is undeniable and manifests itself in countless aspects of daily university life: the widespread perception among language teachers that students, as a rule, tend to take language or skills courses less seriously than other courses; the pervasive attitude among literature professors who frequently consider language teaching at the beginning and intermediate level as beneath them; the lower status of "language teachers" compared with "literature" (or other "content") professors within the profession. The Georgetown German Department curriculum, initially designed to address the divide between skills and content teaching, has also had a significant effect on some of these ancillary issues: in our department, the hierarchies dividing "language teachers" and "literature professors" have of necessity disappeared along with the divide between language and content courses.

3. *Student A:* Der Film spricht viel über diesem Problem zwischen die Bauern und die Obrichkeit. Die historische Hintergrund, als *Der zerbrochne Krug* geschrieben wurde, erklärt dieses Thema. Die Französische hatten

plötzlich ihre Revolution (1789) und zehn Jahre später kam die französische Okupation in Deutschland (mit Napolean als Kaiser). Das deutsche Volk waren natürlich nicht froh darauf und aus diesem Gefühl kam *Der zerbrochne Krug*. Ein passendes Thema hier ist, ob man die Obrigkeit respektieren sollte. Das hat Ruprecht nicht gemacht, und dafür hat er eine Strafe bekommen.

4. *Student B:* Die Aufführung der von Heinrich von Kleist geschriebene Komödie soll sich prinzipiell mit dem Thema Unrecht in der Gesellschaft befassen. Obwohl Unterschiede zwischen den geschriebene und aufgeführne Komödien existieren, bleibt die Handlung der Komödie in den beiden ähnlich. Der kulturelle Hintergrund des Dramas beschreibt ein niederländisches Dorf bei Utrecht während des siebzehnten Jahrhunderts. In den Mittelpunkt dieser Komödie stellt Kleist die Rolle eines korrupten Dorfrichters. Die Handlung des Films entwickelt sich wie folgt. In der ersten Szene wird der Dorfrichter Adam als ein korrupter und unmoralischer Mensch dargestellt. Mithin wird ein Vorfall vor sein Gericht gebracht. Frau Marthe, eine komische alte Frau, klagt an, dass Ruprecht ihren Krug zerbrochen hatte. Demungeachtet behauptet Ruprecht, der mit ihrer Tochter verlobt ist, dass es unmöglich wäre, dass er den Krug zerschlagen hätte, weil er überhaupt nicht in Eves Zimmer gewesen sei.

5. Our Level IV required course, *Text and Context,* particularly targets this threshold and regularly finds students acknowledging that this is a level of language use that they do not necessarily control well in English.

6. NB: Bitte NICHT "der Abtritt" (= antiquiertes Wort für Toilette!)

Works Cited

Bakhtin, M. M. 1981. *The Dialogic Imagination. Four Essays,* edited by Michael Holquist. Austin: University of Texas Press.

Benton, Michael. 1996. The Discipline of Literary Response: Approaches to Poetry with L2 Students. In *Challenges of Literary Texts in the Foreign Language Classroom,* edited by Lothar Bredella and Werner Delanoy, 30–44. Tübingen: Gunter Narr.

Bernhardt, Elizabeth B. 1991. *Reading Development in a Second Language.* Norwood, NJ: Ablex.

Blickle, Peter. 1998. Teaching the Concept of Childhood and Nineteenth-Century German Children's Books in an Intermediate German Course. *Die Unterrichtspraxis* 31: 110–15.

Brumfit, Christopher J. 1985. *Language and Literature Teaching From Practice to Principle.* Oxford: Pergamon.

Byrnes, Heidi. 1996. The Future of German in American Education: A Summary Report. *Die Unterrichtspraxis* 29: 253–61.

———. 1998. Constructing Curricula in Collegiate Foreign Language Departments. In *Learning Foreign and Second Languages: Perspectives in Research and Scholarship,* edited by Heidi Byrnes, 262–95. New York: MLA.

———. 1999. Meaning and Form in Classroom-Based SLA Research: Reflections from a College Foreign Language Perspective. In *Meaning and Form: Multiple Perspectives,* edited by James F. Lee and Albert Valdman, 125–79. Boston: Heinle & Heinle.

———. 2000. Languages Across the Curriculum—Intradepartmental Curriculum Construction: Issues and Options. In *Languages Across the Curriculum: Interdisciplinary Structures and Internationalized Education,* edited by Maria Regina Kecht and Katharina von Hammerstein, 151–75. Columbus: The Ohio State University Press.

———. 2001. Reconsidering Graduate Students' Education as Teachers: It Takes a Department! *Modern Language Journal* 85(4).

———. in press. The Role of Task and Task-based Assessment in a Content-Oriented Collegiate FL Curriculum. *Language Testing* 19(2).

Christie, Frances. 1999. Genre Theory and ESL Teaching: A Systemic Functional Perspective. *TESOL Quarterly* 33: 759–63.

Dykstra-Pruim, Pennylyn. 1998. Independent Reading for Beginners: Using Children's Books in a Reading Lab. *Die Unterrichtspraxis* 31: 101–109.

Freedman, Aviva, and Peter Medway, eds. 1994a. *Genre and the New Rhetoric.* London: Taylor & Francis.

———. 1994b. *Learning and Teaching Genre.* Westport, CT: Heinemann.

Gee, James Paul. 1998. What is Literacy? In *Negotiating Academic Literacies: Teaching and Learning across Languages and Cultures,* edited by Vivian Zamel and Ruth Spack, 51–59. Mahwah, NJ: Lawrence Erlbaum.

Grabe, William, and Fredricka L. Stoller. 1997. Content-Based Instruction: Research Foundations. In *The Content-Based Classroom: Perspectives on Integrating Language and Content,* edited by Marguerite Ann Snow and Donna M. Brinton, 5–21. White Plains: Longman.

Gray, Richard T. 1995. Part One: Materials. In *Approaches to Teaching Kafka's Short Fiction,* edited by Richard T. Gray, 3–18. New York: MLA.

Guidry, Glenn A. 1991. Teaching Critical Response with Goethe's *Werther. Die Unterrichtspraxis* 24: 156–63.

Gumperz, John J., and Stephen C. Levinson, eds. 1996. *Rethinking Linguistic Relativity.* Cambridge: Cambridge University Press.

Haggstrom, Margaret A. 1992. A Performative Approach to the Study of Theater: Bridging the Gap Between Language and Literature Courses. *French Review* 66: 7–19.

Halliday, M.A.K. 1985. *An Introduction to Functional Grammar.* London: Edward Arnold.

———. 1993. Towards a Language-Based Theory of Learning. *Linguistics and Education* 5: 93–116.

Hasan, Ruqaiya. 1995. The Conception of Context in Text. In *Discourse in Society: Systemic Functional Perspectives: Meaning and Choice in Language: Studies for Michael Halliday,* edited by Peter H. Fries and Michael Gregory, 183-283. Norwood, NJ: Ablex.

———. 1999. The Disempowerment Game: Bourdieu and Language in Literacy. *Linguistics and Education* 10: 25–87.

Heath, Shirley Brice. 1982. What No Bedtime Story Means: Narrative Skills at Home and at School. *Language in Society* 11: 49–76.

Holten, Christine. 1997. Literature: A Quintessential Content. In *The Content-Based Classroom: Perspectives on Integrating Language and Content,* edited by Marguerite A. Snow and Donna M. Brinton, 377–88. White Plains, NY: Longman.

James, Dorothy. 1997. Bypassing the Traditional Leadership: Who's Minding the Store? *ADFL Bulletin* 28(3): 5–11.

Jones, Janet, Sandra Gollin, Helen Drury, and Dorothy Economou. 1989. Systemic-Functional Linguistics and its Application to the TESOL Curriculum. In *Language Development: Learning Language, Learning Culture,* edited by Ruqaiya Hasan and James R. Martin, 257–328. Norwood, NJ: Ablex.

Kern, Richard. 1995. Redefining the Boundaries of Foreign Language Literacy. In *Redefining the Boundaries of Language Study,* edited by Claire Kramsch, 61–98. Boston: Heinle & Heinle.

———. 2000. *Literacy and Language Teaching.* Oxford: Oxford University Press.

Kinsella, Kate. 1997. Moving from Comprehensible Input to "Learning to Learn" in Content-Based Instruction. In *The Content-Based Classroom: Perspectives on Integrating Language and Content,* edited by Marguerite Ann Snow and Donna M. Brinton, 46–68. New York: Longman.

Kintsch, Walter. 1989. Learning from Text. In *Knowing, Learning, and Instruction: Essays in Honor of Robert Glaser,* edited by Lauren B. Resnick, 25-46. Hillsdale, NJ: Lawrence Erlbaum.

Knutson, Elizabeth M. 1993. Teaching Whole Texts: Literature and Foreign Language Reading Instruction. *French Review* 67: 12–26.

Koppensteiner, Jürgen. 1990. 'Das schriftstellernde Phänomen in der deutschsprachigen Jugendbuch-Szene': Ein Plädoyer für die Arbeit mit Texten von Christine Nöstlinger. *Die Unterrichtspraxis* 23: 106–11.

Lazar, Gillian. 1993. *Literature and Language Teaching: A Guide for Teachers and Trainers.* Cambridge: Cambridge University Press.

Littlewood, William T. 1986. Literature in the School Foreign-Language Course. In *Literature and Language Teaching*, edited by Christopher J. Brumfit and Ronald Carter, 177–83. Oxford: Oxford University Press.

Long, Michael H., and Graham Crookes. 1993. Units of Analysis in Syllabus Design. The Case of Task. In *Tasks in Pedagogical Context: Integrating Theory and Practice*, edited by Graham Crookes and Susan M. Gass, 9–56. Clevedon: Multilingual Matters.

Long, Michael H., and Peter Robinson. 1998. Focus on Form: Theory, Research, and Practice. In *Focus on Form in Classroom Second Language Acquisition*, edited by Catherine Doughty and Jessica Williams, 15–63. Cambridge: Cambridge University Press.

Martin, James R. 1985. Process and Text: Two Aspects of Human Semiosis. In *Systemic Perspectives on Discourse*, edited by James D. Benson and William S. Greaves, 243–74. Norwood, NJ: Ablex.

———. 1998. Linguistics and the Consumer: The Practice of Theory. *Linguistics and Education* 9: 411–48.

———. 1999. Mentoring Semogenesis: 'Genre-Based' Literacy Pedagogy. In *Pedagogy and the Shaping of Consciousness: Linguistic and Social Processes*, edited by Frances Christie, 123–55. London: Cassell.

Miller, Carolyn R. 1984. Genre as Social Action. *Quarterly Journal of Speech* 70: 151–67.

Moeller, Aleidine J., and Christèle Kunczinam. 1993. *Der Richter und sein Henker*: A Model for the Teaching of Literature and Methodology for Teacher Educators and Teachers. *Die Unterrichtspraxis* 26: 148–61.

Moffit, Gisela. 1998. *Oya?*—O, ja! Reading *Jugendliteratur* in the German Classroom. *Die Unterrichtspraxis* 31: 116–24.

Mohan, Bernard A. 1979. Relating Language Teaching and Content Teaching. *TESOL Quarterly* 13: 171–82.

———. 1986. *Language and Content*. Reading, MA: Addison-Wesley.

———. 1987. The Structure of Situations and the Analysis of Text. In *Language Topics: Essays in Honour of Michael Halliday*, edited by Ross Steele and Terry Threadgold, 507–22. Vol. II. Amsterdam/Philadelphia: John Benjamins.

———. 1989. Knowledge Structures and Academic Discourse. *Word* 40: 99–115.

Murti, Kamakshi P. 1996. Teaching Literature at the First-Year Graduate Level: The Quantum Leap from Language to Literature. In *Challenges of Literary Texts in the Foreign Language Classroom*, edited by Lothar Bredella and Werner Delanoy, 185–204. Tübingen: Gunter Narr.

The New London Group. 1996. A Pedagogy of Multiliteracies: Designing Social Futures. *Harvard Educational Review* 66: 60–92.

Paltridge, Brian. 1995. Analyzing Genre: A Relational Perspective. *System* 23: 503–11.

Patrikis, Peter C. 1995. The Foreign Language Problem: The Governance of Foreign Language Teaching and Learning. In *Redefining the Boundaries of Language Study*, edited by Claire Kramsch, 293–335. Boston: Heinle & Heinle.

Response to Dorothy James, 'Bypassing the Traditional Leadership: Who's Minding the Store?' Part 1. 1998. *ADFL Bulletin* 29(2): 39–76.

Response to Dorothy James, 'Bypassing the Traditional Leadership: Who's Minding the Store?' Part 2. 1998. *ADFL Bulletin* 29(3): 46–68.

Richards, Jack C. 1994. The Sources of Language Teachers' Instructional Decisions. In *Educational Linguistics, Crosscultural Communication, and Global Interdependence (Gurt '94)*, edited by James E. Alatis, 384–402. Washington, DC: Georgetown University Press.

Robinson, Peter. 2001.Task Complexity, Task Difficulty and Task Production: Exploring Interactions in a Componential Framework. *Applied Linguistics* 22: 27–57.

Ronke, Astrid. 1993. Theaterspielen als didaktisches Mittel im Fremdsprachenunterricht: Ergebnisse einer Umfrage an amerikanischen und kanadischen Universitäten und Colleges. *Die Unterrichtspraxis* 26: 211–19.

Schultz, Jean-Marie. 1996. The Uses of Poetry in the Foreign Language Curriculum. *French Review* 69: 920–32.

Skehan, Peter. 1998. *A Cognitive Approach to Language Learning*. Oxford: Oxford University Press.

Slobin, Dan I. 1996a. From "Thought and Language" to "Thinking for Speaking." In *Rethinking Linguistic Relativity*, edited by John J. Gumperz and Stephen C. Levinson, 70–96. Cambridge: Cambridge University Press.

———. 1996b. Two Ways to Travel: Verbs of Motion in English and Spanish. In *Grammatical Constructions: Their Form and Meaning*, edited by Masayoshi Shibatani and Sandra A. Thompson, 195–219. Oxford: Clarendon Press.

———. 1997. Mind, Code, and Text. In *Essays on Language Function and Language Type. Dedicated to T. Givón*, edited by Joan Bybee, John Haiman, and Sandra A. Thompson, 437–67. Amsterdam: John Benjamins.

———. 1998. Verbalized Events: A Dynamic Approach to Linguistic Relativity and Determinism. Unpublished MS.

Stoller, Fredricka L., and William Grabe. 1997. A Six-T's Approach to Content-Based Instruction. In *The Content-Based Classroom: Perspectives on*

Integrating Language and Content, edited by Marguerite Ann Snow and Donna M. Brinton, 78–94. White Plains: Longman.

Swaffar, Janet K., Katherine Arens, and Heidi Byrnes. 1991. *Reading for Meaning: An Integrated Approach to Language Learning.* Englewood Cliffs, NJ: Prentice-Hall.

Swales, John M. 1990. *Genre Analysis. English in Academic and Research Settings.* Cambridge: Cambridge University Press.

Talmy, Leonard. 2000. *Toward a Cognitive Semantics.* Two volumes. Boston: MIT Press.

Tannen, Deborah. 1982. The Oral/Literate Continuum in Discourse. In *Spoken and Written Language: Exploring Orality and Literacy*, edited by Deborah Tannen, 1–15. Norwood, NJ: Ablex.

———. 1992. How Is Conversation like Literary Discourse? The Role of Imagery and Details in Creating Involvement. In *The Linguistics of Literacy*, edited by Pamela Downing, Susan D. Lima, and Michael Noonan, 31–46. Amsterdam: John Benjamins.

Tomasello, Michael, ed. 2000. *The New Psychology of Language: Cognitive and Functional Approaches to Language Structure.* Mahwah, NJ: Lawrence Erlbaum.

Vygotsky, Lev. 1986. *Thought and Language.* Cambridge, MA: MIT Press.

Wells, Gordon. 1994. The Complementary Contribution of Halliday and Vygotsky to a "Language-Based Theory of Learning." *Linguistics and Education* 6: 41–90.

———. 2000. Dialogic Inquiry in Education: Building on the Legacy of Vygotsky. In *Vygotskian Perspectives on Literacy Research: Constructing Meaning Through Collaborative Inquiry*, edited by Carol D. Lee and Peter Smagorinsky, 51–85. Cambridge: Cambridge University Press.

Wertsch, James V. 2000. Vygotsky's Two Minds on the Nature of Meaning. In *Vygotskian Perspectives on Literacy Research: Constructing Meaning Through Collaborative Inquiry*, edited by Carol D. Lee and Peter Smagorinsky, 19–30. Cambridge: Cambridge University Press.

Wertsch, James V., and Norris Minick. 1990. Negotiating Sense in the Zone of Proximal Development. In *Promoting Cognitive Growth over the Life Span*, edited by Milton Schwebel, Charles A. Maher, and Nancy S. Fagley, 71–87. Hillsdale, NJ: Lawrence Erlbaum.

APPENDIX A

German 266
Look who's laughing: German Comedies
Fall 1998

Plays

Gotthold Ephraim Lessing, Minna von Barnhelm, 1767
Heinrich von Kleist, Der zerbrochne Krug, 1808
Carl Sternheim, Die Hose, 1911
Friedrich Dürrenmatt, Der Besuch der Alten Dame, 1955
Patrick Süskind, Der Kontrabaß, 1983

Prose Works

Heinrich Spoerl, Der Tiefstapler, 1921; Der gute Ton am Telefon, 1919
Ernst Heimeran, Der rätselhafte Huber, 1954

Cartoons

Wilhelm Busch, Max und Moritz, 1865

Films

Minna von Barnhelm, 1992
Der zerbrochne Krug (Emil Jannings version)
Der Besuch der Alten Dame (Elisabeth Flickenschildt version)
Doris Dörrie, Männer, 1985
Sketches by Loriot, 1970s and 1980s

Course

German comedies have often been considered a contradiction in terms: most readers, students, and indeed scholars consider German literature the most sinister, serious, and insidiously humorless of all world literatures. In this course, students will map this perception against a close reading of five German comedies, three short prose works and viewing of films and sketches. We will investigate different stylistic forms of "what's so funny," including irony, slapstick, sarcasm, ridicule, as well as recurring themes in comedy, including class-based "humor" and the gender wars. Short theoretical treatises by authors of comedies will help us determine how authors of comedies themselves have sought to differentiate their genre from other dramatic forms like tragedy or *Tragikomödie,* and when, how and why these distinctions have historically occurred.

Writing Assignments As a Level IV course, this course seeks to refine students' perception of literary style through close readings of selected scenes from each drama and analysis of different aspects of the scene (plot/plotting, construction of the scene, characterization, linguistic aspects). Students will be required to produce three papers of approximately five pages each, all in processed writing (outline, paper, re-write); each incorporating vocabulary and stylistic tools presented and practiced in class. Each paper sets a different task: one is an analysis of a scene or character; the second a review of a comedy performance, to be viewed during the semester, the third a short research paper on genre questions in connection with one of the plays discussed in the course.

Diskussionsleitung and Protokolle Students will be required to lead one class discussion in teams of two; for each of these discussions, another student will produce discussion minutes *(Protokoll)*. Guidelines for both *Diskussionsleitung and Protokoll* will be provided in class.

Referate Students will be required, in teams of two or three, to introduce one of the authors read in the course, with biography, his/her most important works, socio-historical background, and remarks on the author's significance for his/her genre. Research for these presentations is to be done collaboratively. The presentations will be held in German, based on notes.

Final Performance Project Each student is required to participate in the production and performance of one scene which will be performed at the end of the semester. Students will divide into working groups (one per scene); each working group is responsible for selecting the scene, distributing parts, and other jobs (such as acquiring the necessary costumes and props), learning and rehearsing lines, and directing the scene. Students will have the opportunity to view videotaped professional performances of two dramas on which they can "model" their own productions. All work connected with the performance, including organizational and instructional (director's instructions, etc.), must be done in German. The goal of these performances is to use German not only in the theoretical/academic, but also in the organizational context acquire a natural feeling for the diction and intonation of spoken German, and to perform the language in the linguistic as well as the theatrical sense.

Gratuitous Fun Occasionally, brief comedy sketches from German TV will be shown in class. These can be treated as listening comprehension exercises, if you're feeling serious, or as time off/time out/gratuitous fun.

Grade Breakdown

In-class Participation	15%	Diskussionsleitung/Protokoll	10%
First two Papers (15% each)	30%	Referat	10%
Third Paper	20%	Final Performance	15%

Weekly Syllabus

Woche 1 (3. September): **Einführung in den Kurs**
Woche 2–3 (8.–17. September): **Minna von Barnhelm**
Woche 4–5 (22. September–1. Oktober): **Der zerbrochne Krug**

Developing Literacy and Literary Competence 65

Hausarbeit 1   1. **Version: 22. September**
                    2. **Version: 29. September**
Woche 6 (6. und 8. Oktober): Max und Moritz
Woche 7–8 (13.–22. Oktober): Die Hose
Hausarbeit 2   1. **Version: 20. Oktober**
Woche 9 (27.–29. Oktober): Prose Works by Spoerl and Heimeran
Hausarbeit 2   2. **Version: 27. Oktober**
Woche 10-11 (3.–12. November): Der Besuch der alten Dame
Outline und Bibliographie für Hausarbeit 3: 10. November
Woche 13 (17.–19. November): Der Kontrabass
Hausarbeit 3   1. **Version: 19. November**
Woche 14 (24. November): Diskussion der Abschlussprojekte
Woche 15 (1.–3. Dezember): Männer & Abschlussdiskussion
Hausarbeit 3   2. **Version: 1. Dezember**
Woche 16 (8. Dezember): Aufführungen: Szenen

APPENDIX B (English)

Discussing a Test

I. General Statements

The text/the drama/the play <u>concerns itself with</u> the theme of
  (love, money, sexual relations)
<u>In this text, the playwright dramatizes (portrays) the following themes:</u>
  (love, money, sexual relations)
<u>At the center of this comedy are</u> . . .
<u>The plot of the drama develops (unfolds) as follows:</u>

II. Formal Analysis

The play <u>is divided into</u> (five acts, fourteen scenes)
<u>Scenes change</u> (when persons <u>enter</u> or exit <u>the stage)</u>
<u>Scenes are sequenced as follows:</u> . . .
<u>The protagonist(s) / antagonist(s)</u>   <u>are characterized as</u> (+ noun)
                                           <u>are characterized as follows:</u> (begin
                                             another sentence)
<u>The historical (cultural) background of the drama refers to</u> . . .
                                <u>describes</u> . . .
The play originated from the following sources: ...
<u>In the play, the following</u>
           gestures
           light effects
           costumes
           gestures
           props etc.
                    are <u>employed</u>
                         <u>emphasized</u>
                         <u>centered</u>

APPENDIX B (German)
Über einen Text sprechen

I. Allgemeine Aussagen
Der Text
Der Roman/die Kurzgeschichte
Das Drama   befasst sich mit dem Thema ...(Geschlechterbeziehungen, Liebe, Geiz)
Die Komödie

In diesem Text (in dieser Geschichte) behandelt der Verfasser das Thema ...

Der Verfasser dramatisiert in dieser Komödie das Thema ...

Bei diesem Text handelt es sich um ... (eine Liebeskomödie, eine Situationskomödie, eine Kriminalgeschichte)

In seinem Text stellt der Autor (etwas) in den Mittelpunkt
betont der Autor die Rolle (+ Genitiv)

Der Inhalt der Kurzgeschichte/des Romans besteht aus ...
dreht sich um (+ Akk) ...

Die Handlung der Tragödie entwickelt sich wie folgt ...

II. Formelle Aussagen
Das Drama (die Komödie) ist unterteilt in   fünf Akte
                                            vierzehn Szenen

Personen treten auf/treten oder gehen ab (der Auftritt; der Abgang)

Szenen wechseln (beim Auftritt oder Abgang von Personen)

Der Szenenaufbau
Die Szenenabfolge   entwickelt sich wie folgt

Die Hauptfigur(en) und Nebenfigur(en) wird wie folgt charakterisiert:

Die Hauptfigur wird charakterisiert als   ein geiziger Mensch
                                          ein unschuldiges Mädchen
                                          ein bitterer alter Herr

Der historische (kulturelle) Hintergrund des Dramas
bezieht sich auf (+Akk)   das Dritte Reich
beschreibt   den Dreißigjährigen Krieg

Im Drama werden (wird) die (der, das) folgende(n)
               Lichteffekte
               Requisiten
               Kostüme
               Gestik
               eingesetzt

angewandt
verwendet
zur Geltung gebracht
benutzt

APPENDIX C (English)

Countering Scholarly Arguments

The author <u>erroneously</u> states that . . .
This depiction is <u>riddled with inconsistencies.</u>
His <u>conclusion</u> is <u>dubious.</u>
<u>This is not based on (rooted in) fact.</u>
One should avoid such <u>erroneous conclusions.</u>
One could raise the following <u>doubts/questions with regard to</u> the author's conclusion:
The author's conclusion <u>rests on a weak foundation.</u>
This portrayal is based <u>on a misunderstanding.</u>
This opinion is <u>attributed to</u> someone.
It can be regarded as <u>obvious/improbable</u> that . . .
A possible compromise <u>is offered by</u> . . .

APPENDIX C (German)

Ein wissenschaftliches Argument widerlegen

Etwas <u>irrtümlicherweise</u> zum Faktum erheben
In dieser Darstellung <u>bestehen faktische Widersprüche</u>
Seine <u>Schlussfolgerung</u> ist <u>zu bezweifeln/zweifelhaft/anzuzweifeln</u>
Eine Aussage <u>beruht auf einem Irrtum</u>
Man sollte derartige <u>Fehlschlüsse vermeiden</u>
<u>Gegen</u> diesen Schluss <u>sind Bedenken zu erheben/lassen sich Bedenken erheben</u>
Diese Schlussfolgerung steht auf <u>schmalem/wankendem Fundament</u>
Seine Darstellung <u>beruht auf einem Missverständnis</u>
Diese Meinung wird <u>jemandem zugeschrieben</u>
Etwas kann als <u>(un)wahrscheinlich/offensichtlich</u> angesehen werden
Als (Kompromiss)Lösung bietet sich xxx an

APPENDIX D

Instructions for Oral Presentations

Materials

1. Please write *the outline* of your entire oral presentation on an overhead (no complete sentences, please). Except for this overhead, you should not take anything with you, that is: you must speak freely, based only on your notes on the overhead.
2. You should discuss your overhead with me the week before your presentation. Please hand in your overhead (hard copy) during the class period before your presentation. I will then correct it and return it to you the same afternoon.
3. You should also have a handout for the entire class, which follows the content of the outline on your overhead but is formulated in complete sentences. Please hand your handout in to me the class period before your presentation for my correction. It is very important that you do not distribute your handout until *the end* of your presentation. Otherwise, the class will read your handout instead of listening to you. The purpose of the handout is to enable the class to read it at home and have a permanent record of your presentation.
4. Please use other materials, such as video and audio-cassettes, www etc. *very sparingly*. You should consider carefully which pedagogical goals you have in mind by using these materials for your presentation, and how much time you wish to invest in them. Remember that you only have 20 minutes (as a group) and that most of this time must be given to you speaking freely, rather than fiddling with technology. If your author was also a painter (W. Busch), it would be appropriate to show some of his work to the class, either via handout or overhead.

II. Content

Your presentation should consist of four parts:
1. Biography and most important works
2. Literary, political or historical background of the play we have read (Lessing and the Enlightenment, Kleist and Romanticism, Sternheim and the Wilhelminian Age)
3. Significance of the *author particularly for his genre* (Lessing and comedy, Busch and cartoons, Dürrenmatt and tragicomedy/the grotesque)
4. Significance of the author in one other field (Lessing as religious philosopher, Busch as painter). This means that you have to research your presentation carefully. You can either research the entire presentation as a group or divide separate parts of it (political background, biography, etc.) among yourselves. **Do be certain that the final result is a coherent whole.**

Developing Literacy and Literary Competence   69

III. Language
I expect that your presentation will utilize both the style and the expressions we have learned. Of particular relevance may be I (General Statements) and III (Authorial Positions).

IV. Grading
Your presentation will be graded according to the following categories:
1. Extensiveness of research   25%
2. Content   25%
3. Free speech   25%
4. Style/Complexity of speech   25%

All members of the group will receive the same grade in the first two categories; categories 3 and 4 will be individually graded. You should therefore, *as a group*, take great care that your research and the content of your presentation are of professional quality.

APPENDIX E

Heinrich Christian Wilhelm Busch (1832–1908)
(excerpt from a student's oral presentation, my translation)

I. Biography

1832:	Birth in Wiedensahl (near Hanover) Four brothers, one sister
1841:	Education through his uncle (Pastor Georg Kleine) Move to Ebergoetzen near Göttingen. Friendship with Erich Bachmann
1847:	16th birthday. Acceptance at Polytechnic University in Hanover—beginning of his study of mechanical engineering
1848:	Unhappiness with his studies of mechanical engineering; vague period of his life. Takes some courses in art.
1851:	Exmatriculation from the Polytechnic University in Hannover. Move to Düsseldorf. Immatriculation at the Academy of Art in Düsseldorf—Teacher Wilhelm von Schadow
1852:	Move to Antwerp; Student at the Academie Royale des Beaux-Arts
1853:	Severe illness (typhoid fever), return to Wiedensahl, beginning of his collection of fairy tales

APPENDIX F
Homework for Tuesday, October 13

Please write, in teams of 4–5, an adaptation of Kleist's drama *The Broken Jug:*
- In twentieth-century German
- Shortened to ten minutes
- In the style of the US-genre "courtroom drama." To do this, you may have to invent characters that do not exist in the original or leave out some that do.

You should take care to retain *all important* elements of the plot and characterizations. Your drama can be a satire or parody of the original.

PLEASE DO *NOT* QUOTE DIRECTLY FROM THE ORIGINAL: Your entire drama must be a paraphrase of the original.

PLEASE WORK TOGETHER AS A GROUP (do *NOT* divide the scenes up among yourselves and write portions of the play separately!).

You will perform your play on Tuesday, October 13, in class. Every member of your team must participate in the performance. You can take the script with you, in other words, you do not need to memorize the lines, but do act the play out and read with dramatic intonation.

Style: The relevance of our new style (cf. handout "Crime and Punishment") is obvious and can help you a great deal when writing your comedy.

Team 1: Hanne, Michelle, Jeremy, Frank
Team 2: Ivan, Ryo, Suzanne, Kirsten
Team 3: Fred, Vivien, Dan, Patrick, Cy

APPENDIX G (English)
Minna von Barnhelm, Excerpt
Written and Performed by Four Students
My translation, mistakes approximated

Dramatis Personae:
007— Major von Tellheim
Q—Just
008—Werner
Hotel Manager—innkeeper
Frenchman who works for M
Zhenia—Minna
Alota Fagina—Franziska
Widdow *[sp]* of an agents *[sp]*
Riccaut
Post[man]

Developing Literacy and Literary Competence

Hotel in Paris.
- 007 — Thanks for your services, but we today *[syntactical error]* will look for a new hotel.
- Hotel manager. — But no. You can have the room up on the fourth floor—with a view of the Eiffel-tower.
- Q — Yeah, probably with a view of the Eiffel-tower that is painted on the backside of the laundermat. *(Hotel manager exits.)*
- Q — I simply can't believe that he has thrown you, an agent *[ending error]*, out of his room. He would never have had the courage to do that if you were still working for the Queen of England.
- 007 — Q, take this ring and pay the bill with it. I don't want to stay any longer in this pigstie *[sp]* than absolutely necessary.
- Q — That the *[gender error]* pig has admitted himself *[lexical error]* the insolence of insulting you like this. He expects of himself *[lexical error]* that you can't pay just because M has fired you.
- 007 — Please don't remind me. Go after the hotel manager. *(Q exits.)*
- Lady in mourning *(knock, knock, knock).* Does the cat sing at noon?
- 007 — Only if it rains.
- Lady — 007, you don't know me. I am the widow of 009. I don't know if you know *[missing object]*, but he was shot last week by the Soviets in Monaco. In his will he said thaat *[sp]* he owes you a million dollars. Here is the account number of a Swiss account. You can find the money there.
- 007 — You say, you are the wife of 009?
- Lady — *Da*, I mean, yes.
- 007 — Does the singing girl wear a blue bow on Sundays?
- Lady — No, she wears her hair open.
- 007 — My lady, please keep the money. Your husband paid me back a month ago. I'm terribly sorry about your husband. Use the money for your children's education.
- Lady — Oh, you are much too generous. Many thanks. *(Exits.)*

APPENDIX G (German)

Minna von Barnhelm, Auszug
Geschrieben und aufgeführt von 4 Studenten

Dramatis Personae:
007—Major von Tellheim
Q—Just
008—Werner
Hotel Manager—Wirt
Franzoser, der für M arbeitet
Zhenia—Minna
Alota Fagina—Franziska
Witwerin eines Agents
Riccaut
Post

Hotel in Paris.

007: Vielen Dank für Ihre Dienste, aber wir suchen ein neues Hotel heute.

Hotel-manager: Aber nein. Sie könnten das Zimmer oben in der 4. Etage haben—mit Blick auf den Eifelturm.

Q: Ja, wahrscheinlich mit Blick auf den angemalten Eifeltum, der auf der Rückseite der Münzwäscherei steht.

(Hotel-manager geht ab.)

Q: Ich kann es einfach nicht begreifen, dass er dich—einen Agent aus seinem Zimmer rausgeworfen hat. Er hätte niemals den Mut gehabt, das zu tun, wärst du noch bei der Königin von England.

007: Q, nimm diesen Ring und bezahl damit die Rechnung. Ich will in diesem Schweinestahl nicht länger bleiben, als es unbedingt sein muss.

Q: Dass der Schwein sich die Unverschämtheit zugelassen hat, dich so zu beleidigen. Er lässt sich zumuten, dass du nicht bezahlen kannst, nur weil M dich entlassen hat.

007: Bitte erinnere mich nicht daran. Geh dem Hotel-manager nach.

(Q geht ab.)

Dame in Trauer *(klopf, klopf, klopf):* Singt die Katze um Mittag?

007: Nur wenn es regnet.

Dame: 007, Sie kennen mich nicht. Ich bin die Witwe von 009. Ich weiß nicht, ob Sie wissen, aber er wurde letzte Woche von den Sowjeten in Monaco erschossen. In seinem Testament stand, daß er Ihnen eine Million Dollar schuldet. Hier ist

	die Kontonummer von einer Konto in der Schweiz. Dort können Sie das Geld finden.
007:	Sie sagen, Sie sind die Frau von 009?
Dame:	Da, ich meine, ja.
007:	Trägt das singende Mädchen eine blaue Schleife am Sonntag?
Dame:	Nein, sie trägt ihre Haare offen.
007:	Meine Dame, bitte behalten Sie das Geld. Ihr Mann hat mir vor einem Monat das Geld zurückgegeben. Es tut mir furchtbar leid, wegen ihres Mannes. Verwenden Sie das Geld für das Studium ihrer Kinder.
Dame:	Ach, Sie sind viel zu großzügig. Herzlichen Dank. *(Geht ab.)*

Crossing the Boundaries Between Literature and Pedagogy: Perspectives on a Foreign Language Reading Course

Joanne Burnett and Leah Fonder-Solano

Introduction

The issue of collegial divisions among foreign language faculty has been a subject of ardent debate within the confines both of professional publications and departmental hallways.[1] As Hoffman and James (1986) would have it, the "split between language and literature" in university foreign-language departments "amounts to a split between 'language faculty' and 'literature faculty'" (p. 29). Indeed, many language professionals have contributed to this ongoing debate (Bernhardt 1995, 1997; Byrnes 1995; Kramsch 1987; Rice 1991). More specifically, Welles (1998) laments the absence of literature in the *Standards* while Kramsch (1995) views differing perspectives in the field of foreign language education as an opportunity for dialogue and intellectual inquiry. Correspondingly, a spectrum of publications exists on the teaching of literature (Birckbichler and Muyskens 1980; Bretz and Persin 1987; Broad 1988; Chaves-Tesser and Long 2000; Kramsch 1985; Lazar 1993; McKay 1982; Moorjani and Field 1983; Muyskens 1983; Ragland 1974).

As colleagues trained respectively in French language education and Spanish literature, we add to this discussion by approaching the issue from an empirical, research-based standpoint. This division between faculty trained in language education and those trained in literature, played out on a national scale, also exists within our department. For this reason, we decided to methodically compare our beliefs, practices, and decision-making processes with regard to a second-language (L2) reading and literature course. We tend to side with Byrnes (1995), who values consensus making between professionals in language departments trained in different fields as "the result of keen, multifaceted exploration of my and others' beliefs, of our presuppositions, our modes and methods of analysis and synthesis; it is a hermeneutics of inquiry that looks at the contexts that have led each one of us to our opinions" (p. 14). With this in mind, the main questions we explored were at the heart of what we truly do for a living:

- How did our former educational training and research backgrounds shape us as teachers?
- What differences and similarities would we find in comparing our classroom syllabi, activities, handouts, exercises, requirements, and teaching approaches?
- What beliefs did we hold about the way in which an upper-level reading/introduction to literature course should be structured and about how the other would structure her course?

We felt that exploring these questions was fundamental to our jobs as tenure-track Assistant Professors and would promote better understanding of each other's work.[2] Thus, in the spring of 1999, we initiated this study while teaching a parallel reading course in French and Spanish.[3] Our findings represent a first step in a much needed dialogue between university language professors trained differently. Moreover, it provides an opportunity to reflect on the impact of former training and teacher beliefs on curricular decisions as well as collegiality.

Theoretical Frameworks and Design of the Study

The design of the study reflects both a phenomenological and process orientation and is inspired by the theoretical frameworks of symbolic interactionism (Blumer 1969; Mead 1934) and social constructionism (Gergen 1985, 1986, 1991). These frameworks permit a focus on the nature of language teaching as it relates to the meaning we ascribed to classrooms in which the focus was on reading and literature. Interpretation, using the symbolic interactionist's lens, evolves with an understanding of how the individual constructs meaning. Likewise, social constructionists see people as molders of their own social world. Using these theoretical perspectives as the backdrop from which to draw interpretations, it was imperative to view the reading/literature classroom as mediating a complex underlying structure of values, motives, and biases. In this vein, the following questions guided data interpretation:

- What meanings, both overt and covert, do we as teachers attach to behavior patterns and objects in the educational institutions of which we are a part and in which we have been trained?
- How do varying interpretations of meaning, expectations, and motivations affect our professional behavior?
- How does the process of constructing meaning take place?

- In what ways do we as teachers act on the basis of meanings we perceive?

Adapted from Le Compte and Preissle (1993).

Our research additionally contributes to a growing body of literature on language-teacher beliefs, decision-making processes, and practices. As Woods (1996) points out, there are three gaps in this research as it pertains to L2 classroom teaching and learning:

- Research has not described the structure of classroom language teaching in pedagogical terms, i.e., in the context of larger units of course structure and the underlying objectives.
- It has not examined the processes by which teachers plan and make decisions about their teaching (both for and in the classroom).
- It has not examined the language teaching/learning process as it is perceived and interpreted by the participants themselves—in particular the teacher (p. 11).

Beliefs are instrumental in shaping how we as teachers interpret what goes on in our classroom. They have an effect on our representation of reality, guide our thoughts and behaviors, and influence what we know, feel, and do. They are grounded in episodic memory built from prior experiences both as teachers and students and are stable and resistant to change. They have a profound impact on the nature of teachers' reasoning and the ways teachers conceptualize themselves (Johnson 1999). Similarly, research in the area of teacher cognition has argued that understanding teachers' interpretations is central to understanding teaching (Clark 1988; Johnson 1994, 1999). Ulichny (cited in Johnson 1999) captures the interpretive qualities of teaching: "The interpretive framework [the teacher] brings to the class is based on her past experiences as a teacher and learner, her professional knowledge and folk wisdom about teaching, and aspects of her personality" (p. 63). Similar to Ulichny, Woods (1996) addresses belief systems and states, "Teachers 'interpret' a teaching situation in the light of their beliefs about the learning and teaching of what they consider a second language to consist of; the result of this interpretation is what the teacher plans for and attempts to create in the classroom" (p. 69).

We chose a qualitative research design and methodology in order to explore these beliefs, processes, and interpretations. The purpose of qualitative research is to understand phenomena in depth rather than generalize to a larger population. In defining qualitative research, Merriam (1988) and others have described it as an intensive, holistic description and analysis of phenomena within a social unit. The qualitative research process occurs in a natural setting, uses the researcher as the data collection instrument, makes use of tacit knowledge in order to arrive at conditions for common understandings, and employs inductive analysis so that theory about human interaction derives from the study itself (Lincoln and Guba, 1985; Merriam, 1988; Yin, 1989).

In keeping with a qualitative research design, methods of data collection included interviews, videotaped classes, and a reflective journal. Spradley (1979), Mishler (1986), and Siedman (1991) have related the benefit of in-depth interviewing both as a research method in its own right and as a complement to other forms of ethnographic research methods. Thus, we completed four audiotaped interviews lasting from two to three hours throughout the semester of data collection (spring 1999). Our classes were also videotaped for a total of four hours in length. As many qualitative researchers recommend (Glesne and Peshkin 1992; Lincoln and Guba 1985), we also kept a reflective journal to record perceptions of and reactions to the class activities, student participation, and course preparation. In addition, syllabi, lecture and class notes, handouts, written activities, assignments, exams, and a representative sample of work from two students were also collected.

Subsequent to data collection, we viewed the videotapes together and separately with each researcher taking notes on the other's practices. Post viewing and analysis provided notes of student and teacher movement, activities, interaction, and dialogue. By the summer of 1999, each of the four interviews had been transcribed for accurate interpretation of emergent patterns and themes. In order to begin the analysis process, we made two copies of each set of data (class materials, interviews, videotape notes, journals) and read them in their entirety. On the second reading of the interview transcripts, we individually wrote comments in the margins as a point of departure for analysis. In this phase, an understanding of the data via symbolic interactionist and social constructionist frameworks was developed. Subsequently, the data were placed into categories through analytic induction (Goetz and LeCompte 1984; LeCompte and Preissle 1993). This technique involved scanning the data for categories of phenomena and for relationships among these categories. The overarching categories that emerged—Course Organization, Course Goals, Teacher Beliefs, Initial Perceptions versus Findings, and Conceptual Change—were further subdivided into topics: Initial Reactions, Educational Training, Reader Choice, and Diverging Definitions of Literature. In both the beginning and final stages of data analysis, emergent patterns and themes were color coded, highlighted, and placed in file folders. In this manner, the data sources were triangulated to provide a richer understanding of our attitudes and behaviors, as well as the meanings ascribed to our course creation and roles as teachers. Data analysis continued until the spring of 2000 when we also began to create grids and tables of overarching thematic units, as well as specific details supporting these units. Due to the scope and nature of this article, detailed discussion of each category is not feasible neither are all data sources cited equally because they do not all specifically address the aforementioned themes.

Most crucial to establishing credibility in a qualitative study, we both wrote and revised drafts of the present article and argued as well as conferred on the descriptions, interpretations, and conclusions we developed. Thus, as a team, we mutually shaped the written product (Lincoln and Guba 1985). Aware that our dual roles as both subject and object of the study (researchers/authors and teachers) could be construed as problematic, we were conscious of the need to follow preestablished data collection and analysis procedures. For the sake of clarity when referring to our experience as individuals we will use "Burnett," "Fonder-Solano" or "she." However, as seen in this section, with regard to the collaborative narrative, the pronoun "we" will be employed. While for some readers this may seem disjointed, this seemed the most reasonable way to resolve the dilemma of the personal in composition. Moreover, we felt strongly that, no matter the issue of narration or methodology, our story would strike a chord with those who work in the same situation as ours and who, like us, seek understanding and acceptance in the midst of departmental divisions.

Although Burnett had seen Fonder-Solano's demonstration class the year she was hired, we had never since observed one another or discussed at length our personal philosophies or approaches to teaching. This research gave us this chance, one which is, frankly, taken too rarely among colleagues whose offices may be right next door, but whose classrooms remain, in some cases off-limits, and in most, simply unknown.

This article adheres to the tenets of a qualitative account and will attempt to shed light on the interpretive frames we used to support the ways in which we envisioned and fashioned our respective courses. In the sections that follow we will focus first on our educational experience, which had enormous impact on shaping the curricular decision-making processes that inform our practice; second, on comparisons of course goals and organization; third, on our beliefs about how this course should be taught, which include our reasoning, rationale, and philosophy of approach; finally, on our perceptions of how each other would handle teaching the course.

Background

Initial Reactions

Faced with the prospect of teaching an introduction to literature course in French and Spanish, the following reactions are taken from our first interview. Fonder-Solano responded quite positively to being assigned, by the department head, the 300-level literature course. One reason was that as a graduate student she had already taught the same type of course:

> This course is a very natural extension of what I do. I was trained in literature. I have my doctorate in literature, so teaching an introduction to literature course is a very, very, natural extension of what I do and the way I was trained. It was my fifth or sixth time teaching this type of course, and because of my experience perhaps, my main concern was how to make this an exciting and accessible course to the student who is just getting out of four semesters of study in the language. (Interview 1)

Having read the course catalogue's description to "FRE 341 Introduction to Literature—An introduction to the study of French prose, poetry, drama; techniques of literary analysis, continued study of French language," Burnett had a very different reaction:

> My reaction was one of fear. Honestly, first of all, the title was "Introduction to Literature" and with my particular training, I did not feel adequately prepared to teach a course entitled "Introduction to Literature." As well, I'll be very honest about this, I didn't want to take a traditional genre approach, although I had a notion about what that meant, I just did not feel comfortable, because my background is not strong enough in textual analysis to take a more literary approach to a course. (Interview 1)

Because the professor who taught it previously had retired, and no other French faculty volunteered[4], Burnett ultimately agreed. But before doing so, she changed its title and course number and shaped it in accordance with her background and training in pedagogy. This will be discussed in the section entitled *Diverging Definitions of Literature*. However, because our divergent reactions may be directly related to each teacher's background and training, we will first briefly outline our educational experience.

Educational Training

Burnett finished her B.A. and M.A. degrees in French with teacher certification by the mid-eighties. During her master's studies, she applied to and was accepted as a graduate teaching assistant at the Université de Liège in Belgium. A year later she found work in a private school teaching English as a foreign language where she stayed another two years. Undergraduate and graduate coursework in literature included at least one course in eighteenth-, nineteenth-, and twentieth-century literature, mainly composed of excerpts, although she had read several complete plays and novels by the end of the master's level. Her M.A. included a range of courses in education, linguistics, literature and civilization. Burnett recalled that the master's program significantly changed her views of language study:

> It wasn't until I got to [the University of] Illinois that I remember being absolutely fascinated by a course that I took out of the Department of Education called Ethnography of Communication, and we began to look at the social aspects of language, language use in different societies, that I began to see, "O my gosh, there's this other thing that one can do in language that interests me more than nineteenth-century poetry," a course I was currently enrolled in. That's when I began to change over to thinking about language education. (Interview 2)

Upon returning from Belgium, Burnett accepted a teaching assistantship in the Department of French at the Pennsylvania State University. Although her doctorate would be in French, she specialized in FLA (Foreign Language Acquisition) with inter-disciplinary course work in French, Spanish, Curriculum and Instruction, Higher Education, and Speech Communication. Courses included work in second language reading and testing, technology, curriculum development, conversation analysis, applied linguistics, language acquisition theory, methods of teaching as well as qualitative research methods (13 courses total). Her training also included mandatory Teaching Assistant meetings, and in her final year, she was appointed supervisor of third semester French. As part of the program, she was also required to take two courses in French civilization as well as two in literature. In literature, she chose "Gender Theory," a course that influenced positively the way she viewed and valued women's writing and feminist criticism:

> I began to see in gender theory that you could take texts and analyze them using feminist criticism and that you could take texts from science, from anthropology, from literature. You could take texts from

Hélène Cixous, who is still living and writing, and differentiate *l'écriture féminine* from phallocentric writing and analyze a whole culture and how it has repressed and subjugated women. And that became a banner for me, that notion of text as liberating by the way you analyze it. I had never, ever been exposed to that before. (Interview 2)

Before this course, she did not remember having been assigned texts by women, although in recalling several of her final projects for courses in French civilization, she sought out and wrote about women's issues. The second course, entitled "Stylistique Avancée," was a requirement for all graduate students in the French Department; it focused on textual and literary analysis. Far removed from either subject, Burnett's dissertation research ultimately entailed qualitative case studies of teaching assistants who taught weekly in computer-equipped classrooms.

Fonder-Solano completed undergraduate majors in Spanish and Latin American Area Studies at the University of Minnesota, Morris and an M.A. and Ph.D. in Hispanic Literature at the University of Arizona. Her undergraduate language study had a strong literary focus, totaling some five courses. Nevertheless, it was only through her master's and doctoral studies (a total of twenty-three literature courses) that she began to engage analytically not only the texts she was reading, but also, through critical theory, larger social and historic conditions.

During this same period, Fonder-Solano was thrust into the reality of teaching first-year language courses as a graduate teaching assistant. To aid in this stressful transition from language student to language teacher, she had one Teaching Methodology course, the examples of her own professors, and the helpful advice of fellow teaching assistants. Guided by Omaggio's *Teaching Language in Context* (1986) as well as peer observations and classroom activities shared among the assistants (although there were no organized Teaching Assistant meetings), she gradually acquired valuable experience in the classroom and was eventually allowed to teach upper-level courses, including "Introduction to Literary Genres." Her dissertation was a feminist analysis of writings by Cristina Peri Rossi, a contemporary Uruguayan author. Upon being hired at the university, Fonder-Solano, like Burnett, was surprised and shocked to be asked to teach a course far outside her range of experience: a master's level course dealing with some aspect of pedagogy. (She ended up teaching a course dealing with issues of oral communication in the classroom.) The introductory literature course that we examine in this study brought her back to very familiar territory.

Course Overview

On the first day of class,[5] Burnett conducted a survey of student L1 and L2 reading habits and interests and announced that the next class meeting would be at the library to familiarize students with French books, magazines, and films available for their use among library holdings. Her course included a primary reader *Liens: Lectures diverses* (Davis 1994). As the semester progressed she supplemented *Liens* with three selections from a second reader, *Diversité: La nouvelle francophone à travers le monde* (Budig-Markin and Gaasch 1995), and two novels, *L'enfant noir* (Laye 1953) and *Les petits enfants du siècle* (Rochefort 1961). The *Liens* text, rather than adopting a strictly "literary" stance, included newspaper articles, film reviews, and folktales. In addition to completing the readings, students were expected to make extensive, regular journal entries on the reading process including (in either French or English) new vocabulary, reactions to the text, and comprehension strategies. Textbook exercises and teacher-designed activities completed in class were also to be turned in for credit. As a final project, students in this course completed a portfolio of five student-selected readings related to the theme of their choice. For each reading, they wrote a one-to-two page summary-analysis in French. For Burnett, it was important that at semester's end students begin to search for texts according to their own tastes in contrast to the teacher-imposed selections they had been working with all semester. She offers further rationale for this final activity:

> For me the whole notion is to help them in becoming lifelong readers and learners of French. So the reason I'm having them do a portfolio of texts and write summaries is for them. I am, in a way, nudging them towards thinking about where it is they're going to access French texts after this class. And they have to write mini-summaries of those texts as well as state why they would or would not recommend that text to a classmate. Because I want them to understand what social practices of literacy are, I want them to reflect on that in their own lives, What is reading for? What is literature for? It's sometimes to recommend [a text] to somebody else so that you have a common experience in reading. That is part of the social practices aspect that I want them to think about developing in the second language as well. (Interview 2)

Burnett's practices and beliefs will be developed in the pages that follow. They later resurface to reinforce differences in approach between the two teachers.

Fonder-Solano began her course by collecting general information about the students (name, major, phone number, reason for taking the course). She spent the first two weeks practicing reading strategies (dictionary skills, using context/background knowledge, skimming, identifying key information, and re-reading) to be used throughout the course. This course used the reader *Aproximaciones al estudio de la literatura hispánica* (Virgillo, Friedman, and Valdivieso 1993) supplemented by narrative and poetic excerpts. Similar to Burnett's class, students kept a notebook, which included class notes in addition to questions, new vocabulary, and their impressions regarding each reading selection. Students did not receive a grade for written exercises completed in class, but included them in their notebooks. Fonder-Solano also set aside a "library day" whose purpose was to enable students to research and collect sources for their final paper. This final research paper, on any student-selected topic relating to one (or more) of the readings, was a minimum of five pages in length.

Goals, Texts, and Beliefs

Reader Choice

The issues dealt with in our first interview delved into teaching philosophies as well as firmly held notions about course construction and implementation. (The syllabi may be seen in detail in Appendix A.) Since we had both already taught this same course the previous spring, and Fonder-Solano had also taught it several times in the past, we had strong ideas what such a course entailed and were able to justify pedagogical decisions such as the choice of a reader and supplementary materials. Fonder-Solano begins by relating her primary goals:

> Making students relate to literature is my main goal...One of the things I feel free to do is organize it not giving equal time to every genre, but because I feel that what's most exciting to me is also going to be what's most exciting to the students, I really feel that what I can show enthusiasm about is what is going to stick in their minds as well. That's why I'm dedicating most time to the short story, the poetry, and the theater, and at the end we're going to do a theatrical production, so they can see the live version of some of the things we're reading. (Interview 1)

Reflecting her training in curriculum development, Burnett, unlike Fonder-Solano, stated course goals explicitly on her syllabus: "This course has as its goal first and foremost to allow students to practice honing their reading skills in French, to participate in the literate skills necessary to becoming life long learners and readers of French...and

Crossing the Boundaries Between Literature and Pedagogy 85

to whet student appetite for continued reading in French." Burnett reiterates:

> As a teacher of this course my goal is to make them life-long readers, but in making them life-long readers, I have to shape the practices and skills that one needs to read in a second language, so that actually is more important. I am hoping, through my choice of texts [*L'enfant noir* (Laye 1953) and *Les petits enfants du siècle* (Rochefort 1961)], one which is about Francophone culture and the other by a feminist writer, to create critical thinking skills as well as offer cultural information. I want them to gain cultural information. But I think that I still have to help them learn to read. (Interview 2)

Fonder-Solano chose a reader (Virgillo et al. 1993) which divides the literary segments into genre and focused on short story, novel, poetry, and theater. The reader also lists chronologically major literary works and gives brief biographies of the authors, although these were not systematically included in course assignments. In terms of support for comprehension, both footnotes and glosses accompany each text as well as comprehension and discussion questions. For some works, the reader also provides a short identification exercise. Commenting on what she particularly valued about *Aproximaciones* (Virgillo et al. 1993), she stated:

> One thing I like about the book is that there are more readings than you could ever use in the course. It's got a wide selection, and just as many female authors as male and from all the time periods, from medieval to the present, so there's a wide selection. I don't try to cover every area. I try to pick out what I feel are the most interesting readings . . . what might appeal most to my students and what might provoke the most interest in discussions in class. (Interview 1)

On the other hand, in response to the text's lack of reading support, Fonder-Solano was obliged to consistently develop a range of activities to supplement what the reader offered. These included vocabulary building activities, matching exercises, true/false statements, character identification, multiple choice and, in a couple of cases, she also had them draw an image of the scene they had just read.

In the following excerpt, Burnett justifies her choice of reader. She was particularly concerned with the reading process and underscored her reasons for organizing the course:

> I was familiar with and comfortable with *Heinle & Heinle* publications and knew *Liens* (Davis 1994) was [part of the] "Bridging the Gap" series. I knew it had been authored by my [former] professor whose re-

search was in reading and who I respected and admired. I had taken a couple classes with him and thought he was a super teacher. And in looking at the book each text was set up in a very thorough fashion. It wasn't just comprehension questions at the end of the text but it was preparing students to truly understand the text. As the students are reading there are also glossed words and phrases in the margins along with questions that students can answer if they want as they're reading. So the text was set up theoretically by someone who had a strong reading research background, and I thought this would be a super text to use in class because I didn't want to do the [literary] genre thing. I didn't feel comfortable doing it. (Interview 1)

Furthermore, Burnett's reader contained prereading exercises in the form of cognate and word-associations; text overviews which asked students to guess, according to the passages given, what might happen next in the reading; and post-reading activities in the form of both oral and written comprehension exercises that, for example, required students to put key phrases in order or respond to true/false statements. Many of the readings included a bibliography of supplemental readings for students who might desire to read more on the same topic. Because *Liens* (Davis 1994) offered substantial help to the student reader, which was not the case for *Aproximaciones* (Virgillo et al. 1993), Burnett did not have to supplement the reader in the same fashion. She felt confident that *Liens* would engage the student readers in the reading process and that its reading activities were consistent with the most recent theories of L2 reading and language acquisition.

Burnett also explains why she had students read two novels and how she made these choices:

This book is set up by genre but it's not genre in the sense of poetry, theater, short story . . . my book is set up by what I call text-types. The first one is called the portrait, the next is a description of a place, followed by newspaper articles on accidents and finally there are film reviews. I personally feel more comfortable with that. [But] we also read two short novels. You know they're at least reading these novels, and at the end they can say, "I read two short novels in French." The text-types are short, mini-texts. Most of them are excerpts. But I also thought that the students would enjoy or have more of a feeling of accomplishment if they could also read complete works. And because I was interested in these two novels, *L'enfant noir* (Laye 1953), which I had never read in its entirety before and *Les petits enfants du siècle* (Rochefort 1961), which I had taught in excerpt form, and which I wanted to read some day, I decided, "I'm going to teach it and that's how I'm going to get to read it." (Interview 1)

As the foregoing shows, we held firmly to our divergent beliefs about what the overarching goals of the course should be. Burnett adhered to her ideal of creating life-long readers of French by shaping reading practices and felt students would enjoy the accomplishment of reading two novels as well as a variety of text-types. It was equally important, however, in terms of the reading process, to start with shorter texts and build to longer ones. At the same time, she stressed the importance of the novels for offering insight on Francophone cultures as well as engaging students in critical thinking. In choosing her reader, Fonder-Solano valued the diverse selection of readings from different time periods and authors. She felt that, by making literature accessible to students through class activities and by concluding with a play, they would become as excited and enthusiastic as she was. This difference in goals and focus stems, in part, from differing notions of what constitutes "literature." The following section will address this issue in greater detail.

Diverging Definitions of Literature

This section will use Burnett's decision to change her existing course title and course content, an issue that generated substantial debate throughout the tape-recorded interviews, as a point of departure for analysis of the beliefs held by each participant about her respective course. Although both courses studied here were originally designed to prepare students for upper-level literature courses, the decision to change the title from "Introduction to Literature" to "Reading in French," stems directly from Burnett's beliefs regarding this course, many of which were at variance with more traditional departmental views. The bureaucratic process for such a change is in itself quite complex, involving substantial paperwork and passing the "new" course through committees at three different levels of university administration. Moreover, Burnett's change met some resistance on the part of the faculty:

> I don't think certain colleagues value and respect what I do. That's been made clear to me ... with faculty members saying in meetings, "Remember, this is a Department of Foreign Languages *and* Literatures." Or comments like, why don't you all [pedagogy faculty] go over to the Department of Education? Or another faculty member having said to me once, why do you all dislike literature so much? ... One of the reasons, I think, that the faculty says I don't like literature is because I changed the course. (Interview 4)

While Burnett felt at times misunderstood, her implementation of this change despite such obstacles underscores the strength of her convictions regarding second-language reading in general and this course in particular.

First, Burnett argues that a literature-oriented course falsely assumes a certain level of student reading competence. Rejecting the more traditional view of this course as an introduction to literary terminology, literary theory, and classics texts, Burnett views the course as an opportunity for students to continue building linguistic skills by practicing reading in a variety of contexts, particularly given that it directly follows the basic language sequence in the French curriculum. Second, Burnett repeatedly expressed a lack of interest in "literature," in the traditional sense of male-authored canonical works, literary terms and textual analysis: "I just couldn't do that to them [the students]. So we practice reading a variety of texts of different types, but not ones that are canonical or that form what is considered literature in French" (Interview 1). This variance from traditional course content stems both from a perceived lack of preparation in literature/literary theory and Burnett's own experiences as a student. Although looking back at her undergraduate and graduate transcripts, she found that she actually had eight courses in literature, she still did not feel confident teaching a literature-oriented course, particularly one organized by genre or time period:

> I also chose the reader approach the first month . . . [because] I felt confident that I could help them build skills in reading . . . vocabulary building, questioning as you're reading, going back, rereading, checking . . . but I wouldn't feel competent teaching medieval literature, for example. I wouldn't do it. . . . Although I had two courses in nineteenth-century, I still wouldn't feel competent to do the nineteenth-century novel. (Interview 4)

Given Burnett's stated background in literature, her negative response to literature courses cannot be adequately explained as stemming from a lack of training. As the emotional ending of this quote infers, Burnett's aversion toward such courses is strongly grounded in her own negative experiences of literature courses as a student:

> I did read poetry, and I did read theater. I did read some Medieval and Renaissance stuff, which I disliked, *La Chanson de Roland, Pantagruel, Gargantua,* in a French civ course. And in undergrad we had these French anthologies called *Lagarde [et] Michard* from which loads of students were taught in the seventies and eighties, and I think I've got the nineteenth century and the eighteenth century volumes,

but what do I remember from them? Nothing. No. Nothing. . . . But what I remember are the literature things I did at Penn State, the gender theory and then a course I audited for fun on women's writing in the nineteenth century. Maybe I'm at a stage where I'm seeking ways to approach and teach literature that are different from the ways, some of the ways I was taught, and that really didn't work for me. (Interviews 3 and 4)

Third, Burnett reiterated in the interviews her view of this course as developing student interest in reading French, potentially creating "life-long readers" in French. She felt that by exposing students to a wide variety of texts in French, students would be more likely to search out French language texts in the future and to find reading material suited to their individual tastes and lifestyles. To this end, Burnett conducted a "library day" to make students aware of library holdings in French, including magazines, newspapers, books, and scholarly journals. Moreover, she gave certain students the addresses, web sites, and phone numbers of American distributors of foreign language publications. To justify these decisions, Burnett explains her view of the student reading process:

I view the student as still something that we're molding and shaping [in terms of linguistic competency] and that they come to a reading course hopefully with a desire for reading literature. But I just think that first of all I'm still helping them build competency, particularly reading competency, and I think we still have to work at things at the word level, at just the acquisition of vocabulary level. We have to prepare them to read. I want to bring them to reading but I guess I don't want them to be of the opinion that there's only one way of reading. (Interview 1)

In summary, Burnett's course title, syllabus, and policy decisions are strongly guided by her belief that traditional introduction to literature courses do not necessarily prepare students for upper-level French language reading. Furthermore, recalling her own educational training and interests, she doubts that all students will pursue the study of French literature. Rather than emphasizing canonical classics, theoretical terminology, or styles of formal analysis, Burnett's course focuses on the development of reading skills and progresses from page-long readings of a variety of text types to short novels. It additionally offers students the necessary knowledge and opportunity to find reading material in French for future reading. In this way, she hopes to promote French-language reading as a continual process that extends far beyond the scope of a one-semester course.

Fonder-Solano had been teaching this course for several years as a graduate student at the University of Arizona, but had only begun to reflect on and articulate her beliefs about it during this study's recorded interviews. Indeed, she had not even been aware that a debate in the field existed between language pedagogy faculty and literature faculty until she started her current job. Her coursework, her preparation, her background, and her interests had simply not prepared her to address curricular issues such as those presented here.

Unlike Burnett, she did not feel the need to officially change the title that appeared in the course bulletin, "SPA 341 Introduction to Spanish Literature," although her syllabus dubbed the course "Introduction to Hispanic Literature" and included readings from throughout the Spanish-speaking world. As revealed in the interviews, her views of literature contrasted markedly with those of Burnett.

Fonder-Solano's training in marginal literatures, testimony, and postmodern theory—a substantial component of both her M.A. and her Ph.D. degrees—imparted a broader view of literature as defying critics' attempts at definition and categorization, including the canon. Because Fonder-Solano did not perceive the "literature" title to impose either a course organization or course content that made her uncomfortable, she did not consider changing the title, despite using many texts that would not be considered "classics" (works by women, lesser-known texts, and predominantly contemporary works) or even "literature" in the traditional sense:

> I [have] a very wide notion of what is literature and we've talked [in class] about how it's socially defined . . . you know, is a letter you write to your mother literature? No. Well, then why is Che Guevara's diary considered literature? . . . Or Christopher Colombus's letter to the Queen of Spain . . . These are social, postmodern evaluations of what [literature] is. Women's literature and minority literatures and international literatures . . . are starting to become very prominent on the world scene, and given positive . . . value. (Interview 4)

Although she did not question the validity of Burnett's course and organization, like faculty trained in literature before her, Fonder-Solano preferred to use class time exclusively for broadly-defined "literary" works as opposed to the articles from popular media found in Burnett's reader and cited several reasons for this choice. First, Fonder-Solano found literature more interesting and rewarding:

> To me, the definition of literature is not the canon, but it's something that students are going to find thought-provoking, that's really going to generate meaningful discussion. That might [give the reader] an

insight or a new understanding of life. Like when we were reading about moral issues, someone who was between belief and doubt and how that affected his whole life, and all of a sudden Sofia [the native Spanish speaker in the class] had this insight that she'd never realized before how the Catholic church has used religion to keep people down and keep people content with their lot in life, that's why I wouldn't teach film reviews, [for instance], in my course. (Interview 3)

Second, while *Aproximaciones* (Virgillo et al. 1993) began with shorter readings (one- to two-page stories), followed by a short novel, poetry and drama, length was not a determining factor in terms of ordering reading assignments. For Fonder-Solano, the "literary" nature of the beginning texts did not necessarily make them more difficult, particularly when accompanied by notebook assignments and class activities. Third, she felt that she was exposing students to an important part of Hispanic society and culture that they would probably not find in the daily course of their lives, even when studying abroad:

The point [of my course] is to introduce students to another kind of reading, something that is also out there. I think that if students go to Spain or if they go to Mexico or if they continue to have any kind of interaction with the language, I think they'll eventually run into newspapers and I think they'll run into film reviews, but I don't think that in the daily course of their lives, unless they take a course in it, that there's much chance that they will have a meaningful interaction with what is considered literature, or even what is noncanonical literature. (Interview 2)

For this reason, in her view, the course exposed students to many different types of literary readings, not only in the sense of genre (poetry, short story, novel, drama), but also from diverse time periods and geographical areas.

Such variety in reading selections also reflects Fonder-Solano's conscious attempt to find readings that would appeal to her students. This desire to make her course exciting and relevant to students came up at several points in the interviews. Fonder-Solano's firm beliefs about her selection of texts likewise stems from her hope to foster not only reading skills, but like Burnett, critical thinking skills and cultural knowledge:

I hope . . . to develop their critical abilities, not, not in the sense of Siskel and Ebert, thumbs up or thumbs down, but in the sense of, do [they] take everything at face value or to question as they read . . . long after they've forgotten a short story in my course, I hope that they continue to use that skill. . . . (Interview 2)

She adds:

> I feel that what we're teaching them is not only literature... [but also] an expression of the way people think. Of the thought and the culture and the traditions. Look at *So Long a Letter*! [A novel by Mariama Bâ that Burnett has taught in her Francophone Civilization course]. Look at all that comes out about being Muslim, about having many wives, about, about the culture. You can't talk about the book, you can't discuss the book without discussing culture. I wouldn't say that the main thing I want to give to my students is cultural information about the Guatemalan Indians, but if they get excited about Rigoberta Menchú, it's great! I believe in opening the course to making it meaningful on as many different levels as possible. (Interview 2)

To recap, Fonder-Solano held a very different view of literature and its role in this course than that expressed by Burnett. She emphasized the importance of literature, broadly defined, in furthering reading skills, and she also subscribed to the important role literary works have in contributing to critical thinking skills and cultural knowledge. In opposition to departmental views, Burnett wanted students to value her course as more than just preparation for higher-level literature courses. Burnett's goals were to create life-long readers in French, to foster interest in a variety of text-types, and to encourage the process of reading. She, like Fonder-Solano, wanted students to view and to participate in the act of second-language reading outside the boundaries of traditional thinking. Before this study, however, we were unaware that we shared this same goal, albeit expressed differently.

Initial Perceptions versus Findings

Based on her experiences with literature and literature teachers, Burnett expected to find that Fonder-Solano's course would probably emphasize canonical, mainstream texts and that her teaching practices would probably be different from her own. In fact, as stated above, Fonder-Solano's textual choices reflect a postmodern education, using as many marginal writers and texts as mainstream works. With regard to Fonder-Solano's teaching practices, video analysis revealed diverse activities, students working in pairs, students reading portions of the text out loud, and in one instance a creative postreading activity in which students pretended to interview the author of one of their texts. In terms of context-building or prereading activities, she attempted to get students to think about ways in which the theme or topic related to their own lives. After listening to Fonder-Solano describe some of her class activities, Burnett realized that their practices as teachers appeared to be similar: "I'm actually beginning to feel that you as a teacher are more like me than I thought you were" (Interview 4). This was confirmed for Burnett after viewing Fonder-Solano's videotapes. In an earlier interview, Fonder-Solano described her inspiration for teaching ideas and techniques:

> Without necessarily taking pedagogy courses, I've learned a lot from you, I've learned a lot from other teachers I've been exposed to. I'm constantly looking for ideas. I learned a lot from just teaching conversation, seeing the excitement and thinking, ok, ways I can communicate that excitement to a different kind of course. (Interview 3)

Other perceptions held by Burnett prior to this study were in fact borne out by the data. Burnett assumed that Fonder-Solano's class, following convention, would have exams and a paper. This perception was confirmed in that Fonder-Solano's class completed a midterm, take-home exam, consisting of identification and essay questions, although the final exam was never given. The class also wrote a final research paper (five pages in length) that explored a student-selected theme related to any of the readings. In Burnett's course, there were no exams because she believed that journaling and the in-class activities, which were graded on a weekly basis, more than satisfied an implicit goal of encouraging students to perceive reading as a process rather than a product that must be tested. Similarly, Burnett felt that requiring students to write a paper was an artificial task, one that imitated what college professors must do in their profession for tenure and promotion but that held little practical value for the average undergraduate language major or minor.

Finally, Burnett thought that Fonder-Solano would likely emphasize periods, literary terms and genre, and to her way of thinking, this would hardly appeal to the average student audience, because as a student this had held little appeal for her. This premise was borne out only in that Fonder-Solano chose a reader organized by genre (Virgillo et al. 1993). However, Fonder-Solano rejected "covering" the reader in favor of putting additional texts on reserve that she felt would be both appealing and thought-provoking.[6]

Based largely on hearsay regarding Burnett's impetus to change the title, Fonder-Solano also held several preconceived notions regarding Burnett's course. First, she thought that Burnett would rely extensively on pragmatic readings such as film reviews and accident reports. Comparing what she understood as Burnett's text choices with her own, she commented in the first interview why she would personally find such an approach unnecessary and underscored her feelings about the importance of literature:

> One of the reasons I set up the course as a literature course rather than a reading course is my perception of what students are already familiar with, what they should be familiar with at the 200 level. The textbooks that I'm teaching from now include bus terminal information, include realia, say movie theater guides and that sort of thing. The reading for practical purposes, the billboards or the announcement that people might come across in every day life, maybe newspaper articles or figuring out what the bus schedule is those are things that are included regularly in lower-level textbooks. With my love of literature and having studied literature, my main focus is to bring this to the masses, to bring literature and make it understandable and make it accessible and make it interesting to the 300 level students and that's why I focus more on "real" literary texts rather than on maybe bringing them up to that starting point with newspaper articles. (Interview 1)

After viewing the videotapes and other data including the syllabus, Fonder-Solano discovered that, in fact, the proportion of "literary" texts (including folk tales, short stories, and two short novels) in Burnett's course far outnumbered practical readings. Fonder-Solano also assumed that the class would probably focus more on comprehension than interpretation. While this was true for the initial pragmatic readings, Burnett implemented both comprehension and interpretation activities with the novels, folk tales, and short stories. Furthermore, she stated that she would do so in her syllabus. In her analysis of Burnett's journal entries, Fonder-Solano exclaimed, "You really do love literature, don't you!?" She had just read the following from Burnett's journal:

> Teaching novels is very empowering because you teach about the world, history, culture, ideologies, beliefs, and you enable students to begin questioning all that. As I wrote in Sue's [a student's] journal, she had said that she, like Josyane [one of *Les petits enfants du siècle's* (Rochefort 1961) characters], "felt disappointed by life." I responded that life is full of *déception* and love. What was necessary was to find the balance. I also wrote about moving one's thinking system from that of ignorant naiveté to critical inquiry because that was how one got the most out of life—that was how one engaged in life to its fullest. Josyane was trapped in a vicious cycle of materialism and an ideology that imprisons her. I get to talk to students about these things because I chose these texts. I get to talk about polygamy versus divorce and Christian beliefs versus Muslim ones. I get to talk about, as one student wrote in her evaluation of me "things that she never knew were so important." (Burnett, Journal excerpt 4/7/99)

Finally, Fonder-Solano assumed that Burnett's choice of texts would not be based on extensive content knowledge. This perception was borne out in that Burnett selected her course reader based on her knowledge of and confidence in the pedagogical expertise of its author (Davis 1994), rather than familiarity with the texts themselves. However, in making this assumption, Fonder-Solano underestimated the extent of Burnett's preparation in literature. In fact, Burnett had been exposed to excerpts of the novels that she selected to supplement her reader in the course of graduate teaching and research.

Discussion and Conclusion

As the preceding examples demonstrate, even though we had worked and socialized together two and a half years before initiating this study, each of us held several erroneous assumptions about the other's teaching. Many of our preconceived notions were in fact not borne out. This led us to the conclusion that we, as professionals in different fields, do not have an accurate understanding of what we do and how we do it.

Differing views on how to teach a reading/literature course may be directly related to former training that, in essence, prepared us to belong to different professional subcultures within the culture of foreign language teachers. Bruner (1990) offers one possible interpretation of this divergence in perspective: "Our culturally adapted way of life depends upon shared modes of discourse for negotiating differences in meaning and shared concepts and depends as well upon shared modes of discourse for negotiating differences in meaning and interpretation" (p. 13). As seen in the sections on *Diverging Definitions of Literature* and *Initial Perceptions versus Findings*, a lack of shared meaning led to the type of dissonance and misunderstanding that Bruner discusses. After all, meanings are only advantageous to the extent that they are shared by others.

Our educational experiences certainly played a role in creating such divergent views as did our personalities. Due to her personal love of reading, Fonder-Solano's course appeared to take on a traditional hue, but in delving underneath the surface, Burnett realized that Fonder-Solano's stance was not as entrenched in the "old ways" as she thought: Fonder Solano's class embraced women and marginalized writers as much as canonical classics. Video analysis revealed that, in terms of activities, she engaged students in play acting, asked them to keep a notebook of reactions to the text, and paired them off to work out textual difficulties, something Burnett, as a student in a literature class, had never experienced.

The divergent ways of thinking about course organization and text selection ultimately underscore implicitly our view of the student, how the course should be experienced, and what students needed and would themselves value as second language readers. In the end, we both deem it important to look again at what students need above and beyond our own firmly-held notions. In her subsequent reading course, Burnett has added more short stories because, according to midterm evaluations, students reacted to them more positively than some of the pragmatic texts. For her part, Fonder-Solano has become far more concerned about students as readers, has incorporated more text-based activities in class. Moreover, as a direct consequence of this study, she has become increasingly discontent with her course reader due to its lack of pedagogical help.

We feel that this study contributes an original approach to the issue of pedagogical/literary divisions and to the field of language teaching, yet we readily acknowledge its limitations in that we are, after all, only two individuals who may not necessarily represent opposing poles of pedagogy and literature in the strictest sense. Further, a study of one's self is necessarily "messy"; it is always subjective and constantly evolving. Nevertheless, as we have discovered, this research opportunity has contributed not only to improvements in our own teaching, but also to a continued interest and dialogue in each other's practices.

Future research endeavors of this kind as well as others are needed to provide a well-rounded picture of university-level foreign language teaching. What educational training, beliefs, decision-making processes, philosophies, and rationales accompany and support the teaching of courses common to most foreign language curricula? What happens in courses regularly taught by those whose background may be in literature or second-language acquisition but who are responsible for courses in culture and civilization or cinema, conversation or composition? In the course of this study, we spent several months talking, listening, often arguing, and disagreeing. Yet in seeking ways to understand what it is we do and why divisions exist in language education, we collaboratively wrote this paper as a beginning of a dialogue. We, like Kramsch and Byrnes, who in their 1995 publications confront the issue of conflict within foreign language departments, are skeptical of simplistic solutions achieved through talk. Yet without such dialogue, might it also be, as Byrnes (1995) suggests:

> that our world, made up of a network of words, can all too easily become our iron cage of inaction? Could we, through working things out on the ground, with all the pitfalls and difficulties that entails, rather than loftily talking about them, find a consensual common

ground that will allow us to move forward intellectually *and* practically, even in untidy ways (p. 14)?

Although we recognize the ways we enact our roles as foreign language teachers may remain divergent, we agree that a better understanding of our respective views is valuable in and of itself. Today we acknowledge that although many of our dearly held beliefs are intractable, our study has yielded positive results. In a preliminary answer to the questions posed both by Byrnes (1995) and by ourselves at the beginning of this article, dialogue, for us, has led to valuable analysis of our own teaching and increased awareness of the other's teaching which has laid to rest formerly held misconceptions. We recognize that no two colleagues will ever reach complete consensus. However, communication has, at the very least, paved the way for collegiality and for supporting rather than undermining each other's work. We now see in each other a potential advocate who can cross, if not overcome the boundaries of departmental divisions.

Notes

1. A version of this paper was given at the March 2000 meeting of the American Association of Applied Linguistics in Vancouver, Canada.

2. Due to the nature of the research, the name of the university where the study was conducted will remain anonymous. Burnett and Fonder-Solano work in a state funded, public university with a student population of approximately 10,000. The department of foreign languages has a faculty of fifteen full-time members. Burnett was hired as an Assistant Professor of Second-Language Acquisition and French in 1996. Burnett's teaching load splits her between the department's educational core curriculum in the Master of Arts in the Teaching of Languages (MATL) program and French, which includes beginning and intermediate French as well as upper-level and MATL content courses in French history, culture, and Francophone civilization. In 1997, Fonder-Solano joined the faculty ranks as a visiting Assistant Professor. The department offered her a tenure-track position the following year. Currently, she teaches beginning and intermediate Spanish as well as upper-level and MATL courses in literature, civilization, and cinema.

3. The Introduction to Literature courses were part of the curricular offerings before either Burnett or Fonder-Solano were hired. For the last ten years they have been taught in the spring semester.

4. Because hiring policies of the last decade brought in French faculty who could teach in TESOL and the MATL education core, two of Burnett's colleagues in French have doctorates in language education; due to other departmental responsibilities, neither one wanted to take on a new course.

5. In terms of size, the courses in our study were similar, French had seven students (all women) and Spanish had five (one man and four women, one of whom was a native speaker); these small course sizes made comparisons between the two much simpler. In both cases, these courses are taken typically after students have completed the language requirement (four semesters of study) and/or by language majors and minors. In the case of French, due to lower enrollments in general, it is the only course offered at the 300-level during the spring semester and has no prerequisite except the completion of the language requirement or its equivalent. However, most students have completed one 300-level course in the fall before taking this one. In Spanish, there is a two-course prerequisite at the 300 level. While enrollment figures for the French course were typical of enrollment patterns of the past four years, enrollment in the Spanish literature course had been low two years in a row. Numbers increased in Fonder-Solano's course the following year by waiving prerequisites and due to changes in the way students were advised: both Fonder-Solano and Burnett advised students to take her course. In the spring of 2000, Fonder-Solano had thirty students; Burnett had ten.

6. Results of Muyskens (1983) questionnaire both reinforce and explain some of Burnett's presuppositions about her colleague. Muyskens found that the most important goals for graduate and undergraduate introduction to literature/survey courses were for graduates: (1) introduction of literary concepts (86%); (2) practice in reading and discussing literature (84.9%); (3) basic understanding of important literary texts (79.6%); and for undergraduates: (1) gaining a broad knowledge of literature (89.2%); (2) the development of critical skills (88.1%). The most common approach to teaching was lecture with some discussion (74%). Grading practices for some faculty members included student performance in the classroom (64.5%) and a paper plus midterm and final (62.4%). For others (74.1%), students were only evaluated by a paper, midterm, and a final (pp. 417–18).

Works Cited

Bernhardt, Elizabeth. 1995. Response to Claire Kramsch. *ADFL Bulletin* 26: 15–17.

———. 1997. Victim Narratives or Victimizing Narratives? Discussions of the Reinvention of Language Departments and Language Programs. *ADFL Bulletin* 29: 13–19.

Birckbichler, Diane, and Judith Muyskens. 1980. A Personalized Approach to Teaching Literature. *Foreign Language Annals* 13: 23–27.

Blumer, Herbert. 1969. *Symbolic Interactionism: Perspective and Method.* Englewood Cliffs, NJ: Prentice-Hall.

Bretz, Mary Lee, and Margaret Persin. 1983. The Application of Critical Theory to Literature at the Introductory Level: A Working Model for Teacher Preparation. *Modern Language Journal* 71: 165–70.

Broad, Yolanda. 1988. Constructing Critical Readers—Pedagogical Approaches to Literature That Make Use of Literary Theory. *ADFL Bulletin* 19: 4–6.

Bruner, Jerome. 1990. *Acts of Meaning.* Cambridge, MA: Harvard University Press.

Budig-Markin, Valérie, and James Gaasch. 1995. *Diversité: La nouvelle francophone à travers le monde.* Boston: Houghton Mifflin.

Byrnes, Heidi. 1995. Response to Claire Kramsch. *ADFL Bulletin* 26: 13–15.

Chaves Tesser, Carmen, and Donna Reseigh Long. 2000. The Teaching of Spanish Literature: A Necessary Partnership between the Language and Literature Sections of Traditional Departments. *Foreign Language Annals* 33: 605–13.

Clark, Christopher. 1988. Teacher Preparation: Contributions of Research on Teacher Thinking. *Educational Researcher* 17: 5–12.

Davis, James N. 1994. *Liens: Lectures Diverses.* Boston: Heinle & Heinle.

Gergen, Kenneth. 1985. The Social Constructionist Movement in Modern Psychology. *American Psychologist* 40: 266–75.

———. 1986. Correspondence Versus Autonomy in the Language of Understanding Human Action. In *Metatheory in Social Science: Pluralisms and Subjectivities,* edited by D. W. Fiske and R. A. Shweder, 136-62. Chicago: University of Chicago Press.

———. 1991. *The Saturated Self: Dilemmas of Identity in Contemporary Life.* New York: Basic Books.

Glesne, Corrine, and Alan Peshkin. 1992. *Becoming Qualitative Researchers: An Introduction.* New York: Longman.

Goetz, Judith P., and Margaret D. LeCompte. 1984. *Ethnography and Qualitative Design in Educational Research.* San Diego: Academic Press.

Hoffmann, Ernst, and Dorthy James. 1986. Toward the Integration of Foreign Language and Literature Teaching. *ADFL Bulletin* 18: 29–33.

Johnson, Karen. 1994. The Emerging Beliefs and Instructional Practices of Preservice ESL Teachers. *Teaching and Teacher Education* 10: 439–52.

———. 1999. *Understanding Language Teaching: Reasoning in Action.* Boston: Heinle & Heinle.

Kramsch, Claire. 1985. Literary Texts in the Classroom. *Modern Language Journal* 69: 356–66.

———. 1987. The Missing Link in Vision and Governance: Foreign Language Acquisition Research. *ADFL Bulletin* 18: 31–34.

———. 1995. Embracing Conflict Versus Achieving Consensus in Foreign Language Education. *ADFL Bulletin* 26: 6–12.

Laye, Camara. 1953. *L'Enfant Noir.* Paris: Plon.

Lazar, Gillian. 1993. *Literature and Language Teaching: A Guide for Teachers and Trainers.* Cambridge: Cambridge University Press.

Le Compte, Margaret, and Judith Preissle. 1993. *Ethnography and Qualitative Design in Educational Research.* New York: Academic Press.

Lincoln, Yvonna, and Egon Guba. 1985. *Naturalistic Inquiry.* London: Sage

McKay, Sandra. 1982. Literature in the ESL Classroom. *TESOL Quarterly* 16: 529–36.

Mead, George H. 1934. *Mind, Self, and Society.* Chicago: University of Chicago Press.

Merriam, Sharon. 1988. *Case Study Research in Education: A Qualitative Approach.* San Francisco: Jossey Bass.

Mishler, Elliot G. 1986. *Research Interviewing: Context and Narrative.* Cambridge, MA: Harvard University Press.

Moorjani, Angela, and Thomas Field. 1983. Revising and Reviving Textual Analysis *ADFL Bulletin* 15: 12–18.

Muyskens, Judith. 1983. Teaching Second Language Literatures: Past, Present and Future. *Modern Language Journal* 67: 413–22.

Omaggio, Alice C. 1986. *Teaching Language in Context: Proficiency-Oriented Instruction.* Boston: Heinle & Heinle.

Ragland, Mary. 1974. A Dynamic Approach to Teaching Literature. *French Review* 47: 917–36.

Rice, Donald. 1991. Language Proficiency and Textual Theory: How the Twain Might Meet. *ADFL Bulletin* 22: 12–15.

Rochefort, Christiane. 1961. *Les Petits Enfants du Siècle.* Paris: Grasset.

Siedman, Irving E. 1991. *Interviewing as Qualitative Research.* New York: Teachers College Press.

Spradley, James P. 1979. *The Ethnographic Interview.* New York: Harcourt Brace Jovanovich College Publishers.

Virgillo, Carmelo, Edward Friedman and, Teresa Valdivieso. 1993. *Aproximaciones al Estudio de la Literatura Hispánica.* New York: McGraw Hill.

Welles, Elizabeth. 1998. Standards for Foreign Language Learning: Implications and Perceptions. *ACTFL Newsletter* 11: 7–9.

Woods, Devon. 1996. *Teacher Cognition in Language Teaching: Beliefs, Decision-making and Classroom Practice.* Cambridge: Cambridge University Press.

Yin, Robert. 1989. *Case Study Research: Design and Methods.* Newbury Park, CA: Sage.

Appendix

SPA 341 Introduction to Hispanic Literature
Spring 1999

Dr. Leah Fonder-Solano
Office: 123 JGB
Office Hours: Wednesdays 9:00–11:00 a.m. *or by appointment*
Office Phone: 260-6255

Attendance This course requires active participation. Absences will result in a reduction of your final grade: for each absence in excess of three (3), your final grade will be reduced by two (2) points. Three late arrivals constitutes one (1) absence.

Participation Because of the nature of this course, class participation is extremely important. Remember: participation involves much more than showing up for class. It includes the following: a positive attitude, active engagement in class activities, advance preparation (completing reading assignments), leadership of activities and volunteering. Each student will be expected to participate DAILY and will receive a bi-weekly participation grade. Above all, don't be afraid to speak up. Your grade does NOT depend on whether you agree with your instructor and/or classmates, but whether you express yourself.

Assignments Expect daily assignments. This class will require approximately two hours of preparation for every hour spent in the classroom. Most assignments are listed in the syllabus. Any changes or assignments not specified in the syllabus will be written on the board.

Notes This is one of the few classes where you get points for taking good notes. I am very interested in the perceptions, ideas, brainstorms, etc. that may occur to you while you are reading but can get lost over the long weekend that separates classes. Jotting down your reactions while you read will prepare you to participate in class and it will tell me immediately whether you've read or not (a less stressful option than taking quizzes, I'm sure you'll agree). I'll hand out a guide to help you in this process. Notebooks will be handed in for a grade every Wednesday.

Research Project Throughout the semester you will conduct research on any subject which relates to one of our readings. You may use many sources of information (Internet, journal articles, books, etc.) but must support your ideas with a **minimum** of three (3) journal articles which closely relate to your project's thesis. (MLA style, please). **Please begin this library research early (the first few weeks of class) because you will most likely need to avail yourselves of Interlibrary Loan.** Lack of available resources will not be an acceptable excuse for incomplete or lower quality projects.

Timeline Your final decision on a topic will be due on Monday, March 15.
Your outline will be due on Monday, March 29.
Your rough draft will be due on Monday, April 19.
The final version will be due May 5, the last day of classes.

Exams There will be two exams, a midterm and a final. These will be very similar in both format and scope, as each will cover half a semester; the final is not cumulative. On each exam there will be a matching section, an identification section and an essay section. The essay(s) will ask you to interpret some aspect of one (or more) of our readings.

Grading Criteria

Class Participation	20%
Notes	20%
Midterm	15%
Final Exam	15%
Topic Statement, Outline, Draft	15%
Final Paper	15%

Grading Scale

90–100	A
80–89	B
70–79	C
60–69	D
0–59	F

Texto: Virgillo et al. *Aproximaciones al estudio de la literatura hispánica.*

SEMANA 1 (11 y 13 de enero) Introducción, EL CUENTO
    tema: Introducción al arte, a la literatura y a la narrativa
    lectura: "Lo que sucedió a un mozo…" 34; "intro a la narrativa" 2–11

SEMANA 2 (enero 20) ¡Feliz día de Martin Luther King!
    tema: aproximaciones críticas; el cuento
    lectura: "el género narrativo" 19–31; Emilia Pardo Bazán, "Las medias rojas" 42

SEMANA 3 (enero 25, 27)
    tema: el cuento
    lectura: Horacio Quiroga, "A la deriva" RESERVA, Juan Rulfo, "No oyes ladrar los perros" 61

SEMANA 4 (febrero 1, 3)
    tema: cuento
    lectura: Luisa Valenzuela "Los mejor calzados" RESERVA

SEMANA 5 (febrero 8, 10) LA NOVELA
    tema: la novela española
    lectura: Miguel de Unamuno, *San Manuel Bueno, mártir,* 74

SEMANA 6 (febrero 15, 17)
  tema: la novela
  lectura: *San Manuel*

SEMANA 7 (febrero 22, 24)
  tema: la novela
  lectura: (extracto) Rigoberta Manchú *Me llamo Rigoberta Menchú y así me nació la conciencia*

Examen Parcial Marzo 1

SEMANA 8 (marzo 3) LA POESÍA
  tema: introducción a la poesía
  lectura "introducción a la poesía" pp. 100–10 "Romance del conde Arnaldos" 138 "Soneto XI" 140

vacaciones de primavera

SEMANA 9 (marzo 15,17)
  tema: la poesía/el lenguaje literario
  lectura: "El lenguaje literario/práctica" 115–24; poemas de Santa Teresa 141–143/Sor Juana 147–48; "Soledad del alma" 149–150/poemas de Bécquer 156–57/poemas de Darío 160–161

SEMANA 10 (marzo 22, 24)
  tema: la poesía contemporánea
  lectura: poemas de Lorca 175–76/"Verbo" 184 RESERVA—ver Neruda; poesía de Palés Matos 177/"Sensemayá" 181; Castellanos RESERVA/Cardenal 189–91

SEMANA 11 (marzo 29, 31) EL DRAMA
  tema: introducción al teatro
  lectura: "introducción al drama" 198–209; "El viejo celoso" pp. 234–42

SEMANA 12 (abril 5, 7)
  tema: teatro
  lectura: "El drama: definición y orígenes del género" 219–31; *por anunciarse;* RESERVA

SEMANA 13 (abril 12, 14)
  tema: teatro
  lectura: $1 \times 1 = 1$, pero $1+1 = 2$ 256–63

SEMANA 14 (abril 19, 20)
  tema: escoger obra y ensayar

SEMANA 15 (abril 26, 28) ENSAYO y OBRA

SEMANA 16 (mayo 3, 5) El examen final

El trabajo final se debe de entregar para el 3 de mayo

FRE 340: Reading in French

Dr. Joanne Burnett
e-mail: joanne@microgate.com
134 JGB
phone: 260-6257

Required Texts
Davis, J. (1994). *Liens: Lectures diverses*. Boston: Heinle & Heinle.
Laye, C. (1953). *L'enfant noir*. Paris: Plon.
Rochefort, C. (1961). *Les petits enfants du siècle*. Paris: Grasset.

It is highly recommended that the student purchase the *Robert/Collins* French-English-English-French Dictionary available at the university book store.

Course Objectives and Description
As this is, for many, the first reading course in French, this course has as its goal first and foremost to allow students to practice honing their reading skills in French and to participate in the literate skills necessary to becoming life long learners and readers of French. Secondly, this course aims to whet student appetite for continued reading in French. In the first half of the course, we will discuss, write about, and interpret, with the help of a reader designed for intermediate high readers of French, a variety of French texts. This reader provides practice at word recognition, global comprehension, and understanding cultural referents directly related to the reading passages. In the second half of the course, we will read, discuss, write about, and interpret two short novels. The first, *Les petits enfants du siècle*, tells the story of a young suburban French woman growing up poor in Paris in the 1950s. The second, *L'enfant noir*, recounts the story of a young African who describes what it was like growing up in his native village of Kouroussa in Haute Guinée during the mid 1950s. Many contrasts, comparisons, and parallels between the two works can be drawn and students will engage in a variety of tasks to aid comprehension and interpretation of both texts.

Class Requirements

1. **Participation** will include attendance and active discussion, questions, and preparation both in small and large groups. More than four absences will result in a failing grade.

2. **Exercises** will be assigned throughout the semester. Those to be turned in need to be neat and legible.

3. **Journal** Your journal may be written in French or English or in a combination of both. **You should write in your journal at least twice a week.** Please date each entry. It should include vocabulary lists, definitions, questions, responses, and reactions to classroom activities, and your ideas and

thoughts about what you are reading. I am most interested in your personal reaction to the process of reading in French. It should **not** be a personal account of your daily activities. I will collect your journal several times throughout the semester.

4. **Student portfolio** will consist of photocopies of **5 texts/articles/ reviews** in French from **four different sources** on the same theme or topic that interests you. You may use excerpts from novels, plays, poems or sources such as magazines, academic journals, and the Internet. For each text you will be responsible for writing in French a **1–2 page (typed) overview/ summary/synopsis**, as well as why you would or would not recommend it to a classmate.

Grading
Participation	20%
Exercises	40%
Journal	20%
Portfolio	20%
Total	100%

Plan du Cours

13 janvier
Introduction, Présentations, Survol du cours

20 janvier
Visite à la bibliothèque: à la recherche des textes en français;
LIENS: Le portrait pp. 2-9. Faites les exercices pp. 9–10. Pour la prochaine classe lisez *Lire en français pour mon plaisir* p. 10 et *apportez un texte français en classe.*

27 janvier
LIENS: Le portrait p. 12–15. Faites les exercices p. 16. *Ecrivez votre autoportrait en une page (exercice 1 p. 17) et apportez-le en classe* (à rendre).
LIENS: La description d'un lieu pp. 20-26. Faites 1–6 p. 27 (à discuter en classe). Préparez *Réactions orales p. 27* (à faire en classe).

3 février
LIENS: La description d'un lieu pp. 29–32; 34–35. Faites les exercices p. 33. Faites l'exercice *Est-ce que j'ai bien compris?* p. 35. Ecrivez en une page *Réactions écrites J'aime/je déteste* (à rendre). *Journal à rendre.* LIENS: Le conte populaire pp. 38-40; 41–45. Faites 1–6 p. 40. Faites *Est-ce que j'ai bien compris p. 45* (à rendre).

10 février
LIENS: Le conte populaire: pp. 51–54. Préparez *Quel est l'essentiel* et *Réactions orales* p. 55. Nous ferons ces exercices en classe.

LIENS: Le compte rendu d'un événement pp. 58–62. Après chaque lecture, faites tous les exercices intitulés *Cherchez le mot*. Nous ferons *Qu'est-ce que vous en pensez* en classe p. 63.

17 février
LIENS: Autour d'un film—Le compte rendu/Le synopsis pp. 92–102. Préparez *Réactions orales* 1–2 p. 103. Nous ferons ces exercices en classe.

24 février
Film français

3 mars
Discussion du film français. Pour la prochaine classe *il faut écrire en deux paragraphes le compte rendu du film français* que vous avez vu en classe.
LIENS: Le récit pp. 126–34. Lisez la définition du récit p. 114 qui se trouve sous la rubrique *Points de repère* et ensuite faites *Qui a fait quoi* 1–5 p. 135 et *A Discuter* 1 et 5. *Journal à rendre*.

8–12 mars vacances de printemps
Commencez à lire *Les petits enfants du siècle*.

Divers exercices seront distribués plus tard

17 mars
Les petits enfants du siècle pp. 5–38. *Un brouillon du Portfolio à rendre*.

24 mars
Les petits enfants du siècle pp. 39–74

31 mars
Les petits enfants du siècle pp. 75–121. *Journal à rendre*.

7 avril
L'enfant noir pp. 9–54. Allez à la bibliothèque pour lire l'extrait interactif sur **CD ROM** de *L'enfant noir*.

14 avril
L'enfant noir pp. 55–101

21 avril
L'enfant noir pp.102–54

28 avril
L'enfant noir pp.155–221

5 mai
Discussion de *L'enfant noir*. *Journal à rendre*

La semaine des examens vous ferez votre présentation du portfolio en petits groupes. *Portfolios à rendre*.

Language, Literature, and Pedagogy

Rethinking Foreign Language Literature: Towards an Integration of Literature and Language at All Levels

Diana Frantzen
University of Wisconsin–Madison

An artificial separation between language-focus and literature courses remains in place in many foreign language departments at universities across the country where literature is the domain of upper-level classes and overt language instruction is the domain of lower-level and advanced grammar and composition courses. Using the instruction of foreign language literature as the focal point, this article discusses ways that the instruction of literature might be altered in undergraduate language and literature courses alike. A broad spectrum of possibilities will be considered that may inspire different attitudes about the use of literature in foreign language classes at all levels. The hope is that the use of literature will not only provide contexts for meaningful classroom dialogues in beginning, intermediate, and advanced foreign language classrooms but will also foster communication and collaboration among diverse faculty, whose goals for their students are essentially the same: that they will learn to speak and write articulately, to appreciate the cultures that speak the languages that we teach, to function in the culture, to value the literature and the broader culture, etc.

The following issues that center on the instruction of literature will be addressed: (1) the use of literature in lower-level and language-focus classes; (2) the value of incorporating second language acquisition (SLA) research findings and language program techniques into literature classes; (3) models for incorporating linguistic analysis of literature into classes at various levels of instruction; and (4) the value of interdisciplinary collaborative research.

Using Literature in Lower-Level Foreign Language Classes

It is by now widely accepted that presenting and practicing grammatical structures and vocabulary within meaningful contexts in beginning- and intermediate-level foreign language (FL)[1] classes is important for language acquisition. Research has demonstrated that authentic reading materials,[2] in addition to their well recognized value as input, can serve as one type of meaningful context in which to practice and present structures and vocabulary. However, for the beginning level, and in some programs and textbooks even for the intermediate level, authentic texts tend to be journalistic readings and short realia items (advertisements, television guides, and the like), usually not literature.[3] This avoidance of literature is due, in part, to the fact that many feel that literature is best left for the higher levels of instruction. Lee (1986), for example, opposes the use of literature to develop reading skills for beginning learners and also questions its use in intermediate-level classes (p. 162). For those who prefer delaying its use, usually the belief is that the students are not linguistically sophisticated enough to handle literature until the advanced level, or perhaps the intermediate level. As Schofer (1990) points out, "although we pay lip service to literature as 'authentic,' we tend all too often to 'save' it for the more difficult levels and to treat it differently" (p. 327). Of late, however, some teachers and scholars have recognized the value of introducing literature at the lower levels of instruction, while acknowledging the challenges that using literature entails (Barnett 1991; Cheung 1995; Fountain 1996; Frantzen 1998; Knutson 1997; Lalande 1988; Rice 1991; Schofer 1990; Shanahan 1997). Rice (1991), for one, argues "that students can and should work with narratives and other literary forms from the earliest levels on" and "that students can work with these texts as literature, not just as examples of language usage" (p. 13).

Shook (1996) also sees benefits in using literature at the beginning level and provides a plan of attack for dealing with what have been seen as its problems:

> While there exist real problems in the introduction of literary works to the beginning FL learner-reader, there also exist real benefits to the beginning reader from such an introduction. Language teachers who inform themselves regarding such problems and benefits will be better equipped to promote to their beginning FL learner-readers not only literary reading but also reading in general (p. 204).

Significantly, he stresses that the key determiner of students' success is what the teacher asks the learners to do with the text. He provides specific suggestions for what an instructor might do to make use of the literature selection, including taking advantage of unfamiliar vocabulary by using it to practice valuable reading skills. He also provides suggestions for dealing with syntax and culture. According to Shook, "The potential difficulties of reading FL literature...can become *opportunities for learning and expansion* not only for language but also for development of the learners' C2 [second culture] framework" (p. 206).

Shanahan (1997) finds additional benefits to the early introduction of literature. He argues that literature has "an important impact on developing communicative competence in the language learners" (p. 166) and that one of the values of literature is its emotional or affective impact on the reader. He contends that "we need to know much more about how to invoke the affective domain as an inducement to learning, especially with respect to the ways in which the affective loading inherent in language can be turned to the learners' advantage" (p. 168).

Clearly, all who promote the use of literature in beginning- and intermediate-level classes promote its judicious use, taking into account what the students can reasonably do, at the same time considering the level of difficulty of the texts. But a cautionary note about difficulty level is in order. Second language (L2) reading research findings indicate that the assumed difficulty of L2 reading material is often faulty (Allen, Edward, Bernhardt, Berry, and Demel 1988 [for secondary learners]; Lee and Musumeci 1988 [for college-level learners]). Although both Allen et al. and Lee and Musumeci investigated nonliterary texts, it is reasonable to assume that their findings would also be applicable to literature, an assumption supported by the findings of Fecteau (1999) who warns about making assumptions as to difficulty levels of literary texts. In her study involving students in an introduction to French literature class, she found:

> Even very similar texts by the same author make different demands on readers' knowledge and skills not only in the L2, but also in the L1. Despite controlling for as many text-based factors as possible, the complex interaction of text- and reader-based factors (including conceptual and linguistic knowledge) renders predictions of text accessibility and comprehension difficult (p. 485).

One factor that helps explain the difficulty of literature selections is that authors of works of literature do not write for an audience of L2 learners, but rather for compatriots, the majority of whom can be assumed to share most of the cultural and historical knowledge necessary to comprehend their work. Consequently, one of the main reasons that students of all levels find literature difficult is because they do not have the cultural and historical knowledge to be able to understand the text. Martin's (1993) questionnaire and interview results showed that students themselves recognize their own gaps in cultural knowledge and how these gaps make it difficult to understand literary texts. The intermediate-level French students in her study reported that they lacked "the cultural background to enable them to relate to a foreign literature" (p. 205).

Instructors can help students overcome their linguistic and cultural shortcomings and thereby help them to understand the texts better. Shook (1997) provides suggestions for the types of exercises instructors might use for this purpose. He recommends the use of very specific tasks that beginning language learners can perform using various reading strategies (prereading, reading, and postreading) to help them fill in their linguistic and cultural gaps in understanding. He stresses the role of the instructor in presenting and practicing these techniques with their students:

> Since beginning foreign language readers do not share the necessary language and cultural background with the author to fully comprehend the text's linguistic and cultural information, instructors need to guide their students strategically in order to overcome this lack of shared background, assumed in literary texts, building from that which is known to that which is unknown (p. 238).

Kern (1995) also does not see as insurmountable the lacunae that FL students have when approaching a text written for native speakers, as his following observation indicates:

> Of course foreign language students often do not possess the relevant social and cultural background knowledge that would allow them to interpret a text in the same way as a native speaker might. But that does not invalidate their reading—it simply justifies the practice of comparing readings among classmates (and perhaps foreign peers) to become aware of the ways that culture, personal experience, and knowledge can influence textual interpretation (p. 72).

Widdowson (1988) even points out that there can be value in having students read a text without directly addressing the cultural associations contained therein:

> A language will obviously be exploited to meet the varying needs of those who use it and as it is it will acquire cultural associations in the minds of the users. But foreign language learners are remote from such associations, . . . and so they can take advantage of this detachment to relate the foreign language to their own familiar reality. You do not have to take the language and the culture together as a package deal (p. 18).

For presenting literature at the intermediate level, Davis (1989) presents a model for instructors to help them prepare materials for their students. In his model, questions are written for each segment of the text that require the students to interact with the text; at the same time, the questions guide them into an understanding of narrative structure as well as linguistic features. He recommends that classroom activities similar to those presented in his model be used at regular intervals when introducing literature to intermediate students. The goal of this regular practice is to get students to apply the self-questioning technique eventually on their own and, in the process, become better readers.

The introduction of FL literature need not be postponed until the advanced level. Using some care in selecting texts and in preparing materials to help students access the texts, both linguistically and culturally, teachers can expose their students to poems, short stories, plays, and novels that will enhance their language learning experience. As Noricks (1986) argues, "studying literature at the intermediate level need not be a frustrating endeavor. In fact, it can be effectively utilized to increase students' control of oral and written Spanish and serve as an excellent point of departure for producing confident and competent language students" (p. 710). Noricks' argument applies to the beginning level as well, and, of course, to any foreign language.

Using Literature in Advanced Grammar and Composition Classes

Just as beginning- and intermediate-level FL classes can be enhanced by the introduction of literature, advanced grammar and composition classes can also be enriched by using short stories, poetry, and other forms of literature because they provide interesting topics for class discussion and writing assignments. They thereby give additional opportunities to practice speaking and writing in the target language, and to incorporate the structures and vocabulary being studied. They also are valuable because they provide meaningful contexts in which to examine grammatical structures for the important meaning they convey. This section will discuss several possibilities for using works of literature in advanced grammar classes.

Lunn (1985) provides one example of how literature can be used in advanced grammar classes for the purpose of leading students to an understanding of more sophisticated and subtle uses of the language. Lunn uses a "focus model" (citing Hopper and Thompson 1980; and Silva-Corvalán 1983) to classify differences in usage of the preterite and imperfect in Spanish. Lunn explains the choice of aspect "as a linguistic reflex of the cognitive ability to confer or withhold focus: preterite usage clusters around focus and imperfect usage around nonfocus" (p. 50). After explaining the focus model and discussing the conventional uses of preterite/imperfect in terms of this model, she discusses the way novelists may use the preterite and imperfect for unconventional uses and demonstrates this by using scenes extracted from several novels. One example she provides is a discussion of Juan Rulfo's use of the imperfect in *Pedro Páramo* to show the mental confusion exhibited by the title character.

Another example involves the use of poetry in Spanish classes to discuss nuances in meaning conveyed by the placement of descriptive adjectives relative to the nouns they describe. (Descriptive adjectives that follow their nouns generally serve to distinguish one noun in the class from another, as in *la casa blanca* [the white house], as opposed to a house of another color. One of the uses of preposed descriptive adjectives is to indicate a characteristic generally associated with that noun or to indicate what the speaker considers an inherent quality of the noun, as in *la blanca nieve* [the white snow].) This can be a rather dry discussion, so one method I have used to bring alive the point in advanced Spanish grammar and Spanish applied linguistics classes is to distribute a copy of a poem by Sor Juana Inés de la Cruz that is often referred to as "*Hombres necios*" [Foolish/Stupid Men], because that is how the poem begins.[4] After the students have read the poem, I address the issue of the type of information conveyed by adjective placement, asking the students to determine by the placement of the adjective in the phrase *hombres necios* whether the poem is criticizing all men or just a particular group of them. I find that the males in the class learn to appreciate the poem more after they realize that the postplacement suggests that the criticism is directed at men who are *necios*, not that all men are *necios*.[5] This type of discussion helps the students appreciate the fact that grammar really does carry meaning.

The discussion of the adjective placement employed in this poem can be expanded by considering the placement of the same adjective used later in the poem: "*Queréis, con presunción necia/hallar a la que buscáis*" [You want, with foolish arrogance/to find the one you are looking for]. Here the adjective follows the noun. One might, therefore, assume that it was the poet's desire to distinguish this type of arrogance from other types, rather than to suggest that foolishness is an inherent characteristic of arrogance (or of the particular arrogance described in this poem), which could be the interpretation had the adjective preceded the noun. Another explanation that can be considered is that a postposed adjective may carry more *semantic weight* than a preposed one (Bolinger 1972).[6] Still another factor must be considered, however: that of the issue of rhyme that comes into play here. Because of the rhyme scheme established in the poem, this line must rhyme with line 71 which ends with the word *Lucrecia*; consequently, placing the adjective *necia* before the noun would not work here. All of these points may lead to a sophisticated discussion of the poem's meaning as well as to a sophisticated discussion of grammar usage because of the inherently interesting context in which the grammatical element has appeared.[7]

If instructors of upper-level grammar/composition or linguistic courses wish to incorporate literature into their classes, they will most likely have to select the literature and prepare the exercises on their own because few grammar books used in advanced FL classes contain literature; those that do often do not contain language analysis exercises already prepared. Two exceptions for the advanced Spanish audience merit discussion.

In *Repase y escriba*, an advanced Spanish grammar and composition book by Dominicis and Reynolds (1994), each chapter's reading (about half of which are literature selections) is accompanied by an *Análisis* section that includes questions about the grammatical structures focused on in that chapter. For example, some exercises instruct students to find instances of certain usage in the text; other exercises ask students to notice or explain the effect caused by the author's use of a particular structure; others ask students to explain why a certain structure was used in a certain context. One example of this approach is an exercise that appears in the chapter where preterite and imperfect usage are reviewed. In the exercise, students are instructed to find instances in that chapter's story of particular preterite and imperfect usage (e.g., for preterite: beginning, end, or interrupted actions; for imperfect: customary actions, actions in progress, etc. [p. 17]).[8]

Lunn and DeCesaris's *Investigación de gramática* (1992) is an advanced Spanish grammar book whose approach provides a good example of how linguistic and literary analysis can complement one another. It covers in detail ten facets of Spanish grammar. At the end of each chapter, the grammatical features are discussed and students are asked to analyze them in the context of Spanish short stories. The seven short stories provided in the text are "revisited" for different grammar topics when the stories provide examples of the structure worthy of discussion and examination.[9]

As these examples have shown, students in advanced grammar classes would benefit by the inclusion of literature as sources of authentic contexts that can be used to present, discuss, analyze, and practice grammatical structures. If, as is commonly the case, the texts used for an advanced grammar class do not contain literature, instructors can use literature of their own preference and develop their own exercises for these purposes using the examples presented here as guidelines.

Incorporating SLA Research and
Language Program Techniques into Literature Classes

Many researchers, including literature scholars themselves, have of late criticized the traditional approach to teaching literature in foreign language literature classes (e.g., Bernhardt 1995; Bretz 1990; Esplugas and Landwehr 1996; Friedman 1992; Kauffmann 1996; Kramsch 1985; Mittman 1999; Nance 1994; Swaffar, Arens, and Byrnes 1991). After reviewing research from the 1990s, Fecteau (1999) concludes, "there seems to be a consensus that the traditional 'transmission model' of literature teaching does little to foster direct engagement with the text or to develop students' literary competence" (p. 475). Students themselves seem to want this engagement, as Davis, Gorell, Kline, and Hsieh (1992) discovered when they investigated students' attitudes toward the study of literature.

One method of engaging students more directly with the text would be to employ techniques that give students more control over the material, something that has occurred at lower levels of instruction. Much SLA research during the last two decades has underscored the importance of incorporating reading skills development in beginning- and intermediate-level foreign language classes. This research has made its way into textbooks for these levels to such a degree that a publisher would not attempt to market a beginning or intermediate FL text if reading strategies exercises did not accompany its reading selections. However, reading strategies exercises have been slow to make their way into literature anthologies directed at the advanced level, perhaps because of cost or because it is assumed that students who take introduction to literature classes are too advanced to need this type of assistance.[10]

These staples of the teaching of FL reading at the lower and intermediate levels should not be overlooked at the advanced level; these types of exercises are also important at the "advanced" level because, despite the label, the language competence of the majority of the students in these classes is not really advanced, and they need guidance to help them extract meaning from the literature they now read (Bernhardt 1995; Bretz 1990; Bretz and Persin 1987; Fecteau 1999; Knutson 1997; Nance 1994). Literature tends to differ considerably from the expository texts and straightforward literary narratives that students are used to reading at lower levels of instruction. As Knutson (1997) notes, "the value of prereading work in terms of both comprehension and interest does not diminish at the advanced level" (p. 54). Bretz and Persin (1987) also stress the importance of prereading exercises for introduction to literature classes. They recommend that teachers of literature develop "prereading exercises through which students are trained to guess about unfamiliar items, make relevant inferences, articulate their own knowledge concerning literary and linguistic conventions, and generally use context in combination with personal knowledge" (p. 168).[11] Others have also recommended the use of prereading exercises in literature classes (e.g., Bretz 1990; Harper 1988; Kauffmann 1996; Keller 1997; Mujica 1997).

Fecteau (1999) stresses the fact that "even students with apparently strong FL skills are apt to miscomprehend when reading literary texts in their L2 because of the greater demands placed on lexical and syntactic knowledge" (p. 489). Her study demonstrates that, in addition to insufficient lexical and syntactic knowledge, many other factors are responsible for learners' inability to comprehend a literary text: gaps in cultural and historical background, ignorance of literary concepts, and the inability to use textual cues. She reports, "The present findings suggest that certain literary features[12] are not apparent to college students in their L1 or L2, whether because they lack background knowledge or cannot activate it, do not focus on key textual cues or perhaps miscomprehend them, or because these elements are not equally apparent in all texts" (p. 489).

Mittman (1999) discusses a model that she has used for a third-year German literature course that includes the use of a variety of authentic reading (including literature), listening, and viewing materials whose goals are "increasing students' cultural knowledge, critical reading skills, and linguistic fluency" (p. 480). A variety of lexical, syntactic, and stylistic patterns contained in the readings (excerpts from legal documents, poetry, magazine and newspaper articles) is used to help develop the students' language skills. She explains that "by directing the students' attention directly at the language of a given text, they not only gain a sense of empowerment over difficult passages, but also find yet another point of access to the fabric of the culture . . . Thus, the lack of linguistic systematicity in the texts can, if dealt with consciously, itself be a tool to help students overcome their inhibitions and gain a sense of their ability as decoders of texts" (p. 485).

Because most texts written for introductory foreign language literature courses have not incorporated many reading strategies exercises,[13] the responsibility lies with instructors to assess the needs of their students and to prepare appropriate exercises. Prereading exercises can be oral or written but in either case are an effective method of incorporating language practice into literature classes while also helping learners better to comprehend the text.

Those of us who teach advanced-level classes must take into account the fact that students cannot reach very high levels of proficiency in the standard two-year university program without also spending extensive time abroad in the target language country. Even students in optimal programs, such as intensive training programs, must have significantly more hours of instruction than students receive in the first few years of language study to acquire high levels of proficiency. Omaggio Hadley (1993), stresses this fact when discussing the amount of time the Foreign Service Institute expects its students to take to reach various levels of proficiency:

> If it typically takes 720 hours of instruction under the rather ideal conditions of intensive study at the Foreign Service Institute for an adult with high aptitude to become proficient at the Superior level in French or Spanish, it is difficult to expect students in a four-year high school program or a four-semester college sequence to reach that same level of competence after 200 or 300 hours (p. 27).

Skills development, a mainstay of the lower level language program, has not typically been a major component of foreign language literature classes. Several researchers have expressed concern that upper-level literature-focus classes do not typically afford students many opportunities to practice speaking (e.g., Bernhardt 1995; Bretz 1990; Esplugas and Landwehr 1996; Friedman 1992; Kauffmann 1996; Kramsch 1985; Mujica 1997; Nance 1994; Schofer 1990; Swaffar, Arens, and Byrnes 1991). Kramsch (1985), for example, presents "a continuing plea for engaging students in the negotiating of meaning in spoken and written discourse. The strategies they learn from oral communication can be put to use for the interpretation, discussion, and personal understanding of literary texts within the group interaction of the classroom" (p. 364). She contends that "the discourse between a literary text and its readers and among readers of the same text can serve as the link between communicative language teaching and the teaching of literature" (p. 364).

Mujica (1997) agrees and, pointing to the fact that most students who take introduction to literature courses are not fluent in the language, she states that "in order to ensure that the survey course[14] remains an integral part of the students' language-learning experience, instructors need to incorporate strategies for developing speaking as well as reading competence. Even when the textbook provides a pedagogical apparatus, it is still up to instructors to integrate oral production into their courses" (p. 211). Others have pointed out the lack of attention to "language needs" in introductory literature classes (e.g., Graman 1986; James 1996; Schofer 1990; Vogely 1997). James (1996) states that "teachers of literature and of literary criticism have to be prepared to see themselves as teachers of language at the higher levels, and universities have to recognize in their reward structures the investment of time that this involves" (p. 26). She further argues that "in order to teach skills and content successfully at a very high level, you have to learn a lot about your students' actual skills, and you have to be prepared to work intensively with them on improving these skills" (p. 27).

Writing is one of the skills that would benefit from more intensive work. The writing skills of FL students would improve if courses at all levels, including those that focus on literature, required students to write multiple drafts of their compositions, a practice which composition texts, both for English L1 and for L2 composition classes, have promoted for years. This is called *process writing* as opposed to *product writing*, which requires only one draft. Process writing involves several steps on the way to the final paper: prewriting exercises, work on separate components (e.g., the thesis statement, the introductory paragraph, etc.), the use of several drafts, and in some models, the incorporation of peer editing as a component. Kauffmann (1996) asks the question: "Why do we have students write a long term paper due the last week of the semester, after it is too late to interact with their thought processes?" (p. 400). Instead of this approach, she recommends that process writing be used in literature classes, in part to help address the problems that may result from the disparate skills and backgrounds of students in the introduction to literature classes (see also Mittman 1999). As professors of composition and literature classes who have incorporated this approach realize, the various steps of process writing—if carried out appropriately—can guide students into becoming better writers, and are more effective than simply assigning one-draft compositions. The feedback that students receive in the one-draft arrangement is limited to the content and structural comments that the instructor gives on each one of these assignments. The chances for improved writing would increase if more than one draft were allowed so that the intermediary feedback would help guide the students into expressing themselves more clearly.

As for other ways to make writing skills a more central component of literature classes, Kramsch (1985) and Cheung (1995) are among those who recommend that students in some way reconstruct a text in writing exercises in order to help them better understand linguistic features such as style, register, syntax, etc. As Kramsch explains it, "The very reconstruction of the text by the students makes apparent to them better than any analysis by a teacher some of its stylistic features" (p. 363). Kramsch (1985), Cheung (1995), Kauffmann (1996), and Esplugas and Landwehr (1996) all provide models.

While it is true that not all faculty who teach literature employ a lecture-only format, when it is the dominant approach, it is unfortunate because the subject matter taught in these courses lends itself so readily to the active development of the oral and written skills. Clearly, many students in introductory foreign language literature classes would benefit from the use of techniques practiced in lower-level classes. Their comprehension of the texts would improve from the continued use of reading strategies exercises, now applied to literature selections, and their language skills would improve if provided more opportunities to interact with the text and the teacher, both orally and in writing.

Incorporating Linguistic Analysis into Literature Classes

Foreign language literature classes can also be enriched by incorporating discussions of authors' use of particular structures, vocabulary, or sociolinguistic features to convey their ideas. Students in these classes would benefit from overt analysis of linguistic features used by authors in composing their works. According to Cheung (1995):

> Any attempt at literary interpretation must begin with an investigation of the grammar of the literary text, its structures and patterns, and their interrelationships. These linguistic features are in fact products of the natural grammar of the language, which needs to be analyzed explicitly if the meaning of the text is to be explained in all its complexity, not just intuited or described. Comprehension of the text is possible only with proper linguistic knowledge (p. 99).

He further contends that "linguistic analysis is a field in which literature students need just as much basic training as language students" (p. 99). One of the reasons that Cheung encourages students to analyze grammatical structures used by authors is because "linguistic analysis may be regarded as retracing the creative process of writing. Students who participate in this retracing have an opportunity to vicariously experience the act of writing the text themselves; their understanding of its structure, themes, and language is often more profound and revealing than what can be achieved in the traditional lecture format" (p. 101).

Vogely (1997) also encourages students in FL literature classes to examine linguistic features as they relate to the meaning conveyed in the work. She argues that "time can be dedicated to identification and function of linguistic elements, such as object nouns and pronouns and their antecedents. Attention should be given to the use of verb moods and tenses, and how they impact the development of the text" (p. 247).

At this juncture, it is important to point out what a linguistic analysis should not be. Some professors of literature may be concerned that the use of literature in an SLA context will focus not on the aesthetic reading itself but on reading as a springboard to a discussion far removed from the text. This is a legitimate concern. Indeed, if the class discussion becomes a discussion of grammar usage with very little impact in the work, it will lose most of its value and, in all likelihood, will end up being counterproductive. The guiding principle should be to discuss items that play an important role in the conveyance of meaning, in particular items where the author seems to have made a deliberate choice.

An example from Spanish will illustrate this point. In Spanish (as well as in many other languages, such as Bulgarian, French, Russian, etc.), separate verb forms are used to indicate differences in social status and differences in degrees of intimacy between interlocutors. By the advanced level, most students of Spanish are aware that a father would use the *tú* [you-familiar] forms when talking to his son. Consequently, the occurrence of these verb forms in a story containing dialog between father and son would not normally be an important point of discussion at advanced levels of instruction. But when a deviation from expected usage occurs, this would be an important linguistic insight to discuss or have students discover. Juan Rulfo's short story "No oyes ladrar los perros" [You Don't Hear the Dogs Barking] provides a good example. The story is written primarily in dialog form with most of the plot emerging from the conversation between a father and his adult son. At the beginning of the story, as the father carries his gravely wounded son to a town where he hopes to get him medical help, the father addresses his son using the *tú* verb forms, which is to be expected. However, at one point in the story, the father begins using the formal *usted* forms. While reading the story, most third- or fourth-year learners probably do not even notice this switch, something that would be immediately apparent to most native speakers. But if encouraged to find the place where the more formal language is used, students will find it, and if instructed to consider what the father is saying at the place where he uses the more formal language, students may discover that it is at the point when the father is discussing his disappointment with the bad life that his son has lead. If asked to explain why he is doing this, the students may realize that it is to show a psychological distance: that this is one way to demonstrate linguistically the distance he feels on an emotional level.

Linguistic analysis need not be limited to grammatical features of the language. It can involve any language usage or language-related devices that the author has used to construct the work. Jordan (1999) provides a pragmalinguistic analysis of the role played by dialogue in literature, such as the effect of immediacy that dialogue creates; in addition, she shows how the use of dialogue is a linguistically more economic form of communication than narrative, which is especially important for the short story because of its short duration (p. 217).

All the examples discussed previously in the section titled "Using Literature in Advanced Grammar and Composition Classes" apply for the literature classes as well. One additional example for incorporating linguistic analysis into literature classes will be discussed in the next section.

Common Ground for Curricular Development and Interdisciplinary Collaborative Research

How literature should be taught in foreign language programs has been a central issue in discussions of curricular changes for the last two decades, as attested by the numerous citations in this article. The value of incorporating literature instruction at the earliest levels of language study is as clear as is the need to modify the instruction of literature at all levels in many classrooms. Henning (1993) advocates a full integration of literature into the curriculum: "Through literature, students can develop a full range of linguistic and cognitive skills, cultural knowledge, and sensitivity" (p. 53). As has been shown, many areas of common concern really unite us. Graman (1986) underscores this fact discussing the common ground between teaching language and literature and literature theory:

> The point here is that cognitive development, including the critical abilities teachers wish to foster, are the same abilities sought by the language instructor at all levels of language development. Linguistic abilities are needed to express developing ideas. Linguistic and cognitive structures in turn provide the bases for further development. Therefore, while the language teacher's primary goal is second language acquisition, and the literature teacher's the development of critical skills needed for the perception and understanding of literary forms and meaning, both rely on the same constructive and cognitive process, and are therefore accommodating related aspects of the same learning entity (p. 178).

Swaffar (1988) echoes these sentiments, also stressing the common ground that should unite our various disciplines:

> Just as literary criticism, L2 reading research in the past decade has stressed the society's or the reader's meaning options rather than

those of the text or of an "informed" professor. We have some things to talk about with our colleagues in literature and language studies. In view of our shared premises about meaning and the reader role, language departments now have opportunities for coherent programming and teaching practices between levels: The earlier use of authentic texts in the elementary program, the broader definition of literature to include cultural and historical readings in elementary as well as advanced work, the shared concern for developing metacognitive interpretive abilities, can result in integrated curriculum planning. Our "language" and "content" schism within the department can be addressed (p. 141).

Many, like Swaffar, have identified the need for a clear articulation between levels and against the artificial language/literature dichotomy (e.g., Barnett 1991; James 1996; Kern 1995; Kramsch 1985; Ruiz-Funes 1999; Shook 1996, 1997; Swaffar 1988; Swaffar, Arens, and Byrnes 1991).

One way to help bridge the divide is through collaborative research in which the authors' areas of expertise in different fields can complement one another's. One area of investigation discussed above involves the examination of the ways authors use linguistic elements to convey meaning in their works. As Cheung (1995) contends, "Successful reading, therefore, requires not only an ability to identify what each linguistic constituent, semantic entity, or grammatical unit, denotes in the immediate textual environment; it also needs a thorough understanding of how these constituents contrast with other possible choices available in the linguistic code" (p. 99).

An excellent example of Cheung's point as well as of the benefits of interdisciplinary research can be found in the work of Lunn and Albrecht (1997) who argue for the use of examination of "grammar as a tool for understanding texts, and against the curricular separation of grammar and literature" (p. 227). Lunn and Albrecht combined their expertise in linguistics and literature, respectively, to demonstrate how Julio Cortázar's use of language (structure as well as lexicon) in his popular short story "Continuidad de los parques" is responsible in large part for the meaning that the story conveys. The authors point out that although this story is popular in intermediate-level texts because of its short length and its "modest" vocabulary, it is not an easy story to understand, and students essentially miss the point at the end. For that reason, they recommend that the text be presented in terms of its preterite/imperfect usage because, "when the story is taught as an example of . . . how the meanings of preterite and imperfect can be manipulated, it is rendered both comprehensible and accessible"

(p. 232). Their analysis of Cortázar's use of aspect (preterite/imperfect) "reveals that its aspectual structure is parallel to [the story's] narrative structure" (p. 227); they note that "the linguistic structure of the story is mimetic to its narrative structure, with the result that the impact of the whole is enhanced" (p. 228). Tracing Cortázar's use of preterite and imperfect, they show how the story can be divided into four parts: they note that "what happens in each of the first three parts of the story corresponds to distinct and describable uses of verb morphology; i.e., the content of the story is mirrored in the verb forms that are used to tell it" (p. 230). The fourth part—the last three sentences of the story— is marked by the absence of verbs. Lunn and Albrecht explain the lack of verbs in the last part as follows: "The morphological categories of person and tense have thus been eliminated, with the result that the end of the story is *literally* impersonal and atemporal: the violation of reality described in the story is not specific to any person or time" (p. 230). In addition to the preterite/imperfect analysis, Lunn and Albrecht analyze other grammatical structures in the story and give several examples of exercises that teachers can provide their students to help them discover on their own the meaning of the story that is revealed by a grammatical analysis. This technique has the benefit of demonstrating to learners that "all grammatical choices have meaningful consequences" (p. 232).

The collaboration of these two researchers has resulted in a type of analysis that can benefit FL students, regardless of whether they are in a course whose focus is on literature or in one whose focus is on grammar. Both types of courses would benefit from such an overlap. As Schofer (1990) argues, "efforts should be made to bring language and literature teachers together as research teams, as participants in nationally sponsored workshops, and on panels at regional and national conventions" (p. 333). Collaboration at all levels and across the separate fields of language instruction, literature, linguistics, and language pedagogy is valuable, not only for curriculum development, but also for gaining an appreciation of each other's fields.

Conclusion

This paper joins many others in encouraging a reassessment of the way we, as departments and as individuals, teach our various courses, and, in particular, a reassessment of how and even whether we teach literature. Many teachers and scholars point to the value of literature for its affective, cultural, linguistic, and critical thinking value, all of which matter at all levels of instruction. Schofer (1990), for example, argues that "today language and literature teachers are in a strong position to integrate literature into the core of language teaching, to the benefit of both language and literature instruction" (p. 326). Works of literature not only provide meaningful contexts for presenting and practicing grammatical structures in language classes, they also provide examples of structures that can be analyzed at more advanced levels for the meaning they convey.

There are many areas of common ground and common interests among the diverse disciplines that make up university foreign language and second language departments. Many of us are calling for an end to the artificial divisions that have developed over the years. In her provocative article of a decade ago, titled "Language and Literature: False Dichotomies, Real Allies," Marva Barnett (1991) gave a "clarion call for parity among language, literature, and cultural studies" (p. 9). She argued that "as professionals specializing in different aspects of language, culture, and literature study, we *must* talk to one another, articulating our programs not only in individual departments but also across institutions, from the earliest language study to the most advanced literary pursuits" (p. 10). If we can retreat from the domains that have developed over recent decades and incorporate relevant elements from one another's content areas, approaches, and research, the artificial separation that has developed between language and literature courses can be diminished and we, as well as our students, will be the beneficiaries.

Notes

1. The terms foreign language (FL) and second language (L2) are used interchangeably in this article.
2. "Authentic" texts are defined as those that were written for native speakers.
3. Two noteworthy exceptions are: (a) the first-year college French textbook, *Paroles*, by Magnan, Ozzello, Martin-Berg, and Berg (1999); and (b) the first-year college Spanish textbook, *Dicho y hecho*, by Dawson and Dawson (2001). Both texts include prereading exercises to help students better understand the literary works.
4. Sor Juana Inés de la Cruz (1648–1695) was a Mexican nun whose poetry, including the poem treated here, is commonly presented in introduction to literature courses. This poem criticizes men for their contradictory behavior: on the one hand, for encouraging woman into bad behavior and then attacking them afterwards for doing precisely what they had encouraged them to do and, on the other hand, also for criticizing the women who do not comply. The poem is widely available; one source is an anthology by Garganigo, De Costa, Heller, Luiselli, Sabat de Rivers, and Sklodowska (1997).

5. Because this is poetry and not prose, the issue of poetic license must also be considered. Indeed, it may not have been the poet's intent to suggest by her use of adjective placement that the poem was addressing a subgroup of men rather than all men. Sor Juana may have placed the adjective after the noun here for other reasons. For example, by beginning the poem with a noun rather than with an adjective makes the poem's beginning more powerful; in addition, the first word being *hombre* focuses the reader's attention on men, not on the attribute. Nevertheless, because the adjective was postposed, it allows the possibility that this poem's criticism is directed at a particular group of men and not at men in general.

6. Stockwell, Bowen, and Martin (1965) use the term "relative informativeness" for this characteristic (1965, p. 89).

7. Others see the value of using literature in linguistics classes. For example, Álvarez (2000) advocates using excerpts from literary texts to teach or present examples of linguistic variation. She suggests the use of novels to examine the ways authors display differences in dialect, register, pronunciation, and other linguistic variation.

8. *El próximo paso* by Bárbara Mujica (1996) is another advanced Spanish grammar and composition text that contains literature (one story per chapter). Although the analysis exercises that accompany the literature selections in this text do occasionally ask questions that involve the grammar focus of the chapter, they generally do not.

9. This type of analysis could supplement intermediate-level language courses as well as advanced-level courses in applied linguistics or literature.

10. It has been suggested that incorporating methods such as those discussed here into literature classes may help to retain students in FL language programs (e.g., Bretz and Persin 1987).

11. Bretz and Persin (1987) describe a model for a teacher preparation course that was designed to train FL instructors to make literature more accessible to their students. Their focus was to train teachers so that they could use various approaches to literature "to involve students actively in the interpretation and enjoyment of literary texts, and by extension, to help students to perceive literature's place within a larger cultural context" (p. 167).

12. Some of the "certain literary features" discussed by Fecteau (1999) are tone, author's aim, and narrative structure.

13. Mujica (1997) states: "Most Spanish anthologies now offer an up-to-date selection of authors, as well as a variety of pedagogical aids" (p. 211). However, in the recent anthologies I have examined, I have not found there to be many pedagogical aids; those included are not very elaborate.

14. Mujica uses the term "survey course" as follows: "The survey is usually the first literature course that undergraduates take" (p. 211).

Works Cited

Allen, Edward D., Elizabeth B. Bernhardt, Mary Therese Berry, and Marjorie Demel. 1988. Comprehension and Text Genre: An Analysis of Secondary School Foreign Language Readers. *Modern Language Journal* 72: 163–72.

Álvarez, Isabel. 2000. Las novelas que hablan: ¿Es posible enseñar lingüística tomando como base textos literarios? Paper presented at the Mid American Conference on Hispanic Literature, Madison, WI.

Barnett, Marva A. 1991. Language and Literature: False Dichotomies, Real Allies. *ADFL Bulletin* 22(3): 7–11.

Bernhardt, Elizabeth B. 1995. Teaching Literature or Teaching Students? *ADFL Bulletin* 26(2): 5–6.

Bolinger, Dwight. 1972. Adjective Position Again. *Hispania* 55: 91–94.

Bretz, Mary Lee. 1990. Reaction: Literature and Communicative Competence: A Springboard for the Development of Critical Thinking and Aesthetic Appreciation. *Foreign Language Annals* 23: 335–38.

Bretz, Mary Lee, and Margaret Persin. 1987. The Application of Critical Theory to Literature at the Introductory Level: A Working Model for Teacher Preparation. *Modern Language Journal* 71: 165–70.

Cheung, Samuel Hung-nin. 1995. Poetics to Pedagogy: The Imagist Power of Language. In *Redefining the Boundaries of Language Study*, edited by Claire Kramsch, 99–122. AAUSC Issues in Language Program Direction. Boston: Heinle & Heinle.

Cortázar, Julio. 1968. Continuidad de los parques. *Ceremonias*. Barcelona: Seix Barral.

Cruz, Sor Juana Inés de la. 1997. Redondillas. In *Huellas de las literaturas hispanoamericanas*, edited by John Garganigo, René de Costa, Ben Heller, Alessandra Luiselli, Georgina Sabat de Rivers, and Elzbieta Sklodowska, 140–42. Upper Saddle River, NJ: Prentice Hall.

Davis, James N. 1989. *The Act of Reading* in the Foreign Language: Pedagogical Implications of Iser's Reader-Response Theory. *Modern Language Journal* 73: 420–28.

Davis, James N., Lynn Carbón Gorell, Rebecca R. Kline, and Gloria Hsieh. 1992. Readers and Foreign Languages: A Survey of Undergraduate Attitudes toward the Study of Literature. *Modern Language Journal* 76:320–32.

Dawson, Laila M., and Albert C. Dawson. 2001. *Dicho y hecho: Beginning Spanish*. 6th ed. New York: John Wiley & Sons.

Dominicis, María Canteli, and John J. Reynolds. 1994. *Repase y escriba: Curso avanzado de gramática y composición*. 2nd ed. New York: John Wiley & Sons.

Esplugas, Celia, and Margarete Landwehr. 1996. The Use of Critical Thinking Skills in Literary Analysis. *Foreign Language Annals* 29: 449–61.

Fecteau, Monique L. 1999. First- and Second-Language Reading Comprehension of Literary Texts. *Modern Language Journal* 83: 475–93.

Fountain, Anne. 1996. Articulating Literature: Concerns and Considerations. *Hispania* 79(3): 539–42.

Frantzen, Diana. 1998. Focusing on Form While Conveying a Cultural Message. *Hispania* 81: 134–45.

Friedman, Edward H. 1992. Effective Stylistics; or, The Pressure of the Text: Foreign Literature and the Undergraduate. *ADFL Bulletin* 23(3): 18–22.

Garganigo, John F., René de Costa, Ben Heller, Alessandra Luiselli, Georgina Sabat de Rivers, and Elzbieta Sklodowska. 1997. *Huellas de las literaturas hispanoamericanas*. Upper Saddle River, NJ: Prentice Hall.

Graman, Tomas L. 1986. A Common Ground for Teachers of Language and Teachers of Literature: The Same Processes Toward Different Goals. *Hispania* 69: 177–79.

Harper, Sandra N. 1988. Strategies for Teaching Literature at the Undergraduate Level. *Modern Language Journal* 72: 402–08.

Henning, Sylvie D. 1993. The Integration of Language, Literature and Culture: Goals and Curricular Design. *ADFL Bulletin* 24(2): 51–55.

Hopper, Paul J., and Sandra Thompson. 1980. Transitivity in Grammar and Discourse. *Language* 56: 251–99.

James, Dorothy. 1996. Teaching Language and Literature: Equal Opportunity in the Inner-City University. *ADFL Bulletin* 28(1): 24–28.

Jordan, Isolde J. 1999. Análisis pragmalingüístico del diálogo literario. *Hispania* 82: 213–19.

Kauffmann, Ruth A. 1996. Writing to Read and Reading to Write: Teaching Literature in the Foreign Language Classroom. *Foreign Language Annals* 29: 396–402.

Keller, Betsy. 1997. Rereading Flaubert: Toward a Dialogue between First- and Second-Language Literature Teaching Practices. *PMLA* 112: 56–68.

Kern, Richard G. 1995. Redefining the Boundaries of Foreign Language Literacy. In *Redefining the Boundaries of Language Study*, edited by Claire Kramsch, 61–98. AAUSC Issues in Language Program Direction. Boston: Heinle & Heinle.

Knutson, Elizabeth M. 1997. Reading with a Purpose: Communicative Reading Tasks for the Foreign Language Classroom. *Foreign Language Annals* 30: 49–57.

Kramsch, Claire. 1985. Literary Texts in the Classroom: A Discourse. *Modern Language Journal* 69: 356–66.

_____, ed. 1995. *Redefining the Boundaries of Language Study.* AAUSC Issues in Language Program Direction. Boston: Heinle & Heinle.

Lalande, John F. 1988. Teaching Literature in the High School Foreign Language Class. *Foreign Language Annals* 21: 573–81.

Lee, James F. 1986. Findings and Implications of L2 Reading Research. *Hispania* 69: 181–87.

Lee, James F., and Diane Musumeci. 1988. On Hierarchies of Reading Skills and Text Types. *Modern Language Journal* 72: 173–87.

Lunn, Patricia V. 1985. The Aspectual Lens. *Hispanic Linguistics* 2: 49–61.

Lunn, Patricia Vining, and Janet A. DeCesaris. 1992. *Investigación de gramática.* Boston: Heinle & Heinle.

Lunn, Patricia V., and Jane W. Albrecht. 1997. The Grammar of Technique: Inside "Continuidad de los parques." *Hispania* 80: 227–33.

Magnan, Sally Sieloff, Yvonne Rochette Ozzello, Laurey Martin-Berg, and William J. Berg. 1999. *Paroles.* Fort Worth, TX: Holt, Rinehart & Winston.

Martin, Anne. 1993. Student Views About the Contribution of Literary and Cultural Content to Language Learning at Intermediate Level. *Foreign Language Annals* 26: 188–207.

Mittman, Elizabeth. 1999. In Search of a Coherent Curriculum: Integrating the Third-Year Foreign Language Classroom. *Foreign Language Annals* 32: 480–93.

Mujica, Bárbara. 1996. *El próximo paso.* Fort Worth: Holt, Rinehart and Winston.

_____. 1997. Teaching Literature: Canon, Controversy, and the Literary Anthology. *Hispania* 80: 203–15.

Nance, Kimberly A. 1994. Developing Students' Sense of Literature in the Introductory Foreign Language Literature Course. *ADFL Bulletin* 25(2): 23–29.

Noricks, Michael L. 1986. Introducing Literature: Some Points of Departure. *Hispania* 69: 709–10.

Omaggio Hadley, Alice. 1993. *Teaching Language in Context.* 2nd ed. Boston: Heinle & Heinle.

Rice, Donald B. 1991. Language Proficiency and Textual Theory: How the Twain Might Meet. *ADFL Bulletin* 22(3): 12–15.

Ruiz-Funes, Marcela. 1999. Writing, Reading, and Reading-to-Write in a Foreign Language: A Critical Review. *Foreign Language Annals* 32: 514–26.

Rulfo, Juan. 1953. No oyes ladrar los perros. *El llano en llamas.* México: Fondo de Cultura Económica.

_____. 1955. *Pedro Páramo.* México: Fondo de Cultura Económica.

Schofer, Peter. 1990. Literature and Communicative Competence: A Springboard for the Development of Critical Thinking and Aesthetic Appreciation or Literature in the Land of Language. *Foreign Language Annals* 23: 325–34.

Shanahan, Daniel. 1997. Articulating the Relationship between Language, Literature, and Culture: Toward a New Agenda for Foreign Language Teaching and Research. *Modern Language Journal* 81: 164–74.

Shook, David J. 1996. Foreign Language Literature and the Beginning Learner-Reader. *Foreign Language Annals* 29: 201–16.

_____. 1997. Identifying and Overcoming Possible Mismatches in the Beginning Reader-Literary Text Interaction. *Hispania* 80: 234–43.

Silva-Corvalán, Carmen. 1983. Tense and Aspect in Oral Spanish Narrative: Context and Meaning. *Language* 59: 760–79.

Stockwell, Robert P., J. Donald Bowen, and John W. Martin. 1965. *The Grammatical Structures of English and Spanish.* Chicago: University of Chicago Press.

Swaffar, Janet K. 1988. Readers, Texts, and Second Languages: The Interactive Processes. *Modern Language Journal* 72: 123–49.

Swaffar, Janet K., Katherine M. Arens, and Heidi Byrnes. 1991. *Reading for Meaning: An Integrated Approach to Language Learning.* Englewood Cliffs, NJ: Prentice Hall.

Vogely, Anita Jones. 1997. Introductory Spanish Literature Courses: An Instructional Model. *Hispania* 80: 244–54.

Widdowson, H. G. 1988. Aspects of the Relationship between Culture and Language. *Triangle* 7: 13–22.

Reading the Patterns of Literary Works: Strategies and Teaching Techniques

Janet Swaffar
University of Texas at Austin

This essay suggests a foreign language (FL) pedagogy for teaching literature to create a strong reader, a reader equipped with strategies to undertake independent interpretations of literary works.[1] The premise underlying these suggestions originates in the conviction that the difficulties foreign language students face stem not only from a language barrier, but also from practices common in *first* language reading (L1). In many English classes, students read for details that support model readings and teacher interpretations. Few teachers train their students to apply independently top-down processes that yield interpretations.

For students who lack advanced language proficiency and extensive FL background knowledge, however, the strategies for interpretive, top-down processing of texts prove particularly helpful (Swaffar, Arens, and Byrnes 1991). Teaching top-down strategies for global processing of textual detail can help FL readers compensate for insufficient language mastery by prompting them to apply the organizing tools found in leading literary theories, notably post-structuralism, semiotics, deconstruction, and reception theories.

Teaching students to apply such tools involves very different approaches than those needed to interpret, however. While this distinction has not been adequately addressed in research, indications support the claim that using theory and teaching others to use it involve different pedagogical strategies. Precisely because literary theory is the mainstay of a great deal of graduate study and subsequent publication for those in the field of literary and cultural studies, our discipline has presumed that teachers know how to instruct students in applying these theories to better comprehend what they read. But often what is taught is the teacher's application of the theory, a finished interpretation, not the operational theory, the theory as reading strategy (Marshall, Smagorinsky, and Smith 1995).

Teachers who use operational theory, who teach students how to apply theory as top-down reading processes, engage students in reading textual information as a system of meaning, as features of textual events, ideas, institutions, or characters that relate to one another.

Many students, whether in L1 or L2 (second language), find their study of literature frustrated by encounters with unfamiliar social and psychological references. Particularly with a work written in a foreign language, readers may find themselves unable to connect ideas even when they understand most of the individual words on the page. Misreading, initial misapprehension of how the gist of a story relates to its details, can distort a reader's entire comprehension of a work (Bernhardt 1990).

Theory becomes operational when, for example, it forestalls misreading by helping students recognize unfamiliar contexts and behaviors as reflecting a macro system different from the one *they* expect, based on *their* experience. If called to the reader's attention, orientation to a story's global patterns, its consistent discourses and narrative structures, can forestall misreading. A misreading of a single word will be less likely to confound an understanding of events or ideas in a literary work when readers grasp its macropatterns.

The suggestions for teaching the reading of literary works presented in this article rest on two interlocking assumptions about how English and FL teachers generally present literature: (1) that we fail to help students learn how to identify and systematize macropatterns of texts in meaningful ways, and (2) that literary messages consequently remain obscure to students because they lack strategies with which to articulate their readings or bridge their own lack of expertise in critical assessment. Another way of making these claims is to assert that, while absolute or ultimate readings do not exist, absolute texts do (*pace* Stanley Fish [1980] who denies the materiality of the text).

And while it is pleasant to react to texts and discuss their emotional impact, speculation and reactive readings generally will, as initial reading responses, ultimately inhibit stronger, more organized perception about what a text says. Rule one of text-based reading: structure classes to avoid misreading by teaching students to attend to one pattern of textual messages. Their own background knowledge can inform those messages, but only *after* they examine what the text actually states and how it organizes those statements—as chronological events, causal arguments, problems and solutions, contrasts or comparisons, and descriptions.

Cognitive scientists have proposed that reading is a process in which the reader reconstructs textual meaning (Rumelhart 1977; Samuels and Kamil 1984). Consequently, in the approach to reading I suggest here, the teacher avoids telling students how to reconstruct the text. Instead, s/he structures reading in-class and out by asking students to find patterns in textual language and structure. In this pedagogy, teachers assist students initially by helping them identify appropriate macropatterns and the details that support and lend dimensionality to those patterns. Their ultimate goal will be to turn readers into independent, articulate interpreters of literary and other texts: that is, readers capable of finding macropatterns without help from an instructor.

In foreign language classes, this approach empowers students as potential strong readers and interpreters by showing them how to uncover the global or macropatterns of a text—the essential first stage in reconstruction of a longer text. The pedagogy involved presents students with an "r + 1" (the reconstruction made in the process of identifying the way the text arranges student-selected detail into consistent patterns), a reader variant of Krashen's "i + 1" (Krashen 1985; Krashen 1989). The "r" component assumes a reading process that reconstructs the macropatterns of a text out of recognizable details. The "+ 1" component is reflected in the discovery process that this reconstruction involves. Students who identify the way the text arranges the detail in its episodes or character depictions will glean new insights into the larger messages of a work.

Importantly, whatever macropatterns the teacher chooses to emphasize, the principle of adding only one additional element to what the students already know must apply. The literary theory behind that macropattern must clarify for students what they can grasp and, implicitly, the unknown language or ideas they need not worry about at this point in their FL reading of literature. For example, the macropatterns might reflect post-structural ideas (institutionalized behaviors and their resultant impact on members of that society), semiotics (characteristics or markers of one group compared to those of another), deconstruction (the presence and relative absence of features and what that implies), or reception theory (coalescing textual information about people or events to identify patterns and the reader's or the public's response to those patterns). Working deductively, I will model a sequence for a beginner or first year FL class that applies semiotic theory.

To forestall the fear that reading literature is a hurdle surmountable only for readers possessing extensive language skills, early, cognitively managed introduction of stories, poems, and even novels helps students overcome this misapprehension before it sets in. Their expertise can be divorced from the fear that they must master all the textual material before comprehension can occur. Because teacher guidance is critical in early stages and because the stages themselves need to be practiced as learning strategies, such reading must, initially, be structured as an in-class activity.[2]

Although the examples below show how to read texts with beginning FL students, the practices recommended here for in-class introduction of reading assignments are applicable for advanced readers as well. These techniques do not separate the act of reading from the act of joining a language community—comprehension and production are linked activities. In the section that follows, I illustrate this claim with a short literary text written in Spanish.

A Case Study in the Pedagogy of Strong Reading

In even a first semester Spanish class, Enrique Anderson-Imbert's (1976) short tale, *La Muerte*, can be introduced as both a literary work and a template for language use (for full text, see Appendix A). Plan for about ten minutes of group activity described below with follow-up stages of homework and a subsequent class- or small-group activity for perhaps fifteen to twenty minutes. Along with having students comprehend the story, teachers might want them to identify and use particular grammar features recently introduced such as adjective endings or verb forms. They would want to integrate such emphases, however, with particular literary features of the story, such as its repetitive or striking language or its use of motifs from established literary traditions. Such activities combine teaching language while at the same time preparing students to undertake strong or independent readings at the upper division level (Kern 1989).

Using such prereading activities, that gap between lower and upper division can be negotiated with a careful look at the "literary techniques" of the story itself. The tale is an example of what the author describes as an everyday, plausible, and familiar situation into which the fantastic can be interjected to cast light on the human condition and the absurd nature of the cosmos (Anderson-Imbert 1979, p. 43).[3] The point of a prereading activity that capitalizes on such expert background knowledge is, of course, not to tell students what to think about the story, but to have them uncover the fantastic in the text in ways that acknowledge what it says to them in conjunction with the objective facts of language use.

To restate, then, teacher guidance and feedback must avoid providing "expert" information but, at the same time, set up a playing field on which students can discover that information for themselves and (re)construct the practices that will enable them, in time, to become strong readers. Particularly when directed at considering options central to engaging in a fruitful reading, the class activity should, thus, first employ verbalized responses to what is understood, partially understood, or guessed at, to help readers identify the process of meaning-making anchored in textual information. If just introducing these techniques in the first semester, the teacher may want to use English initially. After clarifying procedures and goals (one or two sessions), the switch to Spanish should pose no problems.

The Reading Input ("r + 1") of Prereading The directed reading-thinking activity (DRTA) (Stauffer, 1969) is the basic technique for such a feedback-oriented, in-class reading. It offers all the advantages of having teachers provide prereading explanations without having teachers assume the dominant reader role in making those explanations for their students, thereby denying them a strong reading opportunity. Instead, directed reading encourages students to think out loud about what they expect to read and to compare that expectation with the text title or initial paragraph they have just read, an established research strategy that reveals what they know, what they don't, and what they misread or fail to grasp as a result.

Designed to distinguish pure speculation from text-based inferences, directed reading asks students to express their thinking about how a text presents information, confirming and disconfirming what has been said and to make predictions about forthcoming information. A true exercise in reader response in the sense of Iser (1981), this pedagogical approach has no "right" or "wrong" answers because it honors any attempt to draw meaning from the text that is based on any facet of language practice or background knowledge (Carrell 1991). If empowered by students' preexisting knowledge, directed reading allows them to exercise agency, to verbalize their comprehension of text meaning without anxiety about right and wrong answers, and to receive immediate feedback from peers or the instructor to confirm or disconfirm that thinking.

To implement directed reading, the teacher simply asks students to first read the title, then the first paragraph or two, pausing after each title, subtitle, or paragraph to give readers time to make notes about, consult, or simply respond immediately to what they think the segment just read has said, substantiating those views by referring to language in the text. Depending on the teacher's goals, students may also be asked to identify what genre they are reading or what stylistic or linguistic features strike them. On the basis of everyone's observations and the teacher's minimal comments when questions arise, students will then predict what they think will be said in a subsequent paragraph. Commonly, the class as a whole makes at least three or four predictions, only one of which will be subsequently confirmed and possibly modified after further reading.

The title of the story in question, *La Muerte* will elicit even from beginners responses such as "death," "dying," "murder" or possibly some misreadings such as "corpse" [*el muerto*], "sign," or "face" [*la muestra*]. The act of eliminating any initial misreadings will help focus student attention in subsequent reading, an important step towards fostering a strong reader because misreadings made at the outset have been shown to persist as interference factors when the reader progresses through a passage (Bernhardt 1990).

Once students identify that the title has yielded options in a general field of meaning from "death" or "murder," they can read the first paragraph together on a transparency or computer screen to see whether it offers clues for choosing one particular definition over the other and what additional ideas establish the setting or scenario for either meaning. While reading from a book or xerox copy is also effective, the focus on a screen provides immediate pinpointing of what students identify as important in the text. To exemplify, the first paragraph of *La Muerte* and typical responses are illustrated below:

> La automovilista (negro el vestido, negro el pelo, negros los ojos, pero con la cara tan pálida que a pesar del mediodía parecía que en su tez se hubiese dentenido un relámpago) la automovilista vio en el camino a una muchacha que hacía señas para que parara. Paró (p. 47).
>
> [The driver (black her dress, black her hair, black her eyes, but her face so pale that despite the noonday sun it looked as though it had been struck by lightning) saw on the road a young girl who was signaling her to stop. She stopped.][4]

Importantly, the teacher reminds students to work with what they know rather than to worry about what is unfamiliar. Beginners, for example, will not recognize several verb forms, such as the past perfect subjunctive of the auxiliary "to have" [*haber/hubiese*], the imperfect of "to appear" [*parecer/parecía*], or the preterite form of "to see" [*ver/vio*], but should have no trouble identifying the presence of a vehicle with a driver [*la automovilista*] and descriptors of the driver's appearance— black clothes, black hair, black eyes [*negro el vestido, negro el pelo, negros los ojos*] or relatively common nouns such as *el camino* [street or road] and *una muchacha* [a girl or young woman]. Some may even know the verb *parar* [to stop]. They probably will, moreover, sense something odd in the repetition and position of "negro" in the parenthetical phrase as echoing ritual language, not characteristic of normal speech rhythm.

Research findings suggest such tasks prove efficacious for retention of language (Hulstijn 1992). Students' comments typical of those documented in "think-alouds" (research that asks students how they decide about text meanings while reading) often reveal that readers learn through puzzling out words in context (Hosenfeld 1977). If the students are true beginners (i.e., in their first semester exposure to the language), those observations will probably be in English. Teachers can expect comments such as "an *automovilista* is a car or a driver, maybe a woman driver"; "the driver is dressed in black"; and "I think there's a girl on the road." With a record of assertions on a transparency or the blackboard, teachers can prompt other students to agree, disagree, or elaborate.

By waiting until the class has pooled its knowledge, teachers have several pedagogical advantages. First, they know what the class as a whole knows and does not know. Second, they have focused attention based on their students' cognitive processing and hence maintain those students' interest in resolving remaining anomalies as they continue reading ("read on to decide whether *la automovilista* is a vehicle or a driver"). Finally, such teachers have begun to model how an interpretation is constructed, not an interpretation itself.

Rather than continuing to read to resolve anomalies or puzzling information, the teacher may, depending on her pedagogical goals and the text itself, choose in subsequent sessions to ask the class to reread. If her goal is to highlight the value of functional grammar, a brief reminder that often the feminine ending accompanies noun gender addresses any questions about whether the driver of the car is a man or a woman.

To emphasize stylistic features, the instructor might want students to look again for redundancies: "qué se repite?" [what's repeated?]. The "negro el vestido, negro el pelo" [black her dress, black her hair] etc. will doubtless resonate with some students as a trope of folksongs or ballads in their own culture as well. ("Black, black, black is the color of my true love's hair.") In this way a grammatical exercise has functioned, in essence, as the basis for identifying a literary trope.

The "r + 1" of Confirming the Known Whether asking students to reread or to continue reading for specific points, the teacher's objective will be to establish what is known, what is not known, and, on that basis, to encourage predictions about what will happen next—the reader response processes identified by literary critics (e.g., Rosenblatt 1983). Reading on in *La Muerte*, students will discover that it remains unclear whether the reference is to a death or a murder, whether the driver is a man or a woman. On the other hand, they will probably see that *la automovilista* is a person because she talks with *una muchacha*.

Again, rather than telling students the two people are talking to one another, student discovery of this key conversation at the heart of the story can be facilitated by the teacher. No need may exist to clarify this point as the subsequent verbal exchanges between driver and girl reveal as much. If the shift in narrative mode remains unclear, however, highlighting the question of narrative style clarifies whether or not an *automovilista* is a person and whether or not the driver has stopped. As is so often the case in literary works, obscure or peculiar grammar converges with narrative manipulation.

If, for example, students have been directed to look at the first paragraph as (a) a monologue (b) a description in the first person (c) a dialogue (d) a third person description, their continued reading can determine whether that description, dialogue, or monologue continues or not. A portion of the text illustrates the distinction between the first paragraph and the following exchanges:

—¿Me llevas? Hasta el pueblo, no más —dijo la muchacha.
—Sube —dijo la automovilista ... (p. 48).

["Will you give me a ride? Only as far as the village," said the girl.
"Get in," said the driver. ....]

The dashes and question marks in the text illustrate Spanish type-setting conventions that differ from those commonly used in English language texts. Their brevity and the repetition of *dijo* [he/she said] conveys the sense of a dialogue even if students are unable to identify the preterite form of the verb "to say" as *decir* or "get in" as the imperative form of *subir*.

When teachers focus on what their students know, even novice FL learners can confirm or disconfirm predictions. At the same time, they are learning not to stop reading or to rely on a dictionary because of uncertainties that cannot be resolved outside the text taken as a structure. They experience the value of continuing in order to see if subsequent paragraphs clarify what was unclear in previous passages. They are also learning that, in literary texts particularly, initial paragraphs often introduce rather than explicate. First speeches of plays, initial paragraphs of stories, early pages of novels set the stage but rarely identify overtly all the theatrical props that will be essential in Acts Two and Three.

The "r + 1" of Pattern Identification in a Matrix-Guided Reading.
After monitored feedback on their initial reading, the class is ready for rereading (a second, more informed reading) to establish the discourse pattern of the text as a semantic system. I recommend students

use a matrix schema at this juncture because matrices enable reading that reconstructs textual meaning as a visual pattern. Without such a matrix, students have little recourse but to believe they must understand every word in the text before they can "read." The illusion that "understanding every word" yields a meaningful reading is difficult to break without a matrix. Here a word of explication is in order.

A text matrix helps students comprehend the valence or syntax between central or macropropositions formulated by the instructor in the process of prereading and the supporting, elaborating details or micropropositions in the text (Kintsch and van Dijk 1978). Macropropositions are the "main ideas" or gist features of any story—the tokens of heroism, villainy, nurturing—the compass points of human experience. Thus each macroproposition has a topic (fairy princes) and a comment about its nature, goals, or results (rescue princesses). Micropropositions provide the details, the latitude and longitude found when those compass points are identified—the kinds of heroism or villainy fairy princes encounter and how they deal with such obstacles to rescuing their princesses.

For beginners, a partial "fill in the blank" matrix helps students to sort details of textual information (the micropropositions) in ways that foreground their relationship to macropropositions and the language used to express those relations. In the example below, the tokens or macropropositional categories are in bold; the typological details or micropropositions provided by the instructor are italicized; the items to be completed by the students are in block type.

This matrix displays macropropositions as tokens of a binary reading of Anderson-Imbert's (1976) text. Binary readings such as the

Matrix for *La Muerte*

Scenes	Familiar	Unexpected
Picking up a hitchhiker	*la automovilista* [woman driver]	*negro, negro, negros, pálida* [black, black, black, pale]
Conversing	*varias preguntas* [various questions]	Tres veces: "¿pero no tienes miedo...?" "no tengo miedo" etc. [Three times: "But aren't you afraid?" "I am not afraid" etc.]
Dying	*el auto se desbarrancó, la muchacha quedó muerta* [the automobile crashed; the girl lay dead]	*voz cavernosa, automovilista desapareció* [cavernous or sonorous voice; driver disappeared or vanished]

one illustrated here (in this case using a binary "familiar/unfamiliar" behaviors comparison) are generally most informative because they follow a topic/comment logic for textual data—the behaviors, problems, institutions, ideas, persons or events talked about and the contrasts, solutions, features, goals, or causally related events that illuminate the topic's significance. These constitute the most basic forms of propositions (Kintsch 1998).

If reflecting a valid theoretical grasp of the text's macropropositions, even readers with minimal command of the FL will be able to use the matrix to understand a given passage's conceptual fundamentals and to supplement the gaps in their understanding of details of fact or language. Consequently, an instructor's theoretically anchored matrix construction helps students read for meaning without extensive command of language. The matrix for *La Muerte* applied semiotic theory by contrasting a familiar scenario with its attendant supernatural features. That contrast, a central axis of magical realism in Latin American fiction, illuminates the sign system of Anderson-Imbert's (1976) text.

To illustrate the narrower case of how matrix building can foster language learning, consider the grid above not only in terms of answers provided, but also in terms of potential answers, including inappropriate ones, that might well be added in actual practice. Under the category "unfamiliar," for example, some readers might erroneously suggest ¿*Me llevas?* [will you take me/give me a ride?] as an example of an unexpected exchange between a driver and a hitchhiker.

If, for example, classmates do not object to the inclusion of ¿*Me llevas?* in the "unfamiliar" category, the instructor will need to point out the meaning of the verb *llevar* as "to carry; take" and ask the class to speculate about a probable translation in this context. Once students have understood the verb meaning, the question ¿*Me llevas?* [will you give me a ride?] will be reconsidered for the "familiar" category. By associating the question with its appropriate referential system, the micromeanings of individual words are linked to the macropropositions of the passage. Because students make these distinctions to clarify global meanings, memory of the specific meanings of words should be facilitated (Hulstijn 1992).

When the matrix is used for a homework assignment, rather than in-class work or small group efforts to be reported on, then email consultation or a chat room format is useful to continue the strategies of puzzling out how macropropositions operate as larger systems—they can also help students pool their knowledge about the Spanish language. The more words that are used and thought about in such an environment, the greater likelihood of their retention. Regardless of the specific matrix format, student efforts to construct this level of proposition in a foreign language need to be reviewed and discussed as legitimate stages in the process of more complete comprehension. Discussion of misreadings is useful to clarify language use and reinforce ways in which micropropositions support or fail to support one column of main meaning in the matrix.

To repeat, this feedback function, while essential, must emphasize the validity of student effort in thinking about macropropositional meaning rather than focusing solely on dictionary definitions of words or details without regard to the gist of the text. The imperfect reader who is actively constructing propositional systems must still be valorized as a potentially strong receiver of a literary work. Cognitive engagement, identified in research as essential for success in reading comprehension, lays the foundation for identifying the associative strategies the text uses to "mean" (Kintsch 1998).

If students are to read for the global structure of a text (its macrosyntax) and its main meaning, and, if their goal is to acquire language as well as information from that reading, these goals must transcend concern about initial missteps based on insufficient command of language features. Most of us have misread first as well as second language texts. L1 and L2 research strongly suggests that we become better only through extensive reading that focuses on textual concepts rather than our personal responses to that language (Block 1986). Consequently, the matrix task of reproducing a text's micropropositions, its surface language arranged in associative schemata, will be the basis for subsequent tasks that guide students in thinking about the text and expressing that thinking.

The "r + 1" of Articulatory Stages: The Strong Reader Becomes an Authoritative Interpreter Once the matrix has been completed and verified in the classroom, several recycling options exist for the next growth stage to be introduced. Which option will, again, depend on instructional goals. If language practice and a graduated sequence leading to sophisticated written expression are considered desirable, then students can manipulate the language patterns they have found in their matrices, first at the sentence, or possibly even at the paragraph level. They can, for example, write more dialogue between the characters they have met, exchanges reflecting those characters' voices and modes of being.

To ensure practice in sentence building as part of this propositional logic, matrix information must be cued to students' existing command of grammar. Presuming that beginners have been introduced to the ways to use the present tense forms for the verbs "to have" in Spanish [*tener/haber*], the verbs "to be" [*estar/ser*], and matching of gender endings for nouns and adjectives, these students can be instructed to use their matrices to describe the two figures or objects mentioned in the story. They can be instructed to decide which verbs the text uses for "to have" and "to be" and then to think about which of these forms (*tener* and *estar*) are appropriate for their present tense descriptions.

Anchored first in semantics, the drill automatically acquires a morphological component when based on the story's language use. The story itself uses present tense forms of *tener* and *estar* several times, but only in the first and second person. In their descriptions, students take a first step away from repeating the exact language of the text—the linguistic task of the matrix—to talking about the text in the third person. At the same time, any nouns and adjectives used will be drawn from their matrices and observations about those parts of speech must be anchored in the content of the story. Typical answers will be *La automovilista tiene ojos negros* [The driver has black eyes] and *La automobilista no tiene miedo* [The driver is not afraid]. One set of linguistic material thus achieves new dimensions as several different affective purposes—as expressions of reader intent as well as reader recall.

Despite the relatively limited linguistic repertoire of a first-year class, instructors will discover that students prove to be indefatigable players with language and can, if asked to do so, write from six to eight simple sentences using the format above. They might then be ready to write a longer description that contrasts the familiar with the unfamiliar using discourse connectors such as *pero* [but] or *y* [and]. Given the topic sentence, "This story is/is not very mysterious because. . . ." students have the linguistic tools to express a point of view (e.g., *Este cuento es/no es muy misterioso porque la muchacha tiene muchas preguntas peculiares pero la automovilista no tiene miedo* [This story is/is not very mysterious because the young girl asks many peculiar questions but the driver is not afraid]). And they practice the speech act while optimizing their linguistic resources.

For more advanced students, these steps may strike some teachers as too minimal, too redundant to avoid the status of busy work, a concern that will depend largely on the incremental learning an instructor builds into the task by developing elaborated scenarios. The challenge posed by asking students to change verbs from the indicative to the conditional or to introduce negation will depend on the conceptual material those students are poised to master actively, the "+1" of their particular learning level. In minimally revising simple statements as illustrated above, students are practicing their skill in expressing their own point of view. They practice becoming strong readers who are also articulate readers.

Such practice links meaning to grammar features in the spirit of research that argues for the importance of focus on the communicative function of form (e.g., Doughty 1998 and VanPatten 1996). Students engage in an essential intermediary step between comprehension and the kind of text-based, creative language expression that can become literary interpretation. The usual grammar exercises do not contextualize language practice as part of systematic interpretation and reading. Instead, most reading exercises remain unrelated to the messages of a literary text. Small wonder when students guided only by such strategies prove unable to discuss texts at more sophisticated levels. They have been denied the building blocks necessary to achieve sophisticated expression. Even if they have adequate language skills, they do not have the reference tools of larger proposition building with which to ask such questions and begin to develop interpretations.

To be sure, part of their failure to interpret originates in language deficits. Without intermediary practice stages with building-block vocabulary and expressive options, students often resort to English or, particularly in writing about a literary work, to translation from English idioms. Said more practically, they have not practiced modifying textual language to create individual speech acts. Cognitively, reading the text amounts, under such circumstances, to reading input + 2 or + 3, because the tasks of synthesizing new vocabulary, new grammar features, and new narrative information overwhelms learners as a threefold burden, only two of which can be alleviated by language practice per se.

Ultimately, the kind of task redundancy described above can be interesting only as long as it is not purely mechanical. To forestall mechanical drill, creative tasks that underpin even simple uses of language can prevent boredom while reworking language materials. The point is to have students repeat language but vary the task in ways meaningful and consistent with the pedagogy of those students' learning program—to practice the kinds of grammar, discourse, and propositions that they will, at the end of their study, be required to provide.

After the grammar framework for these appropriate expressions is established and validated at the sentence level (tense, mood, voice, morphosyntactic complexity such as appropriate use of verb condition, adjective endings, negation or whatever the + 1 focus), students are poised to use the texts as the basis for self-expression. They can interpret the work through themselves or their own minds through it.

Command of textual language at the sentence level thus must translate into command of more extended discourse. Such dictates will, of course, depend on the pedagogical objectives of the teacher and the desired juncture between practices at the lower- and upper-division levels. Students can, for example, move toward various styles of proficiency if they repeatedly retell stories read in lower division courses, reproduce them as mini-dramas, provide variant stories using the original's themes and stylistic devices, conduct mock interviews of figures in stories, submit police reports, or express a point of view in a written paragraph or short essay.

In lower-division courses, complex speaking and writing tasks such as those just indicated succeed best when preceded by sentence-level practice linked to the propositional meanings of specific reading materials. With sentence-level practice based on discourse patterns in those materials, the story grammar and the matrix for the story provide a safety net for students' linguistic accuracy by setting limits on linguistic innovation and innovation's attendant high risk of introducing dictionary-based infelicities or translation-based anglicisms.

The "r + 1" of Reading the Matrix for Textual Implications I have been arguing that reading and expression are tied to the construction of literary interpretation. In constructing the topic/comment or binary system of the matrix for *La Muerte*, the instructor has designed tasks for identifying student comprehension of the story and constructed a feedback network to confirm readings that reflect the text and its language and to disconfirm extraneous or inaccurate readings. As we have seen, those matrices then operate as the basis for enabling students to take (1) a first step towards communication of minimal language manipulations that reflect the macropropositions of the text and (2) a second step towards more extended variants of those macropropositions.

On completing these stages, students are ready to address the task of interpreting textual meaning on their terms—applying that school of theory or interpretation they deem most suitable for the text or their reader's goals. To this point in time, readers have used their matrices to understand the Anderson-Imbert (1976) story in truncated, linear terms. They have read the binary oppositions as contrasting semiotic patterns. To interpret the story, to identify what the micropropositions "add up to," they must now read their matrices vertically, as well.

To undertake a vertical reading, the familiar features, drivers of cars who ask questions and have car crashes in which their passengers are killed, must be interrogated as much for what they do not say as what they do (what they defer), how they differ from other reports of such events in newspapers or on TV (in attitude, in formal features).

The same must be done for the second column with its strange questions, cavernous voices, and disappearing drivers.

Because vertical reading of the matrix involves higher order analytical skills, no additional linguistic demands should be made on students. They have to learn to generalize (to use details or tokens to illustrate gist or typologies). As illustrated, however, the language necessary to express the differences between the two columns is rarely complex. Most students who complete a matrix for *La Muerte* will see that none of the references to people in the "familiar" column are personalized with names or other specific identities. The driver and the girl remain types rather than particular persons—all insights that involve no more than simple sentences in Spanish. In this sense students will, in other words, begin to construct distinctions between realism and magical realism.

The second column reveals how this absence of the personal blurs even further because of difficulties in keeping track of who is speaking to whom, particularly when, immediately after the driver repeats for the third time that she is not afraid, laughter is suppressed and a cavernous voice declares itself to be death. Only the early, ballad-like description of the driver ("black the eyes, black the hair, black the clothing") and the driver's repeated answer foreshadows her threatening potential as a personification of death—adding up to a domain that evokes magic.

The realization that that potential will prove supernatural, however, has been postponed until the last sentence of the story, when the driver is described as stepping (out of the car) firmly or unscathed and vanishing behind a cactus [*siguió a pie y al llegar a un cactus desapareció*]. If realized and expressed by students themselves, such insights convey their grasp of narrative nuances and, possibly, their affective pleasure in an aesthetic reading of this text. For rank beginners, these insights that synthesize the verbal movement of the matrix chart will probably be most productively expressed in English (see part 3 of Appendix B). But before many months of exposure to the language have elapsed, students should be able to do precisely that kind of synthesis while using Spanish.

Students who mention the story's pattern of presenting the real and the magical through typecast characters rather than particular people have uncovered one key to interpreting Anderson-Imbert's (1979) aesthetic in this short work. They will probably do so in a variety of ways. Some may recognize that the narrative system, juxtaposing as it does the everyday with the surreal, suggests generalizations about attitudes and behaviors. In this case, a young girl possesses the bravado and dangerously overconfident daring typical of youth.

Others may be aware of Anderson-Imbert's tendency toward expressionistic style with its reductive gesture toward basic human experience—hence echoes of ballads and fairy tales in the descriptions and in the repetition of questions often found in these genres. Yet others may simply wonder why the young girl keeps asking the driver uncomfortable and, by implication, intimidating questions. Moreover, who is asking whom may not be immediately clear unless the sequence of the conversation is carefully established—itself an important, and frequently overlooked, strategy for determining agency in a literary text. In the case of Anderson-Imbert (1976) the omission of explicit references to speakers underscores the subtle ways the author evokes uncertainty in the reader.

Any such responses read a story matrix of the familiar and the unfamiliar as vertical as well as horizontal patterns because they penetrate beneath the surface information of the text in a linear reading (the horizontal syntax of their matrices) to the subtext of themes and authorial intentionality. What is Anderson-Imbert implying by playing this series of little tricks on the reader? What do these narrative ploys add up to and how does the reader respond to his or her initial assumptions or questions about the story at the outset of reading (Is the reference to *muerte* one of death or murder? Is the young girl a victim or indirectly complicit in her death and if so, how?). Whether the answers are searched for in-class with directed reading or at home applying this and other strategies learned in class, students are now prepared to think about and argue their own views. Such acts of synthesis begin to be literary interpretations.

For the teacher of strong readers, no "right" answers exist for these paradoxical or anomalous tendencies of the text. Indeed, the teacher must stress that the questions themselves initiate interpretation, that reading literature involves the reader's interrogation of the text's underlying messages and appreciation of how those messages are constructed through consistent patterns in its surface language. No participant expects absolute consensus about *the* meaning of a literary text (*the* right answer), only right processes of reading its multiple dimensions. After a systematic and careful reading of any literary work, readers have earned the privilege of deciding what those patterns say to them, of drawing inferences and articulating implications. As long as their questions are text-based and their answers intelligible, student insights at this stage should be honored.

The "r + 1" of Values and Literary Texts For initial reading of literary texts at early stages in language instruction, teachers will probably conclude discussion or written work about a story by dealing with student inferences about "how" a text means. For more advanced learners in the second or third levels, however, an additional stage will probably be considered essential: the stage that explores the significance of a text in a larger frame of reference.

Any text, and particularly literary ones, can be analyzed as significant with regard to multiple text-extrinsic dimensions: as reflections of timeless truths, particular social or political issues, as cultural documents, or as well-wrought urns of great beauty. The teacher who wants to prepare students for more advanced literary analysis will probably encourage them to consider one or more of these dimensions. Is this story an example of magical realism? Or is it a distinct sub-genre of the fantastic as some critics would have it? Are such stories distinctly Latin American in origin or are there parallels in English or other literatures with which students are familiar? Alternatively, with increased emphasis in many curricula on cultural studies and content-based coursework in a foreign language, such literary texts can be read in conjunction with other cultural documents to encourage students to reflect about multiple facets of given social problems or attitudes.

A variety of textual combinations will foster such goals. To move from reading to research to interpretation, one must move from a text to intertextuality. Parallel fictional and nonfictional accounts of the same events or subject matter can exemplify how literature lends meaning to real-world experience, pedagogically sound choices from the standpoint of L2 research because such comparisons work with redundant vocabulary and contexts. Parallel accounts can, depending on the goals of the course, be from the L1 or the L2 culture. As a case in point, the teacher might select a Spanish- or English-language text about the incidence of fatal accidents among different age groups in the United States. Readers of *La Muerte* might then be poised to consider youthful attitudes of invincibility as promoting disregard for risk illustrated in Anderson-Imbert's (1976) tale—a sociological reading rather than the aesthetic one foregrounded in the tasks illustrated above.

If the course goals stress cultural dimensions, a parallel text might depict social conditions in the Argentinian countryside and the practice of hitchhiking as a socially accepted means of transportation—the reasons for this acceptance and the reasons why hitchhiking is now relatively rare in the United States and increasingly so in Latin America. Student attention would be drawn to economic differences (the greater likelihood of car ownership in the United States, the banning of hitchhikers on North American and Pan American highways) and their impact on social praxis and cultural attitudes.

Should aesthetic features be emphasized, fictional and nonfictional accounts of a hitchhiker's experience could still be compared—but with a different goal in mind, that of distinguishing between literary conventions and the generally more prosaic accounts of actual events. Here, then, the emphasis would be on differences in how information is conveyed and the aesthetic objectives underlying ambiguity in Anderson-Imbert's (1976) story and disambiguity in a newspaper account.

Literature and Language Learning as Allies

I have tried to demonstrate how the teaching of an unknown language in beginning language instruction can be a natural ally in teaching students to become strong readers of a FL or L2, readers who can identify the topic of a literary or nonliterary text: whether it focuses primarily on people, events, ideas, or institutions. Many texts written in western European languages express their dominant themes in initial paragraphs—if not directly, then by implications shared among the literatures of western countries.

Reading for those implications is a matter of practice—assessment of topic and narrative strategies in developing that topic. Consequently, as has been emphasized here, reading literature as a classroom activity for beginning FL learners involves a wide range of acceptability concerning textual messages and relations between textual messages. The instructional goal must not be to find an absolute truth about the text but to establish a focus of attention that gets students looking at what is there in terms of the language. Only these processes turn students of any language into strong readers.

Whether in the first paragraph of a short text such as the one discussed above or the first chapter of the novel, information must be gleaned in stages. Where students misread or disagree, individual, group, or class work with textual language can resolve resultant uncertainties. To become strong readers, students need to learn that judgments about main characters emerge only after they as readers register the ideas that characters express, the events with which they are involved, and the class structures or institutions they represent. For teachers unfamiliar with how to construct such matrices, the yardstick is simply what works—which binary systems yield interesting and informative ideas about the text. As a rule, for realistic literary texts about people, one matrix grid that generally proves useful involves a column for what people do and a column for how they do it or what they say about doing it and to whom.

Key to the pedagogy of teaching literature presented here, for all initial task stages, whether prereading, reading, rereading, or articulating meaning, teachers ask students to look at what the text says, not what they, the teachers, think it says or interpret it as saying. In other words, teaching the strong reader involves designing tasks that have readers use textual language as the basis for expressing what the text says.

The length or type of literature read should depend on a combination of student background and interests coupled with program goals. As an initial exercise that bridges "reading" and "interpretation," the instructional approach outlined in this paper has the further advantage of identifying the "who, what, why, where," the semantics of the text during initial stages of reading. The larger propositional syntax, the "how" and "why," have been bracketed, are "offsides" so to speak, prior to students' development of a matrix.

That postponement, the delay in introducing how and why, eases the FL reader's cognitive load. Answers to why and how questions involve the difficult analytical issues that, unless rooted in command of textual language with which to express relationships, lead students into subjective tangents rather than inferences based on textual material. Initially, therefore, reader attention should focus on semantics. It is the teacher who must provide analytic schemata for syntactic relationships by helping students identify a logical pattern in textual information—setting up the grid for student execution of a matrix assignment. That grid, in turn, will be the basis both for using textual language in spoken or written expression (the linear or horizontal reading of the matrix) and in drawing inferences about what that text means to them (the vertical reading of the matrix).

By establishing what the text says to them on the text's terms (the binary grid of the matrix), students can clarify for themselves and others the difference between what the text says and what they think it says. The space between text statement and reader perception of text statement is identified and becomes available for objective consideration. This availability is essential if students are going to learn to recreate the content of a story or the thinking of figures in literary works. And those are essential abilities for teachers who want their students to appreciate what a text probably said to its original audiences as well as what it says to them as nonnative speakers of that audience's language—whether those students are reading the work in the original or in translation.

If students read foreign language literature without strategies such as those outlined here, research in reading comprehension suggests that what happens is often counterproductive (e.g., Bernhardt and Kamil 1995). Students take pieces of information from texts with which they are unfamiliar or uncomfortable and either distort them (misreading) or fail to note their presence. A proactive pedagogy, having students identify the unfamiliar or uncomfortable moments in the text helps them to register the presence of difference. From that point it is a relatively small step to interpolate such differences as significant if they develop into a pattern of contrasting or causally related details that inform larger categories such as "familiar" and "unfamiliar." As the illuminating parts of the initially obscure whole, these details emerge in a matrix as tokens of typologies, of species or subsets of a genus, of reader-detected micropropositions that construct the text's macropropositional meaning.

Once students are aware of such possible discrepancies between their expectations and the information in the literary work, they can establish the consciousness from which to explore the text as Other, the *automovilista* of Anderson-Imbert's (1976) story as the reality of the mind that literature can transform into the reality of the physical world. When that process starts early in a FL course sequence and is continued as a central strategy for comprehending and articulating meaning, literature can be integrated seamlessly and happily into language acquisition.

Notes

1. I am indebted to my colleagues Dr. Sharon Foerster and Marike Janzen for their assistance with the Spanish language use in this paper and Dr. Katherine Arens and two anonymous reviewers for their editorial suggestions.
2. For suggestions about appropriate in-class reading activities and related assignments, see Kern, 2000, pp. 129–69; for detailed lesson plans used in integrating reading tasks into a first semester German language sequence, see Maxim 1999, Appendix I, pp. 332–94.
3. In the author's words, the story "reveladora del carácter humano y también de la naturaleza absurda del cosmos. . . ."
4. This and all subsequent translations are the author's.

Works Cited

Anderson-Imbert, Enrique. 1979. *Teoría y Técnica del Cuento*. Buenos Aires: Marymar Ediciones, S.A.

———. 1976. La Muerte. *Cuento en Miniatura. Antología*. Caracas, Venezuela: Editorial Equinoccio, Universidad Simon Bolivar.

Bernhardt, Elizabeth B. 1990. A Model of L2 Text Reconstruction: The Recall of Literary Text by Learners of German. In *Issues in L2: Theory as Practice/Practice as Theory*, edited by Angela Labarca and Louise M. Bailey, 21–43. Norwood, NJ: Ablex.

———. 1995. Interpreting Relationships between L1 and L2 Reading: Consolidating the Linguistic Threshold and the Linguistic Interdependence Hypotheses. *Applied Linguistics* 16: 15–34.

Block, Ellen. 1986. The Comprehension Strategies of Second Language Learners. *TESOL Quarterly* 20: 463–94.

Carrell, Patricia L. 1991. Second Language Reading: Reading Ability or Language Proficiency. *Applied Linguistics* 12: 159–79.

Doughty, Catherine. 1998. Acquiring Competence in a Second Language: Form and Function. In *Learning Foreign and Second Languages: Perspectives in Research and Scholarship*, edited by H. Byrnes, 128–56. New York: Modern Language Association.

Fecteau, Monique L. 1999. First- and Second-Language Reading Comprehension of Literary Texts. *Modern Language Journal* 83: 475–93.

Fish, Stanley. 1980. *Is There a Text in This Class?* Cambridge: Harvard University Press.

Hosenfeld, Carol. 1977. "A Preliminary Investigation of the Strategies of Successful and Non-successful Readers." *System* 5: 110–23.

Hulstijn, Jan H. 1992. Retention of Inferred and Given Word Meanings: Experiments in Incidental Vocabulary Learning. In *Vocabulary and Applied Linguistics*, edited by P. J. L. Arnaud and H. Béjoint, 113–25. London, MacMillan.

Iser, Wolfgang. 1981. *The Act of Reading*. Baltimore: Johns Hopkins University Press.

Kern, Richard G. 1989. Second Language Reading Strategy Instruction: Its Effects on Comprehension and Word Inference Ability. *Modern Language Journal* 73: 135–49.

———. 2000. *Literacy and Language Teaching*. Oxford: Oxford University Press.

Kintsch, Walter. 1998. *Comprehension. A Paradigm for Cognition*. New York: Cambridge University Press.

Kintsch, Walter, and Teun A. van Dijk. 1978. Towards a Model of Discourse Comprehension and Production. *Psychological Review* 85: 363–94.

Krashen, Stephen. 1985. *The Input Hypotheses: Issues and Implications*. New York: Longman.

———. 1989. We Acquire Vocabulary and Spelling by Reading: Additional Evidence for the Input Hypothesis. *Modern Language Journal* 73: 440–64.

Marshall, J. D., P. Smagorinsky, and M. W. Smith. 1995. *The Language of Interpretation: Patterns of Discourse in Discussions of Literature*. Urbana, IL: National Council of Teachers of English.

Rosenblatt, Louise M. 1983. *Literature as Exploration.* New York: Modern Language Association.

Rumelhart, David E. 1977. Toward an Interactive Model of Reading. *Attention and Performance,* edited by Stanislov Dornic, 573–603. New York: Academic Press.

Samuels, S. Jay and Michael J. Kamil. 1984. Models of the Reading Process. *Handbook of Reading Research.* New York: Longman.

Stauffer, Russell G. 1969. *Directing Reading Maturity as a Cognitive Process.* New York: Harper & Row.

Swaffar, Janet, Katherine Arens, and Heidi Byrnes. 1991. *Reading for Meaning. An Integrated Approach.* Englewood Cliffs, NJ: Prentice Hall.

VanPatten, Bill. 1996. *Input Processing and Grammar Instruction: Theory and Research.* Norwood, NJ: Ablex.

APPENDIX A

LA MUERTE
Enrique Anderson-Imbert

La automovilista (negro el vestido, negro el pelo, negros los ojos, pero con la cara tan pálida que a pesar del mediodía parecía que en su tez se hubiese detenido un relámpago) la automovilista vio en el camino a una muchacha que hacía señas para que parara. Paró.

—¿Me llevas? Hasta el pueblo, no más –dijo la muchacha

—Sube —dijo la automovilista. Y el auto arrancó a toda velocidad por el camino que bordeaba la montaña.

—Muchas gracias —dijo la muchacha, con un gracioso mohín— pero ¿no tiene miedo de levantar por el camino a personas desconocidas? Podrían hacerte daño. ¡Esto está tan desierto!

—No, no tengo miedo.

—¿Y si levantas a alguien que te atraca?

—No tengo miedo

—¿Y si te matan?

—No tengo miedo.

—No? Permíteme presentarme —dijo entonces la muchacha, que tenía los ojos grandes, límpidos, imaginativos. Y, en seguida, conteniendo la risa, fingió una voz vernosa—. Soy la Muerte, la M-u-e-r-t-e.

La automovilista sonrió misteriosamente.

En la próxima curva el auto se desbarrancó. La muchacha quedó muerte entre las piedras. La automovilista siguió a pie y al llegar a un cactus desapareció.

DEATH

The driver (black her dress, black her hair, black her eyes, but her face so pale that despite the noonday sun it looked as though it had been struck by lightning) saw on the road a young girl who was signaling her to stop. She stopped.

"Will you give me a ride? Only as far as the village," said the girl.

"Get in," said the driver. And the car took off at high speed down the road along the side of the mountain.

"Thank you very much," said the girl, with a gracious gesture, "but aren't you afraid to pick up strangers? Someone might hurt you. It's so deserted here!"

"No, I'm not afraid."

"What if you pick up someone who robs you?"

"I'm not afraid."

"What if they try to kill you?"

"I'm not afraid."

"No? Then allow me to introduce myself," the girl responded; she had large eyes, limpid, imaginative, And therewith, suppressing her laughter, she simulated a sonorous voice. "I am Death, D-E-A-T-H."

The driver smiled uncannily.

At the next curve the car crashed. The girl lay dead among the rocks. The driver emerged from the car unscathed, walked away, and alongside a cactus, vanished.

APPENDIX B

Assignment format for precis—Katherine Arens and Janet Swaffar

There is a difference between a text's facts and the strategy used to present those facts. A "precis" (`pray-see`) reflects this difference. It is designed to reflect the structure of a text's argument, not just a set of notes on the text's contents. A precis is one typed page long.

No matter what type, a precis has three sections:
1) A statement about the text's **FOCUS**. This is the main issue that the text addresses.

   **You write a concise statement (1–2 sentences) of that focus.
   Likely alternatives:
   -issues or problems
   -representative concerns of a group or its interlocked set of beliefs
   -institutions/systems
   -events and their characteristics or repercussions

   e.g.: "The structure of the mind and how it relates to behavior in the social world."

   What <u>not</u> to do: Do not include journalistic commentary, or examples, or evaluations – just state what the topic is.

2) A statement of **LOGIC** and **GOAL** (its **Intent**), which will introduce a **CHART WITH HEADINGS** encompassing the text's data in two parallel columns of notes (usually with page references to the reading).

   **You write a sentence describing the logic pattern (e.g., "By examining the sources of _____, the author shows the consequences of _____"; "In order to _____, the text correlates the _____ and _____ of social behaviors.")

   Typical verbs indicating such logic: compare, contrast, link causally, cause, follow from . . .

   ***After that, you write* two column headings creating classes of information which the author systematically correlates with each other. Under these headings, you typically add three or four examples which fit the content of the text into its form.

   Typical categories of information:
   -characteristics of a model, role, event
   -stages in an event or process
   -sources, conditions, or restrictions on a context
   -participants or interest groups
   -effects, impact, consequences
   -goals, purposes to be realized

3) A paragraph (ca. 3 sentences) indicating the **IMPLICATIONS** of the information pattern. This is **not** a description of the information pattern or focus, but rather an extension of the covert statement implied by the information and pattern. *That is,* what is this text/precis *good for,* especially as seen from the outside? In setting the argument up this way, what is being hidden, asserted, or brushed aside? What is new or old-fashioned about the correlations made? Who would profit most by this arrangement?

Note: Beginning FL students will soon be able to fill in the first two sections in the FL. The instructor may find it useful to have them complete part three in English to facilitate and cross-check readers' comprehension.

Teaching Literary Texts at the Intermediate Level: A Structured Input Approach

Stacey Katz
The University of Utah at Salt Lake City

In this article, it will be taken for granted that it is important for literary works to remain a part of the foreign language curriculum (see Jurasek 1996; McCarthy 1998; Tucker 2000). The question, however, is how to integrate the teaching of literature into the modern foreign language classroom, where teacher-centered activities are discouraged and communication among students is paramount. Perceiving the need for innovative methods to teach literature in the communicative classroom, Virginia Scott (2001) challenges her colleagues "in both language and literature to avail ourselves of the research in SLA in order to rethink the teaching of literature" (p. 547). The goal should be to adapt theories that are shown to be effective in language and grammar instruction to the teaching of literature and hence to make literature a more complementary component within four skills courses.

Lee and VanPatten's (1995) *Making Communicative Teaching Happen* describes a theory of foreign language pedagogy that has the potential to be effective in the literature classroom, especially at the intermediate level. The authors propose that various types of structured input and output activities used for teaching both reading comprehension and grammar can also be applied to the teaching of literature. It is important to stress that reading for comprehension is only one part of the purpose of studying literature; the analysis of literary texts is valuable precisely because of what can be found behind the literal meanings of the words on the page.

In this article, I propose that structured input and output activities can not only lead students to discover the general meaning of a poem or a work of prose but also can help them to become aware of underlying themes, various literary devices, and other elements that enrich literary works; hence, foreign language reading becomes more intellectually stimulating and satisfying.

This article is organized in the following manner: in the first section, I discuss the difficulties of teaching foreign language classes at the intermediate level, and I describe the ways in which the study of literature can be incorporated into the communicative classroom. In the second section, I summarize some of the important tenets of Lee and VanPatten's (1995) theory and demonstrate how it can be applied to the teaching of literature. Last, I provide examples of the kinds of texts and activities that work well within this framework.

The Intermediate Level: Difficulties and Challenges

It has been widely acknowledged that there are problems in the design of the foreign language curricula at the intermediate level. For the past two decades, scholars have debated whether literature should be taught in postsecondary foreign language classes (see Birckbichler and Muyskens 1980; Bretz and Persin 1987; Harper 1988; Jurasek 1996; Knutson 1993; Kramsch 1985; McCarthy 1998; Muyskens 1983; Schultz 1996; Schulz 1981; Tucker 2000). Byrnes (1998) points out that faculty members' disagreements over the role that literature should play in departmental curricula can create much tension within language departments, especially in those that are experiencing dramatic decreases in enrollment.

At the intermediate level, the discussion has become especially heated, primarily for two reasons: first, it is particularly difficult to design and to teach effective intermediate courses, and second, it is at the intermediate level that there exists a real opportunity to increase enrollment and to build programs. Poorly conceived intermediate courses foster the disintegration of language programs. According to Kramsch (1993), part of the problem is that instructors may lack confidence in their ability to teach literature: "Some teachers still feel hesitant to use literary texts in the language classroom. Their hesitation is often a reflex of academic self-defense. As language teachers they are told that they are competent only to teach language, not literature" (p. 7). Similarly, literature specialists may be unsure about how to teach literary texts in a class intended to be communicative.

The typical intermediate foreign-language class at the university level is often difficult to teach because it is composed of two different types of students: those who only want to fulfill their language requirement and do not intend to continue their study beyond the intermediate level, and those who are considering a major or a minor in the language. The students in the first group may have little interest in the subject or in improving their proficiency in the language. In contrast, those in the latter group often have had success in the first-year language courses and are enthusiastic about furthering their studies; sometimes, they have already mastered a foreign language and are eager to learn another. In addition, there are students in this group who have studied the language in high school and, thus, tend to be more fluent and more comfortable with the language.

Because of their varied backgrounds and levels of proficiency and interest, students at the intermediate level might be considered to be in the "adolescence" of foreign language learning. In other words, the intermediate level can be viewed as an awkward, in-between stage. At the elementary level students read easy, usually nonliterary material, acquire a childlike command of the language, and engage in simple conversations about their daily lives. At the advanced level (third year and above), students enter "adulthood"; the advanced courses emphasize complex themes and often focus on literature. At the intermediate level, one finds an identity crisis like that which happens in adolescence: the students are not yet mature nor are they children. In addition, they progress through this stage of development at different rates.

Referring to intermediate courses as "bridges" or as "filling the gap" between elementary and advanced studies, unfortunately implies a disregard for the students who will not continue on to the next level. We must evaluate our intermediate curriculum to determine what will be useful for these students as well as what will inspire those who are considering becoming majors or minors. Although it is generally assumed that oral communication is the most important goal of studying a foreign language, Schulz (1981) points out: "Many educators agree that reading is probably the longest retained skill; moreover, unlike speaking, reading can be developed to a relatively sophisticated level rather early" (p. 43). Reading is also an area in which students who have difficulty communicating in the spoken language may excel.

It is true that some students say that they are not interested in studying literature (see Davis, Kline, and Stoekl 1995; Gonzales-Berry 1996). They regard the study of literary texts as irrelevant in their lives, ineffective for developing their communicative skills, or just plain boring (see Scott 2001, p. 542). The successful integration of literature into the curriculum relies on the selection of intellectually challenging, interesting works with which students of all levels can interact. The themes and topics should be complex, yet the language of the texts should not be too difficult (see Carrell 1984; Jurasek 1996; Knuston 1993; and Kramsch 1985, who discuss the importance of choosing appropriate texts).

After having carefully chosen appropriate readings, the instructor must lead students to awareness of the structures that may impede their comprehension and help them focus on these constructions in order to understand the text's general meaning. As I discuss below, structured input and output activities can be employed to assure that students have a basic understanding of the work (e.g., in a story, recognizing the important characters and following the plot; in a poem, deciding who is speaking and the situation he or she is in). After acquiring this knowledge, they are ready to discover the elements of the text that lie beneath the surface and that contribute toward making it a work of literature. At this point, the types of input and output exercises used to ensure reading comprehension can be employed to take students to a deeper level of understanding and to an appreciation of the richness of literary works.

In the next section, structured input and output are described in greater detail, and I explain how this framework can be applied to the teaching of literature. In addition, specific techniques are outlined and demonstrated, using examples of two French texts that work well in the intermediate classroom.

Structured Input and Output

Lee and VanPatten (1995) present a method for teaching foreign languages that relies heavily on the role of structured input. They contend that when students are acquiring grammatical structures, they should receive a great deal of comprehensible input that contains the given structures. After students have received a substantial amount of input, this input should become what is called intake, which is "a reduced, sometimes slightly altered set of input data" (p. 94). This leads to the students' acquiring a developing system that forms at the stage where they begin to internalize the target structures. Only at this point can students be expected to begin producing the target structures. Lee and VanPatten explain: "Note the contradiction between traditional grammar practice and our model of acquisition. The development of an internal system is input dependent; it happens when learners receive and process meaning-bearing input. Traditional grammar practice, on the other hand, is exclusively output oriented" (p. 94). Lee and VanPatten also postulate that students "must become more active, more responsible for their own learning" (p. 13). The instructor becomes the resource person, or in their terminology, the "architect" of the classroom, while students "become information gatherers and negotiators as well as builders and coworkers" (p. 17). I shall show that both concepts (input leading to output, and making students responsible for their own learning) can be applied to the study of literature.

In recent years, schema theory has become an integral part of foreign language instruction, and many current textbooks employ some of the tenets of the theory in the exercises that accompany readings. These textbooks provide prereading activities that activate appropriate frames of reference that help students understand a reading more easily; for example, they draw attention to the way in which a text is organized so that students gain a better idea of the purpose of the text, which leads to improved comprehension. Relying heavily on research done in schema theory (see Carrell 1984; Rumelhart 1980), Lee and VanPatten (1995) offer many other strategies for teaching students to read. Following the hypothesis of schema theory, that students should incorporate any background information that they already possess into their understanding of the text, an instructor should provide students with an appropriate knowledge base before they begin reading. Lee and VanPatten identify several techniques for activating students' background knowledge and for preparing them to interact with a given text. The authors suggest brainstorming; analyzing titles, headings, and illustrations; activating world knowledge; giving a pretest; and scanning for specific information to help students prepare for reading the text (pp. 200–04).

As mentioned above, however, comprehending the meaning of the words on the page is only one part of studying a literary text. Scott (2001) explains that a major goal of a literature course she recently taught was to have her students "see the text as a creative work with layers of meaning" (p. 542). This objective succinctly distinguishes the teaching of reading from the teaching of literature. The goal of reading is understanding the main ideas of a text. The ultimate satisfaction of studying literature is the discovery of layers of meaning. This idea of discovery is essential. Through interactions with the text, both in pre- and postreading activities, students should be the ones who come up with theories about the deeper meanings of the text, some of which the instructor has led them to formulate, others of which the instructor may not have anticipated.

Once the students have grasped the intricacies of the literary work they are studying and have recognized the techniques used by the author, they are prepared to create output at the discourse level. Lee and VanPatten (1995) emphasize "the importance of allowing learners to access form and structure at the sentence level before proceeding to connected sentences" (p. 122). Students should begin with basic tasks and move to more complex ones after they have understood the structures at hand. Therefore, it is beneficial for students to produce simple sentences before being asked to create longer forms of discourse.

Literary texts, poetry in particular, provide models for students' own writing. Scott (1996) explains: "Because written discourse is culturally determined, reading should be linked to writing. Extensive reading, or reading texts for the gist, can help students to internalize patterns of discourse, levels of register, and links between language and culture. Intensive reading, or close textual analysis, can provide students with models to follow" (p. 155). Thus, after studying a poem, students can try to imitate the writer's style. Kramsch (1993) asserts: "We should not underestimate the pleasure students can derive from experimenting with literary form, nor should we feel bashful, even in language classes, about discussing the craft behind the students' products" (p. 171). As shown in the next section, students can follow the pattern of a poem and come up with creative works of their own. They can also be encouraged to interact with a story by writing letters to the characters or by relating the themes to their own lives and experiences. These types of exercises appear in the following section where I show how to apply Lee and VanPatten's theory to the teaching of literary texts.

Before students begin producing output, however, they must receive a great deal of input about the general meaning of the texts and about the literary themes that they will discover at a deeper level of analysis. For each of the two works discussed below, a poem and a *récit*, students are required to work with the input first. For example, they decide whether or not they agree with lists of statements, first about the text's plot or situation and its top level of meaning, and second, about some of the less obvious aspects of the text (the more abstract, deeper levels). Through doing these exercises, students are led to focus on literary elements (such as imagery and symbolism, figures of speech, allusions to other sources, tone, how the sounds of a poem contribute to its meaning, character motivation, etc.) and to hypothesize what they consider to be the underlying meanings of the text.

Next, students move to the output phase where they are required to support the hypotheses that they have constructed in the input sections. They find appropriate words and phrases in the text to back up their arguments, and they produce short sentences or questions in the target language. Finally, they communicate at the discourse-level, which assumes their having grasped the elements in the text that distinguish it as a work of literature.

Poetry

Jacques Prévert's poem "Déjeuner du matin" [Breakfast] is commonly included in curricula at both the elementary and intermediate levels of study. It is a simple poem with a series of actions written in the *passé composé:*[1]

Il a mis le café	He poured the coffee
Dans la tasse	Into the cup
Il a mis le lait	He poured the milk
Dans la tasse de café	Into the coffee

Il a mis le sucre	He put the sugar
Dans le café au lait	In the café au lait
Avec la petite cuiller	With the little spoon
Il a tourné	He stirred
Il a bu le café au lait	He drank the café au lait
Et il a reposé la tasse	And he put the cup down again
Sans me parler	Without speaking to me
Il a allumé	He lit
une cigarette	A cigarette
Il a fait des ronds	He blew rings
Avec la fumée	With the smoke
Il a mis les cendres	He put the ashes
Dans le cendrier	In the ashtray
Sans me parler	Without speaking to me
Sans me regarder	Without looking at me
Il s'est levé	He got up
Il a mis	He put
Son chapeau	His hat
Sur sa tête	On his head
Il a mis	He put on
Son manteau de pluie	His raincoat
Parce qu'il pleuvait	Because it was raining
Et il est parti	And he left
Sous la pluie	In the rain
Sans une parole	Without a word
Sans me regarder	Without looking at me
Et moi j'ai pris	And me, I put
Ma tête dans ma main	My head in my hands
Et j'ai pleuré.	And I cried.

Since students rarely have difficulty understanding the literal meaning of this poem, it is an excellent text for them to study. First, students should read the poem to understand the general sense of what is going on. Then they should study it to discover the elements that enrich it: tone, form, rhythm, sound, figurative language, and ambiguity.

The students' first reaction to the poem is usually favorable. But why do they like it? What is it about the poem that appeals to them? For one thing, students tend to like the poem because they immediately understand the words. However, if it were just an easy poem with no deeper meanings, it is doubtful that it would leave much of an impression on them. What is remarkable in "Déjeuner du matin" is the depth of the emotion conveyed in the poem. The poet accomplishes this effect by incorporating various literary elements. For example, the repetitiveness and the rhythm of the short lines create a tone that seems matter-of-fact and emotionless, which contrasts with the narrator's sorrow. Another striking contrast is the banality of the ordinary actions that occur against the background of profound grief. Although this emotion is not apparent until the end of the poem, there are signs early on that the narrator is indeed upset. For example, the alliteration of "s" sounds (**s**ous la pluie/**s**ans une parole/**s**ans me regarder) suggests sighing and sobbing. Another literary device that appears in the poem is the idea of the "pathetic fallacy," which refers to a connection between what is happening in nature and a person's emotional state. In the poem, there is a correspondence between the rain that is falling and the speaker's tears and sorrow. Students should be led to consider this connection. (Would the poem be as powerful if, for example, the sun were shining?)

Another literary element is the poem's intended ambiguity, which makes the poem more interesting and more relevant to a diverse group of readers. Is the speaker a man or a woman? A child or an adult? Does the scene take place in a restaurant or in the kitchen of a house? There is really no way to tell from the words on the page. Therefore, the poem can be interpreted in several different ways, depending upon the perspective of the reader.

The structured input and output exercises that are provided below help to lead students along the path of discovering the literary richness of the poem, allowing them to interact with the text and arrive at their own interpretations. All the activities are meant to be done in groups and are intended to stimulate discussion among group members, except for the final, discourse-level structured output exercises.[2]

Exercise 1: Selecting Alternatives (Input)

(This activity should occur before the students read the poem. They are required to choose the most appropriate answer from the list given after each sentence. The exercise serves to provide students with background information about some of the important ideas of the poem, such as quarreling through silence and the pain of being ignored. The questions lead the students to become aware of literary devices, such as the symbolic relationship between an action and an emotion, and the connection between nature and the human situation. After doing this exercise, the students will be ready to read the poem.)

1. When people argue,

They refuse to speak to each other.	Always	Usually	Sometimes	Never
They stare at each other.	Always	Usually	Sometimes	Never
They don't like each other.	Always	Usually	Sometimes	Never

Teaching Literary Texts at the Intermediate Level

They misunderstand each other.	Always	Usually	Sometimes	Never

2. When people are sad,

They run away.	Always	Usually	Sometimes	Never
They cry.	Always	Usually	Sometimes	Never
They talk.	Always	Usually	Sometimes	Never
They smoke.	Always	Usually	Sometimes	Never
They drink coffee.	Always	Usually	Sometimes	Never
They sleep.	Always	Usually	Sometimes	Never

3. When it rains,

People feel sad.	Always	Usually	Sometimes	Never
People feel happy.	Always	Usually	Sometimes	Never
People don't want to go outside.	Always	Usually	Sometimes	Never

Exercise 2: Binary Options
(Input)

(This activity begins with several statements that are designed to ensure that the students have understood the main ideas of the poem. Through questions about setting and tone, it reveals the poem's ambiguity, and it leads students to discover that their interpretations of the poem may differ from those of their peers.)

It is nice out.	Agree	Disagree
The speaker is happy.	Agree	Disagree
The man is talkative.	Agree	Disagree
The man drinks his coffee black.	Agree	Disagree
The speaker is a woman.	Agree	Disagree
The speaker is a child.	Agree	Disagree
This scene takes place in a café.	Agree	Disagree
This scene takes place in the kitchen of a house.	Agree	Disagree
The man doesn't know the speaker.	Agree	Disagree
The man is ignoring the speaker.	Agree	Disagree
The man doesn't see the speaker.	Agree	Disagree
The speaker has a new haircut and looks very different.	Agree	Disagree
Behind the routine of everyday events, there are often deep emotions.	Agree	Disagree
Early in the poem, the speaker indicates that he or she may begin crying.	Agree	Disagree

Exercise 3: Matching
(Input)

(This activity allows students to discover symbolism and symbolic actions as well as the possible correspondence between people's emotions and what is happening in nature. Note: The suggested matches are given on the same line here, but they would be scattered on students' sheets.)

rain	tears
sun	happiness
raining	crying
hand	blocks tears
raincoat	blocks the rain
make smoke rings	indifference
"without speaking to me"	rejection

Exercise 4: Questions
(Output at the sentential level)

(Students are asked to write five questions that they would like to ask the two main characters. This exercise helps them to recognize the poem's ambiguity and the significance of actions and images that may suggest symbolic meanings. For example, they might think about why the poet shows the man drinking coffee sweetened with milk and sugar rather than black coffee. Is there a possible symbolic meaning? Are his deliberate, silent actions of pouring the coffee and the milk, putting in the sugar, and stirring it, symbolic?)

Model:

1. Why won't you talk to your wife (child, girlfriend)?

2. Why do you think your husband (father, boyfriend) is angry (or another emotion, such as disappointed or depressed). Is he leaving you with regret (because of another lover, to go away on a trip, because he lost custody of you)?

3. Where will you (the speaker and/or the man) go afterwards?

Exercise 5: Another Perspective
(Output at the sentence level)

(Students are asked to imitate the style of the poet by rewriting the poem from the perspective of the other person, perhaps in the present tense. In the model below, they will discover a drastic change in tone: what makes the speaker seem amused?)

Model:

Dans un café	In a café
Je bois mon café	I drink my coffee
Elle me regarde sans cesse	She keeps looking at me
Qui est-elle?	Who is she?
Pourquoi me regarde-t-elle?	Why is she looking at me?
Est-ce que je la connais?	Do I know her?
J'essaie de boire mon café.	I try to drink my coffee
Tranquillement.	Peacefully
Mais elle me regarde sans cesse.	But she keeps on looking at me.

Exercise 6: Your Own Poem (Output at the discourse level)

(Students have another opportunity to imitate the poet in their own work.)

Directions:

Write a poem using simple sentences written in the *passé composé*. Possible topics may include leaving home for the first time to go to college or attending a wedding or a funeral. Be sure to convey emotion in the poem; establish a contrast between the speaker's highly emotional state and the matter-of-fact style of the lines. At the end of the poem, there should be an action that clearly shows the speaker's feelings, such as the distraught utterance: "J'ai pris ma tête dans mes mains, et j'ai pleuré."

The Short Story

A short story or an excerpt from a longer work can be effectively employed in the intermediate classroom. For example, "Mère" [Mother], taken from the longer work *La Clé sur la porte* [The Key above the Door] by Algerian author Marie Cardinal, describes a woman's alienation from her mother due to the mother's obsession with an infant daughter who died seventeen years earlier. In this *récit*, which takes place in an Algerian cemetery, the narrator describes a yearly trip to the cemetery with her mother and reveals the jealousy she feels because of the love that her mother has for the dead child.

This story is difficult for students because it contains mostly long, descriptive paragraphs and only five lines of dialogue. There is a great deal of new vocabulary, though it is glossed in the *Liens* (Hammadou 1994) edition. Therefore, it is important that the structured input activities ensure that students understand the general plot of the story before leading them to interpret the deeper levels of meanings of the text. During the structured input exercises, the appropriate frames of reference should be activated; students should be asked to think about literary elements that are not necessarily immediately apparent when reading the text, such as allusions, religious images and symbols, and contrasts.

Recognizing the Christian overtones is essential for students to understand the deeper meanings of the text. Cardinal employs various literary devices that incorporate underlying Catholic themes. For example, there are several biblical allusions in the story. Most important is the Virgin Mary as the archetypal perfect mother, who stands in contrast to the narrator's flawed mother. This opposition is just one of the many striking polarities that students should be led to discover. Some of the other contrasts are listed in Exercise 3 below.

The narrator's using the *récit* as a form of confession is also important in understanding the significance of the story. The narrator appears to be telling the story in order to confess her jealous and unforgiving thoughts. The problem is that she does not really repent; she appears unable to get beyond her anger and her jealousy, and, at the end of the story, her sense of isolation and despair becomes apparent. In the final structured output exercise, students should be encouraged to explore the religious topics of forgiveness and repentance.

Exercise 1: Matching
(Input)

(This exercise, which is done before reading the text, enables students to learn some of the more difficult vocabulary that is essential to understanding the story. It also creates a frame in which students are guided to think about religious overtones, so they will be attentive to religious images, symbols, and allusions when reading the text.)

l'ossuaire [ossuary]	where bones are kept
la dalle [stone]	a piece of marble
un robinet [faucet]	where water comes out
une tombe [grave]	where a body is buried
la Toussaint [All Saints' Day]	a holiday in France when people visit cemeteries
la Confession [confession]	the act of telling one's sins
la Vierge Marie [Virgin Mary]	the perfect mother

Exercise 2: Binary Options
(Input)

(This exercise begins with some basic statements about the plot to ensure that the students have understood the text. Then, it moves on

◈ Teaching Literary Texts at the Intermediate Level **167**

to more subjective ideas, allowing students to explore their own perceptions of the themes of the text, and introduces religious ideas. It also leads students to think about character analysis.)

Do you agree or disagree with each of the following statements?
1. The author has written this story to show her sadness about never having known her sister.
2. The narrator's task at the cemetery is to take her sister's bones to the ossuary.
3. It is a horrible day at the cemetery, rainy and cold.
4. The mother becomes cross with the narrator because she shows no emotion at her sister's grave.
5. The narrator feels ignored and unloved.
6. The narrator is moved by the religious icons found in the cemetery.
7. A mother will never get over the loss of a child.
8. There is no such thing as a perfect mother.
9. It is natural for children to be jealous of one another and to compete for their mothers' love.
10. It is unusual to be jealous of someone who has died.
11. It is easier to love someone who is dead than someone who is alive.
12. It is normal to feel that one's parents prefer one's siblings.

Exercise 3: Finding Examples
(Output at the sentence level)

(As mentioned above, in this story, one of the most striking literary elements is the contrasts, which produce a tension between opposites. Students are asked to find examples in the text that fit the following oppositions. It is hoped that through this activity, students will also discover the religious overtones of the story, such as allusions to angels, the Virgin Mary, the concepts of forgiveness and repentance, and the consequences of making a confession while still filled with anger and resentment.)

life/death
love/hatred
beauty/ugliness
perfect child/flawed child
perfect mother/flawed mother

pleasant smells/bad odors
purity/sin
confession/hardness of heart
forgiving/implacable

Exercise 4: Writing a Letter
(Output at the discourse level)

(This exercise reinforces the students' understanding of the literary elements of tone and character analysis.)

1. Write a letter from the daughter to her mother, explaining why she wants to cut off contact with the family.
2. Write a letter from the mother to the daughter, asking for her forgiveness.

Conclusion

The two literary works presented in this article serve as examples of the ways in which the theory of structured input and output can be applied to teaching literature. In the traditional literature classroom, students are usually asked to read a story, poem, or play and then answer a series of questions based on it to ensure that they have understood it. Then the instructor might facilitate a discussion of the work, asking students about literary elements. In contrast, the type of approach advocated in this article enables students to interact more actively with the text and to discover its many layers of meaning through such interactions. Because of the input activities that the students do both before and after reading, they are led to gain an appreciation of literary style as well as become aware of many of the deeper meanings of the work. After they have attained a thorough understanding of the text and its intricacies have become part of the students' developing system (Lee and VanPatten 1995), students are then ready to produce output and to form their own interpretations of what they have read.

The preparation of structured input and output activities to teach literature is time-consuming for the instructor, but students can be asked to contribute to the development of such activities. For example, after reading a text, students could work in small groups and develop lists of true and false assertions about the text. Then, all the students could decide with which assertions they agree or disagree. The groups could find examples of literary elements, such as irony, ambiguity, allusion, imagery, symbolism, tone, alliteration, and various figures of speech, and the class could try to determine their contributions to the text.

It is important that foreign language textbooks include the teaching of literature, and, to guide instructors, they should incorporate the types of input and output exercises that applied linguists have proposed for the communicative classroom. Especially at large universities where graduate teaching assistants teach literature at the intermediate level, such guidance should be provided since these instructors are in the process of developing and refining their teaching skills. They need materials and methods of instruction. Over the last two decades, most graduate teaching assistants at American universities have been trained how to teach students to communicate in a foreign language, but they have not been trained how to teach students to understand and appreciate literary texts (see Harper 1988; Kramsch 1993; Muyskens 1983). Muyskens (1983) agrees: "It is ironic that those who will spend their lives teaching literature are rarely introduced to methods for doing so" (p. 414). In order to help teachers who are new to the field as well as those who currently limit themselves to teaching only language skills or only literature, there must be further collaboration between applied linguists and literature specialists. In that way, students of foreign languages will benefit from the innovative methods of the communicative classroom, which can make them more sensitive to the richness of literature.

Notes

1. I would like to thank Editions Gallimard for allowing me to reprint this poem.
2. These exercises should be created and performed completely in French. They are provided in English here, however, to make them more accessible to the general reader.

Works Cited

Birckbichler, Diane W., and Judith A. Muyskens. 1980. A Personalized Approach to the Teaching of Literature at the Elementary and Intermediate Levels of Instruction. *Foreign Language Annals* 13: 23–27.

Bretz, Mary Lee, and Margaret Persin. 1987. The Application of Critical Theory to Literature at the Introductory Level: A Working Model for Teacher Preparation. *Modern Language Journal* 71: 165–70.

Byrnes, Heidi. 1998. Constructing Curricula in Collegiate Foreign Language Departments. In *Learning Foreign and Second Languages: Perspectives in Research and Scholarship,* edited by Heidi Byrnes, 262–95. New York: Modern Language Association.

Cardinal, Marie. 1972. "Mère." In *La Clé sur la porte.* Excerpt in *Liens,* edited by Joann Hammadou, 103–06. Boston: Heinle & Heinle.

Carrell, Patricia L. 1984. Schema Theory and ESL Reading: Classroom Implications and Applications. *Modern Language Journal* 68: 332–43.

Davis, James N., Rebecca R. Kline, and Allan I. Stoekl. 1995. Ce que définir veut dire: Analyses of Undergraduates' Definitions of Literature. *French Review* 68: 652–64.

Gonzales-Berry, Erlinda. 1996. Bridging the Gap: A Content-Based Approach. *ADFL Bulletin* 27: 35–38.

Hammadou, Joann. 1994. *Liens: Par écrit.* Boston: Heinle & Heinle.

Harper, Sandra. 1988. Strategies for Teaching Literature at the Undergraduate Level. *Modern Language Journal* 72: 402–08.

Jurasek, Richard. 1996. Intermediate-Level Foreign Language Curricula: An Assessment and a New Agenda. *ADFL Bulletin* 27: 18–27.

Knutson, Elizabeth M. 1993. Teaching Whole Texts: Literature and Foreign Language Reading Instruction. *French Review* 67: 12–26.

Kramsch, Claire. 1985. Literary Texts in the Classroom: A Discourse. *Modern Language Journal* 69: 356–66.

———. 1993. *Context and Culture in Language Teaching.* Oxford: Oxford University Press.

Lee, James F., and Bill VanPatten. 1995. *Making Communicative Language Teaching Happen.* New York: McGraw-Hill.

McCarthy, John A. 1998. W(h)ither Literature? Reaping the Fruit of Language Study Before It's Too Late. *ADFL Bulletin* 29: 10–17.

Muyskens, Judith A. 1983. Teaching Second-Language Literatures: Past, Present and Future. *Modern Language Journal* 67: 413–23.

Prévert, Jacques. 1949. Déjeuner du matin. In *Paroles,* 147–48. Paris: Gallimard.

Rumelhart, David E. 1980. Schemata: The Building Blocks of Cognition. In *Theoretical Issues in Reading Comprehension,* edited by Rand Spiro, Bertram Bruce, and William Brewer, 33-35. Hillsdale, NJ: Lawrence Erlbaum.

Schultz, Jean-Marie. 1996. The Uses of Poetry in the Foreign Language Curriculum. *French Review* 69: 920–32.

Schulz, Renate A. 1981. Literature and Readability: Bridging the Gap in Foreign Language Reading. *Modern Language Journal* 65: 43–53.

Scott, Virginia Mitchell. 1996. *Rethinking Foreign Language Writing.* Boston: Heinle & Heinle.

_____. 2001. An Applied Linguist in the Literature Classroom. *The French Review* 74: 538–49.

Tucker, Holly. 2000. The Place of the Personal: The Changing Face of Foreign Language Literature in a Standards-Based Curriculum. *ADFL Bulletin* 31: 53–58.

A Stylistic Approach to Foreign Language Acquisition and Literary Analysis

William J. Berg and Laurey K. Martin-Berg
University of Wisconsin-Madison

> "Le style est l'homme même."
> —Buffon (1962, p. 258)

Along with the other approaches highlighted in this volume, the notion of style can serve to bridge the gap between foreign language and literature studies that can threaten classroom effectiveness, curricular coherence, and even professional harmony. If literature is the highest form of linguistic expression, it is so in one sense precisely because it causes us to witness the workings of language, the very goal of the foreign language classroom. In literature courses, quite obviously, the notion of style enables the student to recognize, analyze, interpret, and appreciate the linguistic tools and techniques that the writer manipulates to produce meaning and structure. Less obviously, perhaps, yet no less significantly, the notion of style can be used in language courses to allow the student to recognize, analyze, and even practice the varied forms of expression used to convey a message. In both cases, the concept of style permits the student to perceive the difference between ordinary speech acts, intended to communicate a specific message efficiently through transparent expression, and literary texts, designed to suggest an additional or alternative message by highlighting and even problematizing the very means of expression.

We might say that foreign language acquisition, especially with the communicative approach, focuses on the referential function of language (the message itself), whereas literary analysis, as characterized by the seminal study of Roman Jakobson, focuses on the poetic function of language (the means of expression); each focus, however, constitutes an example of style and can be approached stylistically (1963, pp. 209–48). In more traditional terms, language acquisition may well emphasize the content of the message and literary analysis its form, but we must recognize that it is only a matter of emphasis that distinguishes content from form and that ought to distinguish, but not divide, the language classroom from its literary counterpart.[1]

Curriculum and Coordination

At our institution, there are two intermediate-level courses that follow the four-semester basic language program and that serve as prerequisites for the major: a language and culture course and an introduction to literary analysis course. These are both multisection courses, with sections taught by advanced graduate assistants alongside tenure track and adjunct faculty. Both courses are "writing intensive"; that is to say, they involve several types of writing, they approach writing as a process, and they embrace the notion that students should not just learn to write but should learn by writing. Although we recommend that students take the language and culture course first, in practice, the two courses may be taken concurrently or in any order. Thus, while each course has particular goals, to be effective both courses must work in tandem to provide students with a coherent preparation for more advanced study of both language and literature and to provide instructors who may have little or no experience at this level a clear-cut and well-articulated approach that enhances their professional preparation. In a sense, these courses are the ultimate training ground and proving ground for the advanced graduate student, the final courses the student will teach before embarking on a career elsewhere and the most independently-fashioned of the multi-section courses in our program. Although unified by common goals and a core curriculum, each instructor develops his or her own syllabus, prepares and grades testing material independently, adds supplemental material as he or she sees fit, and may replace one of the core texts with a personal preference, usually one being worked on for a research project or the Ph.D. dissertation. Often one or more of the other instructors, including the faculty coordinator, may also choose to adopt the proposed text. Thus, not only does the course framework provide a loose mentoring system for the graduate students, who interact with faculty and staff in course meetings and frequent informal conversations, but it also provides an opportunity for faculty to discover a new text and benefit from the energy and expertise of the graduate student who chose it.

Style

Before proceeding to a demonstration of the application of a stylistic approach to both types of course, it is imperative to define the term "style." As tempting as it is to adopt the common definition of style as a "deviation" from standard expression, this concept simply does not hold up under scrutiny. As Oswald Ducrot and Tzvetan Todorov have noted in their now classic reference work, *Dictionnaire encyclopédique des sciences du langage*, it is impossible, even with the advent of computer studies, to define what is standard expression, and, furthermore, to link it to an author's style, which could well be characterized by adherence to, rather than deviation from, common expression (1972, p. 383). Ducrot and Todorov go on to propose a highly workable definition of style based on "the choice any text must make among a certain number of expressions available in the language" (1972, p. 383), which we reformulate for our purposes as follows: *style is the choice made by a speaker or writer among the various equivalent expressions available in a language for communicating a given potential content.* We would then define the adjective "stylistic" in the broadest possible sense as the application of the above definition of style to the act of reading and interpreting the resultant choice of expressions.[2] As Gérard Genette has noted, "Identifying a unit of speech necessarily involves, at least implicitly, comparing it and contrasting it with what could be, in its place, another 'equivalent' unit, that is to say at once similar and different... perceiving a language, necessarily involves imagining, in the same space or in the same instant, a silence or another expression" (1968, pp. 12–13). Genette's statement provides us with the terms—comparing, contrasting, imagining—necessary for transforming our definition of "style" into an "approach." We can now go on to illustrate this "stylistic approach," first in the intermediate language and culture course, then in the introduction to literary analysis course, before coming to some general conclusions concerning the relationship between the two courses.

The Intermediate Language and Culture Course

The goals of the language and culture course are to provide students with opportunities to improve their proficiency in all four skills and to learn to interpret texts within a cultural framework, thus improving their cultural proficiency as well. It is neither a grammar review course—although it does seek to make students proficient users of tools such as a reference grammar and a dictionary—nor a traditional conversation and composition course, because the goal is not just to have students talk and write, but to encourage them to talk and write about increasingly abstract topics in a less personalized, more analytic way than is often the focus of courses in the basic language program. A variety of texts, both journalistic and literary, are read for a variety of reasons: to enhance the students' historical or cultural background, to serve as springboards for discussion, to provide models for writing, to promote vocabulary acquisition, to illustrate certain grammatical concepts, etc. Thus, while style per se is not an explicit focus of the course, as it might be in a literature course, the notion of style still permeates the course, because all texts become a pretext for talking about language, especially the choices authors make and their impact on the reader.

Folk tales are particularly bountiful sources for language study, because the vast majority of students are already familiar with the characters and the main aspects of the plot and thus can focus more easily on the words with which the text is written as well as the social and cultural implications of the author's choices. Take, for example, Charles Perrault's *La Belle au bois dormant* [Sleeping Beauty] (1697). As an initial reading assignment, students are asked to make a list of the differences they see between the opening lines of Perrault's version of the tale and the beginning of a modern version for children; both versions are glossed for archaic or otherwise unfamiliar vocabulary and usage, such as the imperfect subjunctive.[3] Working through a comparison of the "style" of the two versions in class discussion leads to the discovery of the subtle power of language and numerous insights into the social and cultural values embodied in the stories, which in turn sets the groundwork for a better understanding of each version of the tale:

> Il était une fois un Roi et une Reine, qui étaient si fâchés de n'avoir point d'enfants, si fâchés qu'on ne saurait dire. Ils allèrent à toutes les eaux du monde; vœux, pèlerinages, menues dévotions, tout fut mis en œuvre, et rien n'y faisait. Enfin pourtant la Reine devint grosse, et accoucha d'une fille: on fit un beau Baptême; on donna pour Marraines à la petite Princesse toutes les Fées qu'on pût trouver dans le Pays (il s'en trouva sept), afin que chacune d'elles lui faisant un don, comme c'était la coutume des Fées en ce temps-là, la Princesse eût par ce moyen toutes les perfections imaginables.
>
> [Once upon a time, there were a King and Queen who were so distressed not to have any children, so distressed that it was beyond words. They went to all of the waters in the world; vows, pilgrimages, small devotions, everything was tried and nothing worked. Finally, however, the Queen became pregnant and had a daughter: a beautiful Baptism was held; they chose as Godmothers for the little Princess all of the Fairies that could be found in the Land (there were seven of them), so that each of them giving her a gift, as was the Fairies' custom at that time, the Princess would have by this means every imaginable perfection (Perrault 1981, p. 131).]
>
> Il y a bien longtemps vivaient un roi et une reine qui étaient désolés de n'avoir pas d'enfant. Aussi leur joie fut-elle grande lorsque leur

naquit une petite fille. Ils donnèrent une belle fête pour son baptême et lui choisirent pour marraines toutes les fées du pays. Il s'en trouva sept. Chacune fit un don à la petite princesse.

[A very long time ago lived a king and queen who were sorry not to have a child. Thus great was their joy when was born to them a daughter. They gave a beautiful party for her baptism and chose as godmothers all of the country's fairies. There were seven of them. Each gave a gift to the little princess (Izawa and Hijikata 1967, p. 3).]

When asked during class discussion about differences between the two versions, students invariably begin by noting the greater length of the Perrault version, a distinction that enables the instructor to pursue more substantive questions such as what additional information accounts for this difference. Asking students, for example, to reiterate the content of the second sentence of the Perrault version (missing in the modern text), not only gives the instructor the means of checking on reading comprehension and providing cultural background on concepts such as pilgrimages, it affords the students the opportunity to produce new language through reformulation and to comprehend the extent of the royal couple's efforts to have a child.

Another difference students readily note between the two versions is the use of repetition in the Perrault text, a feature that the instructor can stress by further questioning, which can lead to valuable grammatical and semantic distinctions. The instructor can ask, for example, which word is repeated in the second sentence and what grammatical forms it takes. This leads to the distinction between *toutes* used as an adjective, which agrees with a noun, and *tout* as an invariable pronoun (a point covered in the grammar review for the week). A check on students' comprehension of this distinction can be made by asking them which form of *tout* is repeated elsewhere in the passage, thereby leading them to two further examples of adjectives in "toutes les Fées" and "toutes les perfections." The accumulation of the word *tout*, whatever its grammatical form, reinforces the students' growing perception of the extreme nature of the royal couple's efforts and thus to a definition of their character traits.

Asking the students about other repetitions in the Perrault text will lead them quite naturally to focus on the adjectives used in the first sentence of each version to describe the royal couple's emotional reaction to their childlessness: *fâché* [distressed] in the Perrault version (the repetition itself underscoring the distress), versus *désolé* [sorry] in the other. It should then be pointed out that, although the French word *fâché* does not always connote anger, as it frequently does in contemporary usage, but merely a degree of unhappiness (particularly in the seventeenth century), it is nonetheless a stronger term than *désolé*. This is an important semantic lesson, because students see not only that word usage changes over time, but that synonyms are not exact equivalents and may have different connotations or convey a different sense of force. To emphasize this point, students are asked as a homework assignment to use a dictionary to construct a list of adjectives suggesting unhappiness and then to write a series of sentences illustrating the differences between them. Students thus have the opportunity to broaden their vocabulary in a context that confirms the necessity of consulting a dictionary when reading/writing to distinguish between the connotations of certain words. This discriminatory approach is an important goal of the course, as we attempt to move students from reading for the gist or for precise information to reading in a more analytical way.

A further difference between the two versions that is readily perceived by students is the use of capitalization in the Perrault text. By asking what types of nouns the capitalized words entail, the instructor leads students to note that they refer to certain roles (King, Queen, Princess, Fairies), places (Land), and events (Baptism) that pertain to the royal couple, thus strengthening the notion that Perrault's couple (and perhaps by extension the institution of the monarchy) is self-important and hierarchical. On a cultural and historical level, the self-centered nature of the king and queen and their desperate desire for an heir (even a daughter!) provides the students with an insight, and the instructor with a potential introduction, into the notion of the consolidation of the monarchy that occurred in France during the seventeenth century.

In addition to the greater length of the Perrault passage, students are also struck by the greater length of its sentences, probably because the length and complexity create obstacles for easy reading. This is particularly true for Perrault's third sentence, the content of which (the birth of the princess, the baptismal feast, and the invitation to the seven fairies) is included in four separate sentences in the modern version. By asking what conjunction is used to join sentences in the Perrault passage, the instructor can not only explore the use of the subjunctive with *afin que* [so that] (and point out the archaic use of the imperfect subjunctive here), but can also ask students what it implies about the motives of the king and queen. It becomes clear that they have invited the fairies "in order to" obtain gifts, which is reinforced by the expression *par ce moyen* [by this means]. Thus, it is progressively and readily becoming clear that the Perrault text is not just longer, but that what is included in the additional length affects our perception of the royal couple and the institution of the monarchy as self-centered and self-serving.

When asked about differences between the descriptions of the princess's birth in the two texts, the students note that, in the modern version, "a daughter was born to them," while in the seventeenth-century text the queen "gave birth to a daughter." As subject of the sentence, Perrault's queen is an active participant in the birth, and thus the grammar of the text reinforces that idea that the king and queen took charge, and through their determined, perhaps desperate efforts (vows, pilgrimages, devotions) finally achieved what they desired. At the same time, when asked about the couple's emotional reactions to the birth in the Perrault passage, the students realize that they are not described, but relegated to what Genette (1968) would term a "silence," which is all the more perceptible by comparison with the "joy" expressed in the other version. The modern couple, reduced to the role of indirect object in the sentence describing the birth, seems to play no active part in this seemingly "magical" event, except to rejoice. In fact, the structure of the sentence describing their joy reduces their active role even more, because not they, but the joy itself, is the grammatical subject—a fact that is hard to overlook given the subject/verb inversion necessitated by the opening conjunction *aussi* [thus]. Therefore, this sentence is useful in helping students see differences between the presentation of the king and queen in the different versions of the fairy tale. It also provides a clear and concrete example of a semantic/syntactic notion that bedevils most students at the intermediate level, notably that *aussi* as the first word of a sentence means "thus," not "also," as is does anywhere else in a sentence, and that its use at the beginning of a sentence entails an inversion whose effect is to emphasize the sentences' subject, a stylistic choice that the preceding analysis has shown is not without impact on the reader. To reinforce this point, the instructor can ask the students to rewrite the sentence as homework, using another expression for "thus," and to compare their sentence with the original in terms of its grammatical structure and the impact of that structure on the presentation of the royal couple. They can also be encouraged to find equivalent French expressions for "also," highly useful because it is a key transitional term of high frequency in student compositions.

There are other significant grammatical differences between the two versions of the fairy tale as well, which the instructor can get to by asking the students about differences in pronouns. For example, while the royal couple in the modern version is portrayed in a passive light up through their daughter's birth, after that point they become active, both in terms of what they do and how they are represented grammatically: **They** gave a beautiful party and chose the fairies for the princess's godmothers. Perrault's royal couple, however, after the birth of the princess, share the stage grammatically with the impersonal pronoun *on*, which can mean "one," "they," or even "we," and which thus adds a level of ambiguity that is absent from the modern text. Students can then be asked to consider the implications and effects of the impersonality and ambiguity that result from this pronoun choice. For example, unlike the statement "ils firent un beau Baptême," which contains a personal pronoun whose antecedent is unequivocal, the statement "on fit un beau Baptême," can be read not only as "they held a beautiful Baptism," but also as either "one held a beautiful Baptism," or as "a beautiful Baptism was held." In this particular case, the use of *on* seems to underline the hierarchy of the royal court—for, while the "beautiful Baptism" was undoubtedly the royal couple's idea, it was most likely others who did the work and attended to the details. In another case, the fact that the revelation that all of the fairies "qu'on pût trouver" [that could be found] were chosen as godmothers contains the impersonal *on* might be seen to exculpate the parents for the responsibility of having neglected anyone, because it is not clear that the oversight was directly their responsibility. By analyzing the use of pronouns in this short text, students gain an appreciation not only for the difference between personal and impersonal pronouns, but also for the subtleties and ambiguities introduced by the choice of a pronoun such as *on*.

The instructor can continue to work with pronouns by having the students identify their antecedents, a surprisingly difficult grammar task and an essential skill in reading comprehension. In addition to the rare combination of a noun and a pronoun in tandem necessitated by the inversion in "aussi leur joie fut-elle grande," locating the antecedents for "leur naquit" and "lui choisirent" illustrates the necessity of looking to the preceding sentence and thus reading a block of text, not just a segment. Moreover, the recurrence of "il s'en trouva sept" (in both versions) reminds students of the use of *en* with numbers.

As follow-up activities, students are asked to write a paragraph describing the personalities/attitudes/emotions of the two royal couples and then to write their own introduction to "Sleeping Beauty" based on what they have learned in comparing the Perrault and the modern versions and on their own sense of what the king and queen were like. Next, working individually or in small groups in class, they should be asked to conduct a similar comparison of a different episode from the two versions of this fairy tale or to compare it to a version with which they are already familiar. American students who have seen the Disney movie or read a "sanitized" modern version are surprised, for example, to see that Perrault's tale doesn't end with the princess's awakening and marriage to the prince. Their introduction to the seventeenth-century version of the tale, which ends with the jealous mother of the prince (who is by then the king) throwing herself into a vat crawling with vipers after having been thwarted in her efforts to have the daughter-in-law and grandchildren killed, opens numerous questions as to intended audience as well as cross-cultural and cross-secular differences and thus provides an excellent springboard for further discussion.

In this series of exercises, students have uncovered, in context, a number of lexical and grammatical points, all of which contribute to the readers' understanding, appreciation, and interpretation of the texts—in other words, they have been engaged in an analysis of style. Granted, their focus has been on reading and writing, not on understanding the style of a particular author or the conventions of a given period, but such an exercise effectively prepares them to consider and to analyze style in an explicitly literary context by showing them how to look for and how to interpret the types of choice authors make that constitute their unique styles.

The Literary Analysis Course

Unlike a folk tale such as *La Belle au bois dormant*, which often has several versions whose different styles can be compared, most literary works are unique and have no alternative versions.[4] For any given portion of the work, however, following the implications of Genette's earlier statement that style amounts to a choice, the instructor can simply "imagine" another, equivalent expression. For example, in approaching Gustave Flaubert's masterful short story, *Un Coeur simple* [A Simple Heart], which depicts the bleak life of a country servant in nineteenth-century France, we again decided to focus on the opening sentence, which reads as follows:

> Pendant un demi-siècle, les bourgeoises de Pont-l'Évêque envièrent à Mme Aubain sa servante Félicité. [For a half-century, the bourgeois women of Pont-l'Évêque envied Madame Aubain for her servant Félicité (1952, p. 591).]

At first reading the sentence seems straightforward enough: it introduces the main characters, the servant Félicité and her mistress Madame Aubain, while situating them in time (a half-century) and space (Pont-l'Évêque in Flaubert's beloved Normandy), a hallmark of French realist fiction. It is only when one imagines an equivalent expression for the same information, however, that one comes to appreciate the layers of additional meaning brought out by Flaubert's style.

Based on the stylistic points the instructor intends to bring out (or simply as a means of discovering the subtleties of Flaubert's style), he or she can construct an alternative sentence, such as the following:

> Félicité travailla chez Mme Aubain à Pont-l'Évêque pendant cinquante ans. [Félicité worked for Madame Aubain in Pont-l'Évêque for fifty years.]

As with the examples from *La Belle au bois dormant* explored in the language and culture course, the literature course instructor should assign both glossed texts as an initial reading task and ask the students to make a list of differences they perceive between the two versions in preparation for class discussion.[5] Since we contend that a literature course is also a language course, we believe strongly that the instructor should avoid lecturing as much as possible at this level (always a temptation when "style" is involved) and instead have the students work through the passage in order to encourage their ongoing practice of all four language skills and to develop their own techniques of literary and cultural analysis. Whereas the language instructor often uses questions involving content (at a simple level) to get at points of language, the literature instructor can often use questions involving grammar to get at points of content (at a deeper level). Indeed, we have found that notions of grammar provide a highly effective ordering principle for discussing a text as dense and complex as the one in question from Flaubert's *Un coeur simple* and its imagined alternative.

In order to begin with an overview of the entire sentence and to provide an overall organization for the discussion, the instructor first asks the students to focus on the difference in **syntax** or sentence structure between the two versions. The fact that the servant Félicité is last in Flaubert's version and first in the imagined one is obvious, and, when asked about possible implications, the students invariably draw a link between the concrete detail of position in the sentence and the more abstract notion of position in society, an important perspective for reading the rest of the tale and, indeed, much of French realist fiction.

The instructor then asks what Félicité's **grammatical role** is in each sentence, and the students readily note a change from Flaubert's sentence, in which she is a direct object, to the alternative, in which she is the subject. Prompted by further questioning about implications, the students easily seize the connection between the dominant role of a subject and secondary role of an object in both the sentence and society. The main literary question involves, of course, the effect or function of Flaubert's choices of expression, the very style of which paints Félicité as a mere object whose subordinate place in society is mirrored by that in the sentence, both syntactically and grammatically.

Further aspects of grammar can be explored by asking the students what differences they see between the way the relationship between Félicité and Mme Aubain is depicted in each case. They have little trouble in seeing, grasping, and expressing the notion that the verb *travailla* [worked for] in the alternate sentence implies a degree of action and even freedom that Flaubert's nominal expression "her servant" denies to Félicité, because the noun points to a fixed role. When asked about the implications of the possessive pronoun "her," the grammatical nomenclature itself leads students to the conclusion that Félicité is no more than a "possession" to Mme Aubain.

By this point in the discussion, since a main direction has been established and has gained some momentum, the order of subsequent points is less important. Based on our experience, however, the instructor may now want to ask about the difference in the use of names (not between the sentences, but between the two characters), that is, a **vocabulary** distinction. Students can be guided by comparison with the very classroom situation in which the discussion is taking place and in which the students are likely referred to by first name and the instructor by title and last name. When asked why this is so, the students perceive and articulate notions of social distance and hierarchy that also pertain to the relationship between Félicité and Mme Aubain (but in far more permanent fashion, the instructor should be quick to point out or tease out!). In short, for the servant, the first name alone is used, implying a life-long reduction in identity, whereas Madame Aubain's social status warrants a title and a last name.

The value of the two names, Madame Aubain and Félicité, can also be approached in its own right. Even though they were not changed in the alternate version of the sentence, to maintain a necessary degree of similarity, Flaubert had to choose the two names, and they thus fall under the notion of style. At this level, students do not have enough language at their disposal to judge the suggestiveness of proper names (onomastics), but again in this case the notion can be explored with careful questioning: When reminded that Aubain might mean "in the bath" [*au bain*] and asked what that might imply, some students will see an allusion to her idle lifestyle and dependency on Félicité's attentions. If the instructor uses a dictionary entry to point out that the name Félicité has connotations of religious bliss, the students can then use the theme of religion, also suggested in the toponym Pont-L'Évêque [Bishop's Bridge], as a guideline for further reading, and, at the same time, they will be introduced to the essential (yet often overlooked) necessity of using the dictionary for reading any type of text, especially literature.

To this point the student has already witnessed six examples where the style alone, the linguistic features of syntax, grammar (twice), and vocabulary (three times), beyond the overt content, has suggested the strict hierarchy governing class relationships in nineteenth-century France along with the presence of religion that permeates this highly Catholic country. Highlighting the linguistic terms, which the students have already used in language courses (even those prior to the intermediate level), gives them the confidence that they already possess the essential tools of literary analysis. At the same time, this focus on language lends continuity to the foreign-language curriculum: in short, the literature course is also a language course.

We can next turn to another difference between the two sentences, involving what Genette (1968) terms a "silence" or what may more commonly be called an "absence," by asking students what is missing in the alternative version. They readily recognize that the subject of Flaubert's sentence, the "bourgeois women," has disappeared altogether from the alternate text and with it the suggestion of class content that it entails. Furthermore, as the instructor may point out or work through with further questions (depending on time), Flaubert's verb, "envied," suggests a significant aspect of the motivations and mechanisms governing the bourgeois class: the desire for someone else's "possessions," a desire based more on what someone else has than on what one really wants.

Seen now in its entirety, Flaubert's sentence structure mirrors the social structure of provincial France, in which the servant is dependent on the mistress, who herself exists in function of the group or class to which she belongs and which determines the prevailing value system, based on possessions, fueled by jealousy, and sustained by gossip.

Another lexical difference that strikes the students but whose function or meaning proves more difficult for them to explain involves the distinction between "a half-century" in Flaubert's sentence and "fifty years" in the alternative version. Unlike the countable units (years), which imply the possibility of difference and change, a "half-century" seems more uniform, permanent, and static. The instructor may point out, as an introduction to further reading of the tale, that Félicité's duties, like her wages, remain the same throughout her life. Even the events and encounters of her life betray a remarkably consistent pattern of attaching herself to someone, who then leaves her. This pattern is reinforced, then transcended by the parrot, Loulou, the stuffed remains of which Félicité is able to keep and idolize even after it dies, finally becoming confused, then conjoined with the Holy Ghost in Félicité's religiously rich imagination.

To this point, the discussion has focused on the ideas suggested by Flaubert's linguistic choices, what is signified, rather than on the "signifiers," the material properties of the words themselves, the **sounds**, **rhythm**, and **typography** of the sentences that constitute their "poetry." If the students have already studied poetry in the course, as ours have, or if the instructor would like to use this sentence to introduce poetic properties, it is necessary to use considerable guidance. We propose that the instructor begin by aligning the different word groupings of the sentence one above the other, as in a poem:

Pendant un demi-siècle,
les bourgeoises de Pont-l'Évêque
envièrent à Mme Aubain
sa servante Félicité.

The arrangement itself causes the students to note that the sentence is divided somewhat equally into four segments of roughly eight syllables each (pronouncing Mme as Madame and counting the mute e's, as one does in French poetry). The instructor can point out that the regular rhythm may well suggest the regularity and monotony of Félicité's life, but at the same time it creates a sense of harmony that elevates the text above that life into the realm of art. This "poetic" quality is further suggested by the internal rhyme in French between *siècle* and *Pont-l'Évêque*, the occurrence of which is highlighted by the comma after *siècle*. Even Félicité's name, when viewed in terms of its phonemes, has a certain harmony based on the repetition of the vowel [i] inserted between that of the vowel [é]. Although Félicité is relegated to the lowest and last place in the social hierarchy, she stands out in the text. The instructor can point out that this tension between life and literature is necessary to a full appreciation of Flaubert's vision of human existence, a vision that emerges only through consideration of his style, which he himself defined as "an absolute manner of seeing things" [*une manière absolue de voir les choses*] (1926, II, p. 346).

At this point, just when we have seemingly extracted every drop of substantive marrow from the text, we can apply the stylistic approach from a different angle. Having focused on the **differences** between Flaubert's sentence and our alternative expressions, we can nonetheless explore essential **similarities** between the two versions. In "dialectical" fashion, we can now use the similar points between the alternate expressions to imagine another alternative that differs from both. When asked to describe similarities, students find both versions, for example, to be "objective," and, indeed, both are devoid of overt commentary by the narrator on the one hand and of figurative speech on the other. If the students have already studied other authors, the instructor can ask them to draw a parallel with, say, a Balzac story, where the narrator might claim that Félicité "ressemble à toutes les femmes qui ont eu des malheurs" [resembles all women who have had problems] and proclaim that "ce drame n'est ni une fiction, ni un roman. All is true . . ." [This drama is neither fiction nor a novel. All is true [sic] . . .].[6] Here Balzac's generalizations ("All"), the conclusions ("problems"), allusions to the text itself ("this drama"), and use of another language ("All is true") help the student to appreciate the subtlety of Flaubert's famous impersonal narration. Victor Hugo, on the other hand, might well characterize Madame Aubain as *un mastodonte* [elephant] or *cette montagne...de chair* [this mountain of flesh].[7] Here the flagrant use of simile and hyperbole can serve to illustrate Flaubert's more restrained use of figurative language.

In continuing our comparison of Flaubert's text with our initial alternative, the instructor can now ask the students what similarities they see between the verbs in both versions. The rather obvious answer that both are in the simple past (a literary tense) and in the third person leads students to an important discovery about the conventions of nineteenth-century narration and their foregrounding of the narrator; as Roland Barthes puts it: "Le passé simple et la troisième personne du Roman, ne sont rien d'autre que ce geste fatal par lequel l'écrivain montre du doigt le masque qu'il porte" [The simple past and the third person of the novel, are nothing more than the fatal gesture by which the writer points his finger at the mask he is wearing] (1964, p. 37). Following this lead, the instructor can write on the board a transformation of the alternative sentence or ask the students to do so, using the first-person and the present tense of the verb *travailler* [to work]; unlike rewriting Flaubert's initial sentence, a task simply too complex for most students at this level, rewriting the alternative in the present is within their reach, with a little coaching on the use of *depuis* [for] for actions continuing into the present:

> Je travaille chez Mme Aubain à Pont-l'Évêque depuis 50 ans. [I've been working for Madame Aubain in Pont-l'Évêque for fifty years.]

When asked about the effect of this change, the students readily note that the loss in information (the character's name) is more than compensated for by a gain in intimacy (through the first person) and freedom (the present tense, unlike the past, implies a future open to change). Once again the instructor can reiterate the notion that differences in literary technique amount to matters of language, primarily grammar, involving different verb tenses and pronouns. Because a distant third-person perspective that nonetheless produces privileged insights into an individual's personal life is not to be had in reality (after all, just who has been watching Félicité from a distance during fifty years?), the student can appreciate Barthes' statement above that such a narrative stance suggests literature not life. Barthes' statement was itself prefigured by Jean-Paul Sartre's judgment that such a position reflects a religious, bourgeois vision of life that deprives the character of existential freedom.[8] More important, from our standpoint, the students can appreciate Flaubert's use of these conventions to create a certain distance, replicate a feeling for the individual's isolation and impotence in human existence, and produce a sense of the narrator's god-like power that Flaubert sought in the realm of art:

> L'artiste doit être dans son œuvre comme Dieu dans la création, invisible et tout-puissant; qu'on le sente partout, mais qu'on ne le voie pas. [The artist should be like God in creation, invisible and all-powerful; one should feel him throughout, but see him nowhere (1926, IV, p. 164).]

To give students a further appreciation for the suggestive power not only of Flaubert's style but of language in general, we suggest a follow-up writing exercise, even if only a brief one. Students are assigned or asked to pick any sentence or complete clause from Part I of *Un Coeur simple* and to rewrite it. Having several students put their alternatives on the blackboard enables the instructor to work through grammatical and lexical points, as well as stylistic features, with the class. We frequently assign the clause "Elle se levait dès l'aube, pour ne pas manquer la messe..." [She would get up at dawn so as not to miss mass]. Among the numerous responses we have received, two are quite typical: "Elle s'est levée le matin pour aller à la messe..." [She got up in the morning to go to mass] and "Elle ne voulait pas manquer la messe, parce qu'elle était très religieuse..."[She didn't want to miss mass because she was very religious]. Several linguistic points in the original are brought out by comparison with the alternatives, namely, the necessity of using the imperfect tense for describing repeated actions (and Félicité is a creature of habit) and the early hour denoted by "dès l'aube"(and Félicité is an early riser). Among additional stylistic features that emerge from comparison of the alternatives to Flaubert's text are the differences between "aller à la messe" [to go to mass] and "ne pas manquer la messe" [not to miss mass] (which implies a sense of duty typical of Félicité) and "elle était religieuse" [she was religious] (which implies an explicit judgment that Flaubert usually leaves unstated, engaging the reader to draw the appropriate conclusion from the factual detail). This brief exercise thus enables students not only to work through the subtleties of language but to witness its power when wielded by a master like Flaubert.

In addition to the understanding of Flaubert's art that emerges from the stylistic approach based on alternative expressions, the students are also exposed somewhat painlessly to all of the elements of the dreaded "explication de texte." In effect, they have seen firsthand how literary analysis involves the notions of *situation* (the expository function of the first sentence), *narration* (the effect of third-person narration), *vocabulary* (Flaubert's suggestive use of names), *syntax* (the order of the first sentence, which replicates that of society's hierarchy), *composition* (the order of the passage in the first example, the same as syntax, since the passage is but one sentence), *grammar* (the effect of the past tense in limiting the character's freedom), as well as *sounds* (the symmetry of the vowels in Félicité's name), *rhythm* (the regular divisions of Flaubert's first sentence), and *typography* (the highlighting created by capitalization and punctuation), which elevate the prosaic sentence to the level of poetry.[9] Furthermore, rather than learn these categories a priori, then impose them like a cookie cutter on the text, the students have seen the notions emerge inductively from the concrete examples in the discussion, an approach to learning that, in our opinion, should find its way throughout the entire foreign-language curriculum. The students have also seen that all of the elements of literary analysis are defined by linguistic terms and concepts they have already encountered in their language courses, which gives them a sense of personal confidence and curricular continuity.

Conclusion

By utilizing a simplified yet rigorous and effective approach to texts, based on the comparison of two versions of the same textual segment, either from preexistent or imagined sources, we can open up the notion of style to make it accessible to students at the intermediate level. Such a stylistic approach empowers students, because it enables them not only to witness, analyze, and appreciate the workings of language but also to practice various forms of expression. The stylistic approach enhances the development of all five skills—reading, writing, listening, speaking, and culture—while encouraging students to utilize the reference grammar and the dictionary, the two most essential tools for making their way beyond the intermediate level. Although the notion of style is primarily studied in language courses to point out linguistic usage and in literature courses to uncover patterns of expression that lend the work its meaning and structure, the language course instructor invariably points out the literary function of the expression, and the literature instructor the linguistic basis of the expression. The similarity of approaches points to the compatibility of the courses and helps bridge the potential gaps between the two parts of the curriculum, while fostering exchange between faculty and graduate students of various types of training and persuasion, and thus promoting a unified vision of the profession.

Notes

1. Numerous scholars, some trained in second-language acquisition, others in literature, have examined this question of the importance of establishing connections between foreign language learning and foreign language literature. For example, see Barnett 1991; Kramsch 1985; Rice 1991; Rochette-Ozzello 1978; Schofer 1984; Schultz 1996. For a list of further studies that focus on "style, form, and voice within a student-centered pedagogy," see Kramsch and Kramsch 2000, p. 569.
2. This definition of "stylistic" stands apart from more specific definitions of the field of stylistics by, for example, Charles Bally (1909) and Leo Spitzer (1970) or the term as it is applied to advanced courses designed to polish off a students' command of the language.
3. Indeed, the reader we use, *Images* (Martin and Berg [1990] 1997), has both versions of the tale's beginning, along with questions involving language and style.
4. Nonetheless, some literary scholars study the linguistic variations in different editions of the same work, and one can always compare similar works or adaptations of a work in different media, such as a story and a film version of it.
5. The reader we use, *Poèmes, Pièces, Prose* (Schofer, Rice, and Berg 1973), has a glossed version of the entire tale, along with questions involving style.
6. These examples come from the narrator's description of Madame Vauquer at the beginning of *Le Père Goriot*.
7. These examples are from the narrator's description of Madame Thénardier in Hugo, p. 419.
8. See *Qu'est-ce que la littérature*, pp. 177–79 and "M. François Mauriac et la liberté" in *Situations I*, pp. 36–57.
9. One could now study the sentence in terms of its relations with other parts of the text. See, for example, Berg and Martin 1995.

Works Cited

Bally, Charles. 1909. *Traité de stylistique française*. 2 vols. Heidelberg: Carl Winter.

Balzac, Honoré de. [1834] 1963. *Le Père Goriot.* Paris: Garnier.

Barnett, Marva. 1991. Language and Literature: False Dichotomies, Real Allies. *ADFL Bulletin* 22(3): 7–11.

Barthes, Roland. 1964. *Le degré zéro de l'Ecriture.* Paris: Editions Gonthier.

Berg, William J., and Laurey K. Martin. 1995. Teaching Reading Tactics in *Madame Bovary.* In *Approaches to Teaching Flaubert's* Madame Bovary, edited by Laurence M. Porter and Eugene F. Gray, 137–43. New York: Modern Language Association.

Buffon, Georges-Louis Leclerc de. [1753] 1962. *Discours sur le style.* In André Lagarde and Laurent Michard. *XVIIIe siècle.* Paris: Bordas.

Ducrot, Oswald, and Tzvetan Todorov. 1972. *Dictionnaire encyclopédique des sciences du langage.* Paris: Seuil.

Flaubert, Gustave. 1926. Letter to Louise Colet, 16 January 1852. *Correspondance II*, 346. Paris: Conard.

_____. 1926. Letter to Mlle Leroyer de Chantepie, 19 February 1857. *Correspondance IV*, 164. Paris: Conard.

_____. [1877] 1952. *Un Coeur simple* in *Oeuvres II*, 591–622. Paris: Gallimard, Editions de la Pléiade.

Genette, Gérard. 1968. Introduction. In Pierre Fontanier, *Les Figures du discours*, 5–17. Paris: Flammarion.

Jakobson, Roman. 1963. Linguistique et poétique. In *Essais de linguistique générale*, translated by N. Ruwet, 209–48. Paris: Editions de Minuit.

Hugo, Victor. [1862] 1951. *Les Misérables.* Paris: Gallimard, Editions de la Pléiade.

Izawa, Tadasu, and Shigemi Hijikata. 1969. *La Belle au bois dormant (d'après Perrault).* Paris: Editions des deux coqs d'or.

Kramsch, Claire. 1985. Literary Texts in the Language Classroom: A Discourse Perspective. *Modern Language Journal* 69: 356–66.

Kramsch, Claire, and Olivier Kramsch. 2000. The Avatars of Literature in Language Study. *Modern Language Journal* 84: 553–73.

Martin, Laurey, and William Berg. [1990] 1997. *Images.* New York: Harcourt Brace Custom Publishers.

Perrault, Charles. [1698] 1981. *La Belle au bois dormant* in *Contes*, 131–40. Paris: Gallimard (Collection Folio).

Rice, Donald. B. 1991. Language Proficiency and Textual Theory: How the Twain Might Meet. *ADFL Bulletin* 22.3: 12–15.

Rochette-Ozzello, Yvonne. 1978. Contraintes et créations: Pédagogie de la production poétique. *French Review* 51: 626–43.

Sartre, Jean-Paul. 1948. *Qu'est-ce que la littérature.* Paris: Gallimard.

_____. 1947. M. François Mauriac et la liberté. In *Situations I*, pp. 36–57. Paris: Gallimard.

Schofer, Peter. 1984. Theoretical Acrobatics: The Student as Author and Teacher in Introductory Literature Courses. *French Review* 57: 463–74.

Schofer, Peter, Donald Rice, and William Berg. 1973. *Poèmes, Pièces, Prose.* New York: Oxford University Press.

Schultz, Jean-Marie. 1996. The Uses of Poetry in the Foreign Language Curriculum. *French Review* 69: 920–32.

Spitzer, Leo. 1970. *Etudes de style.* Trans. Eliane Kaufholz, Alain Coulon, and Michel Foucault. Paris: Gallimard.

From Scholar to Teacher

Research into the Teaching of Literature in a Second Language: What it Says and How to Communicate it to Graduate Students

Elizabeth Bernhardt
Stanford University

Literature Learning and Teaching?

While the phrase "language learning and teaching" is a perfectly idiomatic expression in contemporary pedagogical circles, the phrase "literature learning and teaching" seems somehow awkward and hollow. Few published research studies exist on the act of foreign-language literature *learning* (Bernhardt 1990; Chi 1995; Fecteau 1999; Tian 1991) in contrast to the thousands of empirical contributions regarding the learning of second languages. By the same token, few empirical contributions on foreign-language literature *teaching* exist (Tian 1991). In fact, Marshall (2000b) notes: "We have had virtually no systematic studies of how literature teaching at the university proceeds" (p. 396). Admittedly, there are a number of technique-oriented books, such as *Literature and Language Teaching* (Brumfit and Carter 1986); *Teaching Literature* (Carter and Long 1991); and *Literature in the Language Classroom: A Resource Book of Ideas and Activities* (Collie and Slater 1987). Of course, frequent discussions of the role of literature in the contemporary foreign-language curriculum (e.g., Kern 2000; Kramsch and Nolden 1994) are to be found. These focus on the relationship between language and literature—not on literature learning and teaching per se. Questions that would parallel the *language* learning and teaching base such as ones that probe the development of an interpretive capacity in foreign-language literary interpretation; the mapping of improvement in learning; the valid assessment of literary learning; or investigations of effective practice within literature classrooms; are not actively presented in the research literature.

There are several bitter ironies here. In actuality, the most substantial portion of the postsecondary foreign-language curriculum is taken up by literature learning and teaching. In parallel to other elementary versus more advanced educational settings, this curriculum is focused on text or on content, not on students (Bernhardt 1995). This text focus may, in part, explain the lack of research in the area. The language curriculum has been profoundly influenced by research on human language development and has, by and large, adapted its curriculum accordingly; the literature curriculum, in contrast, remains focused on texts as objects. Adding to the irony is that, in spite of an interest in scholarship and research that breaks the literary canon, an almost ritualistic pedagogical and curricular pattern seems to be held firmly in place. Marshall (2000a) comments: "Years of anecdotal teacher reports suggest that the literature instruction teachers receive in college—the texts they are taught, the discussions that are held, the writing that is assigned—profoundly affects the instruction they provide when they begin teaching" (p. 396).

A final layer of irony restricting questions in the area of literary teaching is rooted in contemporary literary theory itself. Contemporary literary theory resists the notion of guiding student readers or of criticizing their interpretations. Reader response theory, for example, virtually guarantees that students cannot be "taught" in the conventional sense. Affective response coupled with a relatively unbridled process of relating texts to other texts shirks the notion of norms. Marshall argues the point:

> If texts are selected for instruction precisely because they may represent worlds, cultures, values, and beliefs that are significantly different from what students already know (as in much recent African American, Caribbean, Latino/a, and Asian American literature), then new pedagogies seem called for. Teachers and students, in such a context, cannot rely on a process of identification with characters or situations (these characters are like me and therefore I can identify with them). Instead, students must work through a more difficult and possibly more austere relationship with the text—and this will require a very different kind of classroom practice (p. 397).

Marshall puts his finger precisely on the major issue in foreign-language literature learning. Students are in a curriculum with which they cannot, by definition, identify—if this were not the case it would not be "foreign" to them. By their very nature, students in the foreign-language literatures come to the task of reading foreign-language literary texts from knowledge bases that are incomplete, lopsided, and, perhaps crassly stated, simply inaccurate. These knowledge bases are incomplete, lopsided, and inaccurate *linguistically/grammatically* and *conceptually* precisely because they are foreign. Yet, this linguistic and conceptual foreignness gets read in instruction (by both professors and by future professors or professors in training that is, graduate students) as the need for more grammar courses. Further, a subtext about unsophisticated Americans who just do not know any better or who do not care all that much about the Humanities is often at play (Bernhardt 1995; Shumway 1995).

The question for this article becomes one of understanding what research has to say about these issues and then of formulating a way to integrate this research information into the professional preparation of graduate students who will become teachers of language and literature in postsecondary institutions. The central thesis of this article is the following: *graduate students must learn that they are to teach students not literature; they must understand the linguistic and conceptual framework that individual students come with; and they must learn to see that the acts of language and literature teaching are far more alike than they are different—each is an act of text construction and reconstruction based on the conceptualization of available linguistic and cultural data.*

What Research Says

The only substantial database to look toward regarding second-language literary reading is the set of studies on reading comprehension in a second language that place a particular emphasis on studies that employ literary texts. Much research in second-language reading comprehension tries to probe, from the comprehender's point of view, the nature of the knowledge structures that the nonnative actually needs in order understand texts, but probably most crucially, literary texts, in an authentic way. The first critical feature of the research base is that *the reader's current knowledge base—meaning the first-language knowledge base—is a major contributing factor to the reconstruction of a second-language text.* There are several dimensions to this contribution. First, at the linguistic level, the more literate a reader is in the first language, the higher a given second-language performance is (Bernhardt and Kamil 1995; Brisbois 1995). In other words, the higher any given literacy score (such as a Scholastic Aptitude Test [SAT] or a Nelson Denney literacy test) in the native language, the greater the probability of high second-language performance. About 20 percent of any given second-language reading performance is related to first-language ability (for a complete review, see Bernhardt 2000). In addition, this research indicates that grammatical ability matters: the better second-language readers are in the second language, the better their reading performance tends to be. While this finding might seem to be incredibly obvious, grammatical ability accounts for only 30 percent of second-language reading performance. On this note, the "more grammar courses" argument will account for and enhance only a third of any given second-language performance.

The interaction of the first-language base with the second also continues at the conceptual level: second-language learners are able to retrieve the information from a second-language story that is compatible with first-language cultural patterns, but may not be able to retrieve incompatible information (Steffensen, Joag-Dev, and Anderson 1979). In other words, readers read from their first-language conceptual base and understand what "makes sense to them." Undergraduate readers have been known to read German literary pieces and to respond with "This isn't like Lonesome Dove" or "This isn't the triumph of man over nature as in American literature." Further, second-language readers use the sociohistorical factual knowledge that they have with second-language texts. At times, this is extremely helpful (e.g., a Vietnam veteran being able to identify with the *Trümmerliteratur* of 1950s Germany). However, it can also be destructive (identifying a married couple arguing over food as the late twentieth century American obsession over dieting versus understanding it in the context of war and starvation) (Bernhardt 1990). These examples are not meant for comic relief. They are meant to illustrate the very real cognitive consequences of reading literature in a second language. Readers will use their knowledge base; that knowledge base does not always match the knowledge base necessary for the understanding of a particular text. This is a cognitive issue, not an ignorance issue.

The second critical point from second-language literacy research is that *the knowledge base interacts with second-language linguistic abilities*. The interaction takes the form of knowledge being able to override linguistic deficiencies (meaning that readers with low-level second-language skills can in some contexts exhibit high-level comprehension abilities), but also being able to denigrate or negate actual language skills (meaning that readers with high-level language skills can doubt their own abilities when the text does not match their knowledge) (Bernhardt 1985).

As summary, the act of reading in a second language is extremely tricky—it is even trickier with *literary* texts that are inherently ambiguous, full of metaphor and intertextual relations to texts to which the readers also have no access. This is not the trickiness of the dative case or of appropriate pronunciation or even of capturing sociocultural nuances of oral language. At most levels those are directly teachable "rules" from directly observable norms. It is critical that all who teach have an appreciation of the complexity of understanding the moving target of literature.

Dilemmas of Graduate Student Pedagogical Preparation

The explosion of research and scholarship in the field of language teaching and learning experienced over the past twenty years is stunning, remarkable, and daunting. At one time, it may have been possible to boast that one had read everything there was to read in the field; such a statement is no longer realistic. This explosion, of course, is a great opportunity to understand more precisely the teaching/learning process in second-languages and to develop new ways of bringing learners to higher and more sophisticated levels of language knowledge and use. The clear downside is, however, that the graduate curriculum in language and literature departments has not expanded to accommodate this volume of new knowledge. By and large, within traditional language and literature departments, the applied linguistics contribution to the graduate curriculum is "the methods course"(i.e., a course on the learning and teaching of second languages that includes a discussion of second-language acquisition) which includes practice of the instruction in the four skills, a section on tests and assessment, and some version of field experience—either microteaching or field observation. The more modern the methods course, the less focused it is on methods and techniques, such as how to conduct a rapid-fire pattern drill or how to present the *passé composé,* and the more focused it is on linguistic development and learner performance.

A curricular structure based on an analysis of and a sensitivity toward learner development and learner performance leaves little time for a discussion of literature teaching. Another dimension to the dilemma—a dimension far beyond sheer volume of material to be practiced and mastered—is the uneasy relationship between language and literature teaching. It is indeed within the context of "the methods course" that the (future) profession is socialized into the "lang-lit split." In other words, if the only teacher preparation available is language teacher preparation a clear message is sent that language gets taught, but the corollary collocation for literature remains awkward. A further part of the message communicated within the structure of the traditional methods course is that *language* and *literature* are clearly separable units. As long as this message is sent from the outset of the graduate student socialization process, the "lang-lit split" will remain entrenched in graduate departments because those graduate students are indeed professors in training.

This situation calls for an integration of perspectives. Students need to be set on a path which enables them to think, first, about the *act of teaching* and the *process of learning.* Only after beginning to think about teaching and learning should they begin to think about the specific subsets of teaching and learning in which they will be engaged throughout their professional lives: namely, *language teaching, language learning, literature teaching,* and *literature learning.* The remainder of this paper focuses specifically on the latter subsets, *literature teaching* and *literature learning.*

A Teaching Perspective

Graduate students must understand, first, that teachers teach and students student. Through their vehicle of studenting, students learn. The point is that there is only an indirect relationship (i.e., a mediated relationship) between what the teacher does and student learning. Most graduate students believe in a very direct relationship. Second, they must understand that for young teachers, teaching is a performance often guided by being "liked" and by the principle of being "survival oriented and activity-driven." Most graduate students believe that teaching is about *them* and the *literary text*; in other words, the text-preservation agenda seems to be foremost for graduate students and that undergraduate students just sort of happen to be there. Third, graduate students generally believe that the undergraduate students are like they are and that they are in the course to enhance their ability to analyze foreign-language literary texts. Graduate students must come to understand that this does not seem to be the case. Rather, students report that they are in undergraduate literature courses to enhance their foreign-language abilities and because they like the stories—for them it is not about literary analysis (Davis 1992; Davis, Gorell, Kline and Hsieh 1992). Fourth, inexperienced teachers must come to understand that instruction is guided by the context in which the instructional performance takes place—that institutional norms and resources play a crucial role in what can be accomplished in instruction (Bernhardt 1987). Graduate students generally think they will simply employ the model that they have been exposed to at their graduate institution to other institutions, a point documented by Marshall (2000b). This could be a reason why the teaching evaluations for young Assistant Professors suffer at the beginning stages of their careers. They are perhaps replicating their experience from their previous institution and that experience may simply be incompatible with their new institutions. Finally, graduate student-learners must understand that teachers are guided by belief systems and that their beliefs about learning—language learning *and* literature learning—will guide what happens in their classrooms. It is clear that learners (undergraduates and graduates) will rely on their previous knowledge and culturally determined beliefs. Hence, graduate methods courses must enable graduate students to reveal their folk wisdom—about teaching, about learning, about the goals of instruction, about the ethical demands of their jobs, and so forth—and ask them to question that folk wisdom in light of research-driven knowledge.

A Literature Learning Perspective

The next topic area that should be addressed is learning. Graduate students in foreign-language departments should be made aware of the generalizations in the research literature on human learning; should be asked to relate that literature to the language learning research literature to which they are exposed; and then should be given tasks to relate that conceptualization of research to the act of literature learning and teaching. From this conflation of knowledge bases, they can develop a literature learning perspective. The learning literature (not just language learning, but learning in general) can be synthesized under seven rubrics (Kamil 1998, personal communication; Pressley and McCormick 1995): *time on task, appropriate feedback, prior knowledge, situated learning, task difficulty, multiple solutions, and release of control*.

Time on task in learning is arguably the most crucial feature in human learning. It refers to the total amount of time spent learning to do a task; it also focuses on the nature of the task. Exemplified simply, the longer one spends practicing the task of piano playing, the higher the probability of getting better at playing the piano. Further, lots of time spent practicing the piano implies improvement at playing the piano—not necessarily at playing the violin. To return to the matter at hand, time on task in literature learning means spending significant amounts of time reading and interpreting literature. It does not mean spending lots of time doing grammar exercises and then turning to literature; it also does not mean listening to someone else interpret literature. It literally means for students that if they are to become able learners and readers of literature, they must spend significant time doing whatever good readers of literature do.

A second dimension to human learning is receiving appropriate feedback. Appropriate feedback means working with a knowledgeable coach, tutor, or teacher who can make comments specific to the task at hand. Telling foreign-language students in literature classes that their language is "not very good" and that they "should spend a semester abroad" is vague and unhelpful criticism. Pressley and McCormick (1995) note: "Feedback provides information about what has been learned and what remains to be learned. The more that feedback stimulates the learners to reflect on errant responses in comparison to correct alternatives, the more likely it is to be effective" (p. 249).

Appropriate feedback in the context of literature learning has to focus on two primary dimensions. First, it refers to the nature and appropriateness of the language used to express interpretive comments; second, it focuses on interpretation itself. The former need is substantially linguistic in nature. Either in oral or written texts, students' language use needs to be monitored for its discourse features and levels of sociolinguistic appropriateness. When the discourse structure is wanting (either from the microgrammatical level or from the structure of paragraphs), literature teachers must point out the areas that are in need of work and practice and provide targeted opportunities for such practice. Whether this means commentaries such as "I'll be looking in your next paper/class presentation for a clearer and more refined use of literary-analytic vocabulary. Please refer back to the article X that we read in class and integrate some of the literary terms I called to your attention there" or comments such as "I'd like you to replace the words I've underlined in your draft with ones that we learned in X's article," the point is that literature learners are to understand that their language use needs to become aligned with interpretive language. The instructor is there to help the learner work on the development of that language.

The greater challenge with respect to appropriate feedback is providing feedback regarding interpretation. How does a teacher tell a student that he or she is off track in the interpretive process without sounding too controlling? How does one tell a student that his or her interpretation is too simplistic, too naive? Perhaps this is indeed where the science of teaching gives way to its art. Extended individual discussion with students to grasp how individual students problematize or, perhaps, whether they can problematize is central to providing them with constructive feedback that will make them better at understanding and interpreting literature. Bangert-Drowns, Kulik, Kulik, and Morgan (1991) provide convincing evidence that having learners examine their responses and comparing them with more reasonable or appropriate responses is more effective than other types of feedback. Maintaining an archive of effective responses that students can reference perhaps on a course website is a way of managing this type of feedback in a nonthreatening way.

Prior knowledge is a third critical variable in the learning process. Research indicates that learners will use the knowledge that they have already acquired as a basis for interpreting and understanding the new knowledge they are to acquire. In literature learning, this means that learners will use their knowledge of American literature, for example, to interpret Spanish or French literature and that they will use the interpretive skills that they have acquired in other educational settings (such as twelfth-grade English) for their interpretive tasks. There is much positive to be said about the store of knowledge that learners bring to the foreign-language literature setting. It is not as if they have never encountered difficult texts with multiple meanings. Indeed, they have, and have practiced this kind of reading. That is, they come to their foreign-language literature class with a set of useful strategies. The question becomes whether these useful strategies are the most appropriate.

The interpretation of a foreign-language literature from a native-language literature can be relatively useful, but it is frequently inappropriate. As noted above, inappropriate interpretations are often received in college foreign-language literature classes as moral failings (i.e., not having enough cultural sophistication to get it "right"). In fact, research evidence indicates that when the knowledge base is off-target or nonexistent, learners often resort to the overuse of strategies (Pressley and McCormick 1995, p. 83). Bernhardt (1991) provides evidence for this from her interviews with literature students. They admit to not understanding many foreign-language texts, but readily acknowledge that they have sufficient strategic knowledge to look up interpretations in the secondary literature and to parrot them back in order to prepare and complete classes and assignments. The point is that the task of the literature instructor is to enable learners to acquire the knowledge structures they need for authentic interpretation.

Research also indicates that for effective learning to occur, that learning should be situated. In other words, learning should be relevant to the task at hand, that is, it should be in a context in which performance normally takes place. One can learn lots of techniques from practice and can learn many strategies from books. But, to be a good golfer, one must go out on the golf course. To be a good researcher, one must conduct research. What does situated learning with respect to literature look like? In its most fundamental sense, literature learning is about interpretation. If students are not asked to interpret in some authentic way, their learning will be of the most superficial kind. Questions posed to students situate the learning. The vague assignment of "Write a five-page reaction paper to the text" is nonsituated and most probably a grammar and composition task in disguise. When literary critics are asked to conduct a text analysis, their task is not to complete a grammatically correct five-paragraph essay. Rather, the task is to provide some novel insight into a particular text, referring to other texts to build an effective argument. Pressley and Mc-Cormick (1995) note:

> The real challenge is to make schooling sufficiently like the real world, so that reading, writing, and problem solving learned there are tied to important real-world situations. Many believe school should be reconstructed so that students serve as apprentices to people doing real reading of real books, real writing for real purposes, and solving of real problems (p. 182).

In other words, making the task match the real world task as closely as possible will produce a higher level of learning in students. Contextualizing an interpretation task by asking students to write a book review; to follow the development of an essay that the instructor herself is composing; or to take on the personae of a "critic" are means of situating the students' learning.

A fifth learning principle is the easy to hard principle. The question here is how to define easy versus hard within a literature perspective. Historically, a rule of thumb has been to choose texts for literature courses that are linguistically easy (i.e., subject-verb-object-easy with lots of short words). But what of conceptual ease? For example, a text with a plot, (i.e., a text where there are clear answers to *Who? What? Where? Why?,* and *How?*) may lighten the learning burden versus a text that is based on an internal monologue or one that begins at the middle of a story with anaphoric and cataphoric references. The structure of the literature curriculum is a key to unlocking several dilemmas related to difficulty. If the literature curriculum is indeed structured around an author, a theme, a genre, the text types and structures themselves become more and more familiar and, therefore, easier. Random sets of short prose pieces from multiple authors, multiple time periods, and diverse themes force students to begin again with each new text rather than being able to build systematically on what they know. The systematic build up of background knowledge will contribute significantly to lightening the cognitive load.

Next, effective learning also appears to be a result of having the learner perceive multiple solutions. In other words, in order to learn something, a learner must try things out in different contexts. Within a literature context, the tired essay form that is used to learn interpretive skills in a foreign language might not be the only solution. Other opportunities to use interpretive skills need to be provided. Dramatic readings or the placing of narrative into a dialogue form and vice versa may help learners to understand how to interpret and may provide instructors with knowledge about the interpretive directions and skills of their learners.

A seventh principle is release of control. This means that the learners must be given a chance to try literary interpretation in a foreign language on their own. In other words, a culminating task that allows a learner to put everything together without too many guidelines for essays, too many restrictions, too much hovering feedback and grammatical correction is required to insure appropriate learning. Indeed, multiple drafts with lots of instructor feedback are important, but at some point learners need to understand that they will be responsible and on their own for an individual product ready for scholarly assessment.

In summary, graduate students should come away from a discussion of these principles with the following understandings. First, learners will develop their interpretations within the context of the sociocultural knowledge that they carry with them. This knowledge is *not* necessarily appropriate or relevant. It is, however, all that they generally have as an interpretive base. This is not a moral failing; it is a background knowledge issue. Second, learners' linguistic level will influence their interpretation. Learners are not generic, but carry with them semideveloped arsenals of word knowledge, syntax, and morphology. Third, learners' literacy level in their first language will also influence their interpretations. Some learners will be better at analysis than others. That is separate from their linguistic ability and separate from their relevant or irrelevant sociocultural knowledge. Literature instructors must learn to distinguish between "excellent written French" and "excellent interpretive skills" and insure that they are not blinded by linguistic acumen. Instructors will find excellent language expressing trivial ideas and will find spotty language depicting serious analysis on the part of their students; it is the instructor who will have to make a judgment about which of these to value.

A Literature Teaching Perspective

Marshall (2000a) argues that any literature curriculum that focuses on the Other calls for a new pedagogy—one that enables learners to cope with the "austere" relationship that they find in texts from cultures other than their own. This perspective, wedded to notions of linguistic and conceptual development gleaned from the second-language acquisition and human-learning literature, calls for a pedagogy that is focused on reader conceptualization, how that conceptualization is constructed and developed over time, and how it can be modified.

Student-readers are learners. This means that when they arrive in their literature classrooms, they will rely on prior knowledge, will respond to feedback, and will see to construct their understanding based on the classroom context in which they find themselves, and so forth. The task of the foreign-language literature instructor is to uncover the conceptual representations of literary text that student-readers construct. Further, after uncovering the representations, the task of the instructor is to realign the representations when they are inappropriate. This task is much the same as the task of the language instructor who must try to listen for and to understand how a student has conceptualized a particular linguistic rule within automatic speech and who must then try to set contexts for the correct use of the form.

How do these conceptualizations get uncovered in a literature classroom? How can a literature instructor listen? A vehicle for uncovering representations is recall in the native language and at higher fluency levels, recall in the foreign language. The key point is that an instructor must find a way to tap the individual student's conceptualization of a literary text. There should be no interrupting questions, no interfering interpretations on the part of the instructor. What is in the text from the conceptualization of the individual reader must be the pedagogical point of departure. Whether this uncovering process is conducted in the classroom, retelling a story in writing, or by email, the point is the students must be permitted to provide an individual interpretation on which the literature instructor can base a subsequent class hour. The point of departure must be what the student understands is in the text, not what the teacher tells him or her it is about.

How does a literature instructor in training learn to listen to students? The obvious answer is by listening to students in authentic classroom settings. Yet, while the observation of literature teaching is a possibility within graduate methods courses, it is difficult to arrange literature teaching field experiences—frequently because there are not many literature classes taught at any given time in a language department, and because professors often do not wish to relinquish class hours to graduate students for practice teaching. Hence, simulation is an efficient alternative. Graduate students can be given learner-generated conceptualizations of literary texts and be asked to then conduct an analysis of these learner-generated texts using standard text-analysis techniques. Below is an example of the written recall in English of the German-language text from Franz Kafka, *Vor dem Gesetz* (1996). The learner was asked to read the text in German and then to recall the text in the language in which he or she felt most comfortable. The student, a freshman with 30 weeks of German, recalled the following:

> A doorman stands before the entrance of his building. He wears a warm fur coat, has a distinctive nose, and has a long black beard. A man from the country (he seems like a country bumpkin) asks the doorman if he can enter the building. The doorman will not let him enter. A conversation ensues between the two and the bumpkin leaves.

The man from the country travels a great deal and after some time, he returns to the building. Meanwhile, the doorman had remained day in and day out at his mundane job. Another conversation ensues.

Generally, a set of recalls from individual students of a particular literary text like the one above are given to each graduate student. (Recalls from five separate students are enough to simulate a class.) The graduate student in the course is to imagine that each individual student is in his or her literature class and is coming to the class having read and understood the story in the manner exemplified by the recalls. The task for the graduate student is to look for and to diagnose misunderstandings arising from cultural misconstructions, linguistic deficiencies, or both. This exercise permits graduate students to use the primary research tools that they have–literary skills–for text analysis. After they complete this kind of analysis of student-generated texts from multiple perspectives, graduate students are asked to design lessons for the group of learners whose recalls they analyzed. They are asked to answer the following question: *Given what your students believe about this text, how will you proceed—in terms of sociocultural knowledge, in terms of linguistic knowledge, in terms of literary analytic skills—keeping in mind what you know about human learning?*

Implications

This approach to lesson planning for the literature classroom has rarely if ever been discussed in the foreign-language research literature. Such an approach is, however, critical in bringing about programs that are consistent with the second-language research base and that bring students to higher levels of linguistic proficiency and cultural appreciation. The end-result should be twofold. First, changing graduate students' understandings of literature learners radically changes their teaching attitudes. Graduate students often believe that their literary study and its methodology is somehow distinct from the pedagogy that they will and should use in their own teaching. The language/literature split is partially to blame for this, of course. As long as graduate students believe that language learning happens in two years and that, after two years, students can discuss great literature, there can be no claim that graduate students will naturally become successful literature teachers. Changing their beliefs changes what they believe they can accomplish in their literature teaching. Second, this approach—one that integrates notions of human learning, second-language development, and literary study—potentially leads to greater professional job satisfaction. Graduate students will begin to perceive the literary methodologies they currently have as useful pedagogy and feel more comfortable as instructors. They will begin to have a grasp on the inextricable link between language and literature study and no longer perceive one as a necessary evil and the other as the real goal.

Research and theory in all fields has become increasingly more sophisticated and complex. This increased complexity implies a need for new means and modes of communicating the information to graduate students and enabling them to take ownership of it. The field is at the point that a one-size-fits-all-for-all-teachers-and-all-courses approach to teaching is woefully inadequate. A course on the teaching of literature must be added to and required within the standard graduate curriculum in language departments. Structuring a course on the teaching of foreign language literature according to the belief systems and knowledge structures with which graduate students come to their own learning process should make for a satisfying experience and for more sophisticated and attentive future foreign literature instructors.

Works Cited

Bangert-Drowns, R.L., C.L. Kulik, J.A. Kulik, and M. Morgan. 1991. The Instructional Effect of Feedback in Test-Like Events. *Review of Educational Research* 61: 213–38.

Bernhardt, Elizabeth B. 1985. Reconstructions of Literary Texts by Learners of German. In *New Yorker Werkstattgespraech 1984: Literarische Texte im Fremdsprachenunterricht,* edited by M. Heid, 254–89. Muenchen: Kemmler & Hoch.

_____. 1987. The Text as a Participant in Instruction. *Theory into Practice* 26 (1): 32–37.

_____. 1990. A Model of L2 Text Reconstruction: The Recall of Literary Text by Learners of German. In *Issues in L2: Theory as Practice/Practice as Theory,* edited by A. LaBrea and L. Bailey, 21–24. Norwood, NJ: Ablex.

_____. 1990. Knowledge-Based Inferencing in Second-Language Comprehension. In *Linguistics, Language Teaching and Language Acquisition: The Interdependence of Theory, Practice and Research,* edited by J. Alatis, 271–84. Washington: Georgetown University Press.

_____. 1991. *Reading Development in a Second Language: Theoretical, Research, and Classroom Perspectives.* Norwood, NJ: Ablex.

_____. 1995. Teaching Literature or Teaching Students? *ADFL Bulletin,* 26(2): 5–6.

———. 2000. Second-Language Reading as a Case Study of Reading Scholarship in the 20th Century. In *Handbook of Reading Research* (Vol. III), edited by M. Kamil, P. Mosenthal, P. Pearson, and R. Barr, 791–811. Mawwah, NJ: Lawrence Erlbaum.

Bernhardt, Elizabeth M., and Michael L. Kamil. 1995. Interpreting Relationships Between L1 and L2 Reading: Consolidating the Linguistic Threshold and the Linguistic Interdependence Hypotheses. *Applied Linguistics* 16(2):16–34.

Brisbois, Judith. 1995. Connections between First- and Second-Language Reading. *Journal of Reading Behavior* 24(4): 565–84.

Brumfit, Christopher J., and Carter Ronald A. 1986. *Literature and Language Teaching.* Oxford: Oxford University Press.

Carter, Ronald, and Michael N. Long. 1991. *Teaching Literature.* New York: Longman.

Chi, F-M. 1995. EFL Readers and a Focus on Intertextuality. *Journal of Reading* 38(8): 638–44.

Collie, Joanne, and Stephen Slater. 1987. *Literature in the Language Classroom: A Resource Book of Ideas and Activities.* Cambridge: Cambridge University Press.

Davis, James, Lynn Gorell, Rebecca Kline, and G. Hsieh. 1992. Readers and Foreign Languages: A Survey of Undergraduate Attitudes Toward the Study of Literature. *Modern Language Journal* 73(3): 320–32.

Davis, James. 1992. Reading Literature in the Foreign Language: The Comprehension/Response Connection. *French Review* 65(3): 359–70.

Fecteau, M.L. 1999. First- and Second-Language Reading Comprehension of Literary Texts. *Modern Language Journal* 83(4): 475–93.

Kafka, Franz. 1996. Vor dem Gesetz in Franz Kafka Erzählungen und andere ausgewählte Prosa, 162–63. Frankfurt: Fischer Taschenbuch Verlag.

Kern, Richard. 2000. *Literacy and Language Teaching.* Oxford: Oxford University Press.

Kramsch, Claire, and Timothy Nolden. 1994. Redefining Literacy in a Foreign Language. *Die Unterrichtspraxis* 27(1): 28–35.

Marshall, James. 2000a. *Closely Reading Ourselves: Teaching English and the Education of Teachers. Preparing a Nation's Teachers: Models of English and Foreign Language.* New York: Modern Language Association.

———. 2000b. Research on Response to Literature. In *Handbook of Reading Research* (Vol. III), edited by M. Kamil, P. Mosenthal, P. Pearson, and R. Barr, 381–402. Mawwah, NJ: Lawrence Erlbaum.

Pressley, Michael, and Christine McCormick. 1995. *Cognition, Teaching, and Assessment.* New York: HarperCollins.

Shumway, Nicholas. 1995. Searching for Averroes: Reflections on Why It Is Desirable and Impossible to Teach Culture in Foreign-Language Courses. In *Redefining the Boundaries of Language Study,* edited by C. Kramsch, 251–60. Boston: Heinle & Heinle.

Steffensen, M.S., Joag-Dev, and R.C. Anderson. 1979. A Cross-Cultural Perspective on Reading Comprehension. *Reading Research Quarterly* 15:10–29.

Tian, G. S. 1991. Higher Order Reading Comprehension Skills in Literature Learning and Teaching at the Lower Secondary School Level in Singapore. *RELC Journal* 22(2): 29–43.

Contributors

William J. Berg (Ph.D., Princeton University) is Professor of French at the University of Wisconsin–Madison. His current interests include the relationship between literature and painting and the use of technology in foreign-language education. He has authored or co-authored two books on Flaubert, two books on Zola, and three textbooks in the field of French language, literature, and culture.

Elizabeth B. Bernhardt (Ph.D., University of Minnesota) is Director of the Language Center and Professor of German Studies at Stanford University. She has spoken and written on second-language reading, teacher education, and policy and planning for foreign- and second-language programs. She teaches undergraduate German language courses and offers graduate seminars on second-language learning and teaching and second-language literacy. Her book, *Reading Development in a Second Language*, won the Modern Language Association's Mildenburger Award as well as the Edward Fry Award from the National Reading Conference for exceptional research in foreign language and as an outstanding contribution to literacy research.

Joanne E. Burnett (Ph.D., The Pennsylvania State University) is Assistant Professor of French and Second Language Acquisition in a mid-size university. She has published and is a frequent conference presenter on technology and the language classroom and has recently begun to present on topics related to culture and reading. She teaches undergraduate and graduate courses in language teacher preparation and French language and civilization. Her research interests include teachers' beliefs, conceptions of practice, and decision-making processes.

Heidi Byrnes (Ph.D., Georgetown University) is Professor of German/Linguistics at Georgetown University. Her research focus within second language acquisition (SLA) is the advanced instructed learner of German, particularly the learners' acquisition of academic literacy in a second language, as well as discourse analysis and cross-cultural discourse. Her interest in instructed learning by adults has led to a complete restructuring of the undergraduate curriculum in the German Department at Georgetown University with a content-focus, a project on which her contribution in this volume is based. Her most recent book-length publication is an edited volume entitled *Learning*

Second and Foreign Languages: Perspectives in Research and Scholarship (New York: MLA, 1998) which provides an overview of the field, including curricular recommendations regarding content-based approaches to second language learning. She has recently expanded this work with a number of articles that explore the possibility of using genres as a foundation for conceptualizing advanced L2 learning and teaching, and is currently working on a book on principles and practices for curriculum construction within collegiate foreign language departments.

Leah Fonder-Solano (Ph.D., The University of Arizona) is Assistant Professor of Spanish at a mid-sized university. She teaches Spanish courses which have ranged from basic language to graduate courses on Latin American civilization, film, and the pedagogy of literature. She is director of the university-wide Committee on Services and Resources for Women. She has spoken and written on contemporary Latin American women's literature and reading in the classroom.

Diana Frantzen (Ph.D., Indiana University) is Assistant Professor of Spanish and Director of the Spanish Language Program in the Department of Spanish and Portuguese at the University of Wisconsin–Madison. She teaches courses in foreign language teaching methodology, applied linguistics, advanced language practice, phonetics, and second language acquisition. Her research interests include lexical and grammatical acquisition in L2 writing, error correction, culture, and the integration of literature at all levels of instruction.

Stacey Katz (Ph.D., University of Texas at Austin) is Assistant Professor of French at the University of Utah at Salt Lake City, where she is supervisor of teaching assistants and coordinator of the lower division language program in French. She teaches courses in French language, linguistics, and teaching methodology. Her research interests include the grammar of spoken French and applying pragmatic theory to the teaching of French. Her articles have appeared in the *French Review* and *Foreign Language Annals*.

Susanne Kord (Ph.D., University of Massachusetts Amherst) is George V. Roth Professor of German at Georgetown University. She has authored four books and over thirty articles on women's literature, reception history, and the social history of literature and aesthetics. Among the books she has edited or co-edited is the acclaimed *Feminist Encyclopedia of German Literature* (co-edited with Friederike Eigler). She is the recipient of numerous awards, including the Brentano-

Preis of the Free University of Berlin and the Robert-Kahn Award for Poetry. In 2001, she served as Chair of the Executive Division of Eighteenth- and Early Nineteenth-Century Literature of the Modern Language Association.

Laurey K. Martin-Berg (Ph.D. University of Wisconsin–Madison) is Distinguished Lecturer of French at the University of Wisconsin–Madison. Her current interests include articulation between language and literature courses, language teacher training, and the use of visual media in foreign language instruction. She has co-authored a first-year textbook program and an intermediate-level anthology, as well as monographs on Flaubert and Zola. She has also written and spoken on second language reading, teaching literature, and the use of new media throughout the foreign language curriculum.

Jean Marie Schultz (Ph.D., University of California at Berkeley) holds a Ph.D. in Comparative Literature from the University of California at Berkeley where she directs the Intermediate French Program and is currently the Academic Coordinator for the Berkeley Language Center. She works in the field of Second Language Acquisition Theory and Applied Linguistics, focusing particularly on issues of foreign language writing and language-through-literature approaches to teaching. Her most recent publications include "Toward a Pedagogy of Creative Writing in a Foreign Language" in *Pedagogy of Language Learning*, ABLEX 2001; "Computers and Collaborative Writing in the Foreign Language Curriculum" in *Network-Based Language Teaching*, Cambridge UP 1999. She has also published in the *Modern Language Journal* and in the *French Review*. She is an ACTFL certified Oral Proficiency Tester of French.

Virginia M. Scott (Ph.D., Emory University) is Associate Professor of French at Vanderbilt University. She has served as Director of the French language program, supervisor of the graduate student TAs, and Chair of the Department of French and Italian; she is currently Associate Provost for Academic Affairs. She teaches undergraduate-level French language and literature as well as graduate-level courses on theory and research in second language acquisition, foreign language pedagogy, and applied French linguistics. In 1996 she was awarded a Vanderbilt University Chair of Teaching Excellence. Her research has focused on foreign-language writing and technology in language teaching and research. In addition to her teaching and research, she is active in state and regional professional organizations; she served on the Board of Directors of the Southern Conference on Language

Teaching (SCOLT) and participates actively in the Tennessee Foreign Language Teaching Association (TFLTA). Her recent interest in the teaching of FL literature is reflected in her co-editing of this AAUSC volume.

Janet Swaffar (Ph.D., University of Wisconsin) is a Professor of Germanic Studies as well as the programs in Foreign Language Education and Comparative Literature at the University of Texas at Austin. She has written widely about an approach to reading for meaning that integrates speaking, writing, and listening comprehension with the cultural implications of fiction and non-fiction texts. Her workshops, presentations, and publications have stressed styles of input and intake that lead to creative language use and independent student interpretation of textual implications. She also writes about contemporary literature and film and is currently completing a book illustrating the application of her reading theories for the teaching of English.

Holly Tucker (Ph.D., University of Wisconsin-Madison) is Assistant Professor of French at Vanderbilt University. She has published articles on Pierre Corneille, Charles Sorel, the French literary fairy tale, as well as on the place of literature in the Standards. She is also author of *Pregnant Fictions: Tales of Childbirth in Early-Modern France* (forthcoming), which explores the intersections between medicine and seventeenth- and eighteenth-century literature. Her interest in the teaching of foreign-language literature flows from graduate work in SLA and her experiences as an Editorial Assistant for the *Modern Language Journal*. At Vanderbilt, she has also served as coordinator of the first-year language program.

AAUSC Style Sheet for Authors

In-Text Citations

The *AAUSC Issues in Language Program Direction* series uses the author-date citation system described in *The Chicago Manual of Style*, 14th ed. *(Note that here and elsewhere a number of these references do not refer to a real work; they are for illustration purposes only.)*

1. Basic reference: If, from the context, the author is clear, use only the date within parentheses. If not, use the last name of an author and the year of publication of the work, with no punctuation between them. Note that no designation of "ed." or "comp." is used.

   (VanPatten 1993)

   Benseler and Cronjaeger (1991) provide the first comprehensive listing on the topic of TA development in foreign languages in their extensive bibliography.

   Although exhortations to the contrary are easily found (Allwright 1981), the textbook, particularly the introductory textbook . . .

2. For a reference with page numbers, use a comma to separate date and page number. Precede the page number(s) with p. or pp.

   (Byrnes 1990, p. 42)

3. For a reference with volume and page numbers, use arabic number for volume, colon, and arabic number for page:

   (Weinberg 1952, 2: p. 129)

4. For a reference to volume only, add volume number to avoid ambiguity:

   (Weinberg 1952, vol. 2)

5. For works by two or three authors, use this form:

   (Smith and Jones 1991)

   (Smith, Jones, and North 1993)

6. For works by more than three authors, use "et al." If there is another work of the same date that would also abbreviate to "et al.," use a short title identifying the work cited.

   (Mitchell et al. 1992)

   (Mitchell et al., Writing Space, 1992)

7. For a work by an association or agency without a specific author, use the organization name in full. If the name is particularly long, you may abbreviate but be sure that the reader will be able to easily find it in the works cited and that it is used consistently throughout the text.

   (ACTFL 1994)

8. For two or more references, separate them by using a semicolon. Add a comma for page numbers.

   (Jones 1992; Light 1990; Smith 1991)

   (Jones 1992; Light 1990, pp. 72–74; Smith 1991, p. 6)

9. For multiple works by the same author, do not repeat name and separate by comma if there are no page numbers. If there are page numbers, separate by semicolons and use commas for page numbers:

   (Kelly 1896, 1902a, 1902b)

   (Kelly 1896, p. 4; 1902a, pp. 120–22; 1902b, p. 45)

10. For a new edition of an older work, put the original date of publication in square brackets:

    (Piaget [1924] 1969, p. 75)

11. For a personal communication, do not include the reference in the Works Cited section. Write the prose of the text to indicate personal communication, with the year given in parentheses:

    *In a personal communication (1994), Tucker indicated that . . .

Works Cited Section

The AAUSC series uses *The Chicago Manual of Style* (14th ed.) "B" reference style. Consult Chapter 16 of *Chicago*.

Order of Entries

Always alphabetize by last name of principal author; for questions of alphabetization, see *Chicago* Chapter 17.

1. If an author has both individual and coauthored works, all individual works precede coauthored ones.

    a. By date: oldest first

    b. If more than one work in the same year, order by alpha and add lowercase a, b, c, etc.: 1993a, 1993b

2. Coauthored works:

    a. cluster together groups containing the same coauthors. Groups of 2 precede groups of 3, which precede groups of 4, etc.

    b. within each group, organize by date (oldest first)

    c. if more than one work with same date, organize by alpha using a, b, c.

Clément, Richard. 1980. Ethnicity, Contact and Communicative Competence in a Second Language. In *Language: Social Psychological Perspectives*, edited by H. Giles, W. P. Robinson, and P. M. Smith, 147–54. Oxford: Pergamon.

Clément, Richard, and Bastian G. Kruidenier. 1983. Orientations on Second Language Acquisition: 1. The Effects of Ethnicity, Milieu, and Their Target Language on Their Emergence. *Language Learning* 33: 273–91.

———. 1985. Aptitude, Attitude, and Motivation in Second Language Proficiency: A Test of Clément's Model. *Journal of Language and Social Psychology* 4: 21–37.

Clément, Richard, Zoltán Dörnyei, and Kimberly A. Noels. Submitted for publication. Motivation, Self-Confidence, and Group Cohesion in the Foreign Language Classroom.

Three-em Dashes (———) for Repeated Names:
Do not use when a coauthor is first added. If the same author is used again, add 3-em.

> Dörnyei, Zoltán. 1990a. Analysis of Motivation Components in Foreign Language Learning. Paper presented at the Ninth World Congress of Applied Linguistics, Greece.
>
> ———. 1990b. Conceptualizing Motivation in Foreign-Language Learning. *Language Learning* 40: 45–78.
>
> Dörnyei, Zoltán, and Sarah Thurrell. 1992. *Conversation and Dialogues in Action*. Hemel Hempstead: Prentice-Hall.
>
> ———. 1994. Teaching Conversational Skills Intensively: Course Content and Rationale. *ELT Journal* 48: 40–49.

Special Notes

1. Personal names beginning with "Mc" or any abbreviated forms of "Mac" should be indexed under "Mac" as though the full form were used.

2. For all state abbreviations, consult *Chicago* 14.17.

3. There is always a comma separating the names of authors, even if there are only two authors:

   Bernhardt, Elizabeth, and JoAnn Hammadou. 1987.

4. There are no quotation marks around article titles. Use quotes only when there is a title within a title. Books are in italics.

5. Abbreviate page-number spans according to 8.69.

Journal Article: One Author (16.104)

Note that identification of the issue is used *only* when each issue is paginated separately (in contrast to the common practice of consecutive pagination throughout a volume).

> Lange, Dale. 1986. The MLA Commission of Foreign Languages, Literatures, and Linguistics: Comments and Advice. *ADFL Bulletin* 17(1): 28–31.

Journal Article: Two or More Authors (16.104)

Allen, Wendy, Keith Anderson, and Léon Narváez. 1992. Foreign Languages Across the Curriculum: The Applied Foreign Language Component. *Foreign Language Annals* 25: 11–19.

Organizations, Associations, or Corporations (16.52)

If a publication issued by an organization bears no personal author's name on the title page, it should be listed by the organization, even if the name is repeated in the title or in the series title or as the publisher.

American Council on the Teaching of Foreign Languages. 1986. *ACTFL Proficiency Guidelines.* Hastings-on-Hudson, NY: ACTFL.

Edited Book (16.46):

Byrnes, Heidi, and Michael Canale, eds. 1987. *Defining and Developing Proficiency: Guidelines, Implementations, and Concepts.* Lincolnwood, IL: National Textbook.

Article in an Edited Book

James, Dorothy. 1989. Reshaping the "College-Level" Curriculum: Problems and Possibilities. In *Shaping the Future: Challenges and Opportunities,* edited by Helen S. Lepke, 79–110. Burlington, VT: Northeast Conference.

Book in a Series (16.86)

Magnan, Sally Sieloff, ed. 1991. *Challenges in the 1990s for College Foreign Language Programs.* AAUSC Issues in Language Program Direction. Boston, MA: Heinle & Heinle.

Johnson, Carl L. 1944. *Professor Longfellow at Harvard.* Studies in Literature and Philology, vol. 5. Eugene: University of Oregon Press.

Article in Edited Book that Is Part of a Series

Lee, James F., and Bill VanPatten. 1991. The Question of Language Program Direction Is Academic. In *Challenges in the 1990s for College Foreign Language Programs,* edited by Sally Sieloff Magnan, 113–27. AAUSC Issues in Language Program Direction. Boston, MA: Heinle & Heinle.

An Edition (16.79)

Pedhazur, Elazar J. 1982. *Multiple Regression Behavioral Research: Explanation and Prediction.* 2d ed. New York: Holt, Rinehart, and Winston.

Publisher's Information Implies a Special Publishing Division

Light, Richard J. 1992. *Harvard Assessment Seminars Second Report.* Cambridge: Harvard University, Graduate School of Education.

Unpublished Thesis (16.132, if published see below)

Tucker, Holly. 1996. Strategies of Rewriting in Charles Sorel's *Histoires Comiques.* Ph.D. diss., University of Wisconsin-Madison.

Published Thesis (16.96 if microform; treat as normal book if otherwise. Note use of italics.)

Jones, Mildred. 1962. *Il Pastor Fido: Sheep and Their Shepherds.* Chicago: University Microforms.

Papers Read at a Meeting (16.133)

Magnan, Sally Sieloff. 1990. Preparing Inexperienced TAs for Second-Year Courses: Are Our Orientations and Methods Courses Adequate? Paper presented at the annual meeting of the American Council on the Teaching of Foreign Languages, Nashville.

Forthcoming or In Press (16.57)

Knight, Susan. Forthcoming. Dictionary: The Tool of Last Resort in Foreign Language Reading. A New Perspective. *Modern Language Journal.*

Waldman, Lila. In press. Bilingual Administrative Support Personnel in United States Corporations. *Modern Language Journal* 78.

ERIC Docs

Rubin, Joan, and Irene Thompson. 1992. Material Selection in Strategy Instruction for Russian Listening Comprehension. ERIC Doc. No. ED349796.

Membership in AAUSC

AAUSC
The American Association of University Supervisors, Coordinators, and Directors of Foreign Language Programs

Purpose
Since its inception in 1980, the AAUSC has worked
- to promote and improve foreign and second language education in the United States
- to strengthen and improve foreign language curricula and instruction at the post-secondary level
- to strengthen development programs for teaching assistants, teaching fellows, associate instructors, or their equivalents
- to promote research in second language acquisition and on the preparation and supervision of teaching assistants
- to establish a forum for exchanging ideas, experiences, and materials among those concerned with language program direction.

Who Can Join the AAUSC?
Membership in the AAUSC is open to anyone who is interested in strengthening foreign and second language instruction, especially, but not exclusively, those involved with multi-section programs. The membership comprises teachers, supervisors, coordinators, program directors, faculty, and administrators in colleges and universities that employ teaching assistants. Many members are faculty and administrators at undergraduate institutions.

How Do I Join the AAUSC?
Please fill out the following application for membership, and send it with annual dues to Janine Spencer.

Dues (including yearly volume)
    Regular $15.00
    Student .... $15.00 for two years
Please make checks payable to:

    Janine Spencer
    Secretary/Treasurer, AAUSC
    Multi-Media Learning Center
    Northwestern University
    Evanston, IL 60208

AAUSC Application for Membership

New ☐   Renewal ☐

Name _____

School Address _____

_____

City _____ State _____ Zip _____

Telephone (work) _____

Fax _____

E-mail _____

Home address _____

City _____ State _____ Zip _____

Telephone (home) _____

Languages taught: Chinese ☐   ESL ☐   French ☐
Italian ☐   Japanese ☐   Portuguese ☐   Russian ☐
German ☐   Spanish ☐   Other ☐

Are you a: Teacher ☐   Program Director ☐
            Dept. Chair ☐   Graduate Student ☐   Other ☐